Toward a Biopsychosocial Welfare State?

Nadine Reibling • Mareike Ariaans
Editors

Toward a Biopsychosocial Welfare State?

How Medicine and Psychology Transform Social Policy

palgrave
macmillan

Editors
Nadine Reibling
Department of Health Sciences
Fulda University of Applied Sciences
Fulda, Germany

Mareike Ariaans
Department of Social Sciences
University of Siegen
Siegen, Germany

ISBN 978-3-031-32792-6 ISBN 978-3-031-32793-3 (eBook)
https://doi.org/10.1007/978-3-031-32793-3

This Palgrave Macmillan imprint is published by the registered company Springer Nature Switzerland AG.
The registered company address is: Gewerbestrasse 11, 6330 Cham, Switzerland

Preface and Acknowledgments

"Toward a Biopsychosocial Welfare State?" summarizes five years of research that we conducted within the research group "Medicalization and psychologization of social problems—Challenges and chances for social policy" (MEPYSO). In 2017, I (Nadine) applied for a research grant for cutting-edge research in social policy offered by the German Federal Ministry of Labour and Social Affairs. To me, this call for proposals as part of the newly established FIS Network (Fördernetzwerk Interdisziplinäre Sozialpolitikforschung) was the chance to do something that I had wanted to do for years: namely, to study the link between medicalization and social policy. This link lies at the heart of my two core research interests: welfare state research and medical sociology. As a graduate student, I met Sigrun Olafsdottir, my later PhD supervisor, whose dissertation research on medicalization is among the most inspiring pieces of sociological research that I have ever known. My fascination with medicalization was in good company within the MEPYSO project, where my colleagues and I were able to examine medicalization in the context of three fields of social policy: unemployment, poverty, and childhood (problems). We were interested in finding out how the medicalization of social problems impacts existing ideas, institutions, and actors in the welfare state. Moreover, we argued that aside from medicalization, psychology has become increasingly relevant to these issues. The development of these processes—as well as their integration with existing social accounts in order to deal with social problems—led us to argue that over the last decades, we have borne witness to the development of a biopsychosocial welfare state in which medical and psychological ideas and interventions for social problems have been an important addition to (traditional) social policy in various fields.

This book summarizes the collaborative research effort of the MEPYSO project team. The team behind the book is composed of Nadine Reibling, who is the leader of the project, Mareike Ariaans, who has served as co-leader of the group and the book project since 2021, and research associates Stephan Krayter, Philipp Linden, Lisa Bleckmann, and Lucas Hamel.

Many people have supported our team over the years, and we would like to thank them for helping us to make our research and this book possible. First, we would like to thank our interdisciplinary academic advisory group, which accompanied us over the years and helped us to reflect on our work: Harald Gündel (medicine), Sabine Walper (psychology), Thomas Gerlinger (political science), Pia Schober (sociology), Traugott Jähnichen (social ethics), Stefan Huster (law), and Bernhard Boockmann (economics). Next, we would like to thank the Department of Social Sciences at the University of Siegen, where our project was based and where we received support for our research in multiple ways. Specifically, we would like to thank Claus Wendt, our department chair and the supervisor of the PhD theses that developed within this project. Furthermore, this work would not have been possible without the help of our secretary, Susanne Müller, who supported us with all the administrative tasks that go hand in hand with such a large research project. Furthermore, we would like to thank Torsten Schneider, who helped us with various research and organizational tasks for finalizing the book. Next, we would like to thank Ryan DeLaney, who proofread the book as well as many other manuscripts from the project. Any errors that remain are our own. A big "thank you" also goes to our student assistants, Julia Brase, Tamara Bernhardt, Elisabeth Funk, Theresa Nink, and Maria Rudenko, whose continuous effort and support over the years made this book possible.

We also received important inspirations and feedback on multiple conferences at (1) the RC 19 Poverty, Social Welfare and Social Policy as part of the International Sociological Association, (2) the European Social Policy Network (ESPAnet), and (3) FIS Network Meetings. Moreover, we had the opportunity to discuss our ideas and results in two focus groups with various professionals (e.g., pediatricians, teachers, unemployment agency officers). We thank these professionals for sharing their views and for engaging with our ideas. Their in-depth insights were invaluable to this book.

Special thanks also go to our colleagues Patrick Sachweh, Timothy Bartley, and Simone Leiber, who were vital discussion partners and provided valuable comments on the ideas of the project and the book. We would additionally like to extend our gratitude to Sharla Plant and Liam Inscoe-Jones for their continuous and friendly support, which convinced us that Palgrave Macmillan was the best possible publisher for our book. Last but not least, we would like to thank the German Federal Ministry of Labour and Social Affairs, which made all of this work possible by funding our project through the FIS Network (Fördernetzwerk Interdisziplinäre Sozialforschung) between 2017 and 2022 (Grant Nr. Ia4-12131-1/15).

Fulda, Germany
Siegen, Germany

Nadine Reibling
Mareike Ariaans

Contents

1 Introduction 1
Nadine Reibling
1.1 Moving Toward a Biopsychosocial Welfare State? 5
1.2 An Academic Dialogue 6
1.3 A German Case Study 9
1.4 Medicine and Psychology in Germany 12
1.5 The Book 14
References 15

2 The Biopsychosocial Welfare State: A Theoretical Framework 23
Nadine Reibling and Lisa Bleckmann
2.1 Making Things Medical… 25
2.2 Making Things Psychological? 30
2.3 Similarities, Differences, and Suggestions for an Integrated Analysis 37
References 48

3 Medicine, Psychology, and the Welfare State 55
Mareike Ariaans, Nadine Reibling, and Lisa Bleckmann
3.1 Medicalization and Psychologization as Processes in the Welfare State 56
3.2 The Welfare State and Its Relation to Medicine and Psychology 57

3.3 Welfare State Theories and Dimensions of Medicalization and Psychologization 59
3.4 Welfare State Restructuring as a Catalyst for Processes of Medicalization and Psychologization 64
3.5 The Model of the Biopsychosocial Welfare State 66
3.6 An Integrated Model of Medicalization and Psychologization in the Welfare State 70
References 71

4 Unemployment: A Case for Medicine and Psychology? 77
Philipp Linden and Nadine Reibling
4.1 Medicalization and Psychologization of Unemployment: A Closer Look at the Phenomena 80
4.2 Medicalization of Unemployment in the German Welfare State: How Institutions Shape the Form and Dynamics of the (De-)medicalization of Unemployment 81
4.3 Institutional Complexity and Competing Organizational Actors as Mechanisms of Medicalization 83
4.4 What Are the Consequences of the Medicalization of Unemployment? 92
4.5 Conclusion 101
References 103

5 Poverty: More Than Just a Lack of Material Resources? 107
Stephan Krayter and Mareike Ariaans
5.1 Poverty Revisited: From Economic Measurements to the Concept of Multidimensionality 108
5.2 Scientific Actors in the Medicalization and Psychologization of Poverty 110
5.3 The Role of Political Actors in the Medicalization and Psychologization of Poverty 115
5.4 The Role of Institutions in Medicalizing and Psychologizing Poverty: Medical Status as a Determinant of the Eligibility for Benefits 119
5.5 Poverty: A Medicalized and Psychologized Issue in the Welfare State, But to What Extent? 122
References 124

6 **Childhood in Crisis: Are Medicine and Psychology Part of the Problem or Part of the Solution?** 129
Nadine Reibling, Mareike Ariaans, and Lucas Hamel
6.1 Children and the Welfare State 129
6.2 Medicalization and Psychologization of Childhood in Germany 133
6.3 Childhood Discourses: How Pediatricians and Educators Construct Problems in Childhood 137
6.4 Medicine and Psychology in the Public's View of Children with Problems 144
6.5 Learning Difficulties and the Medicalization and Psychologization of the German Educational System 149
6.6 Conclusion 154
References 155

7 **Neoliberalism and Social Investment: Paving the Way for Medicalization and Psychologization** 165
Mareike Ariaans and Nadine Reibling
7.1 Neoliberalism and the Individual Responsibility for Health 167
7.2 Social Investment and the Turn to Health and Personality as Assets 175
7.3 Conclusion 181
References 183

8 **The Biopsychosocial Welfare State: A New Perspective on Social Policy** 191
Nadine Reibling
8.1 Medicalization, Psychologization, and Welfare State Research 197
8.2 Policy Implications 199
8.3 A Glance into the Future 202
References 204

Appendix 209

References 214

Index 217

List of Contributors

Mareike Ariaans received her PhD in Sociology from the University of Mannheim in 2021. Her dissertation focused on the professionalization of long-term care work in Germany, and her research focuses on the institutional comparison of long-term care and healthcare systems. Within the MEPYSO research group, Mareike Ariaans works on qualitative and quantitative policy analysis as well as on preparing policy recommendations. She holds an MA in Social Policy from the University of Bremen.

Lisa Bleckmann is a research associate in the Department of Social Policy at the University of Siegen and is also a member of the MEPYSO project. Her research topic is the political discourse on employees' mental health in a changing working environment. Lisa Bleckmann studied Social Sciences at the Universities of Siegen and Lancaster.

Lucas Hamel is a research associate in the MEPYSO project. His focus lies on the qualitative and quantitative collection and evaluation of survey data that involve the medicalization and psychologization of early childhood developmental disorders. Lucas Hamel received his MA in Political Science from the University of Cologne.

Stephan Krayter is a research associate at the University of Siegen and is also a member of the junior research group MEPYSO. His research interests lie with the topics of medicalization and psychologization in both media and scientific discourses. Stephan Krayter holds an MA in Social Science from the University of Siegen.

Philipp Linden received his PhD in Social Sciences from the Department of Social Sciences at the University of Siegen and is also a research associate in the MEPYSO project. His research analyzes the consequences of medicalization and psychologization for both the welfare state and its recipient groups by using data from different cross-sectional and longitudinal surveys as well as from a vignette study that was developed especially for the project. Philipp Linden holds an MS in Sociology and Empirical Research from the University of Cologne.

Nadine Reibling is a professor at the Fulda University of Applied Sciences and heads the MEPYSO research group at the University of Siegen. She received her PhD in Sociology from the University of Mannheim in 2014. Nadine Reibling's research focuses on the institutional comparison of healthcare systems and on social inequalities in both health and healthcare-seeking. Since 2017, medicalization in the welfare state has been her primary field of study as it unites her passions for medical sociology and social policy research.

Abbreviations

Abs.	Absatz (English: paragraph)
ADHD	Attention-deficit/hyperactivity disorder
AFET	Bundesverband für Erziehungshilfe e. V. (English: Federal Association for Educational Aid)
AWStG	Gesetz zur Stärkung der beruflichen Weiterbildung und des Versicherungsschutzes in der Arbeitslosenversicherung (English: Act for Strengthening Continuing Vocational Training and Insurance Coverage in Unemployment Insurance)
BayEUG	Bayerisches Gesetz über das Erziehungs- und Unterrichtswesen (English: Bavarian Law on Education and Schooling)
BaySchо	Schulordnung für schulartübergreifende Regelungen an Schulen in Bayern (English: School Code for Inter-School Regulations at Schools in Bavaria)
BMAS	Bundesministerium für Arbeit und Soziales (English: German Federal Ministry of Labour and Social Affairs)
BMFSFJ	Bundesministerium für Familie, Senioren, Frauen und Jugend (English: Federal Ministry for Family Affairs, Senior Citizens, Women and Youth)
BVKJ	Berufsverband der Kinder- und Jugendärzte e. V. (English: Professional Association of Pediatricians and Adolescents)
DAK	Deutsche Angestellten Krankenkasse (English: German Employee Health Insurance Fund)
Destatis	Statistisches Bundesamt (English: Federal Statistical Office of Germany)
DSM	Diagnostic and Statistical Manual of Mental Disorders
ECEC	Early childhood education and care

GBE Bund	Gesundheitsberichterstattung des Bundes (English: Federal Health Reporting)
GDP	Gross domestic product
IADL	Instrumental activities of daily living
ICD	International Classification of Disease
ILO	International Labour Organization
KMK	Kultusministerkonferenz (English: Standing Conference of the Ministers of Education and Cultural Affairs of the States of the Federal Republic of Germany)
MEPYSO	Medicalization and psychologization of social problems (research project title)
NICE	National Institute for Health and Care Excellence
NZFH	Nationale Zentrum Frühe Hilfen (English: National Center for Early Childhood Intervention)
OECD	Organization for Economic Co-operation and Development
OLS	Ordinary least squares
PASS	Panel Arbeitsmarkt und Soziale Sicherung (English: Panel Study Labour Market and Social Security)
PISA	Programme for International Student Assessment
PPP	Public Private Partnership
PsychThG	Gesetz über den Beruf der Psychotherapeutin und des Psychotherapeuten (English: Psychotherapy Code)
SAD	Social anxiety disorder
SE	Standard error
SGB	Sozialgesetzbuch (English: German Social Security Code)
SSCI	Social Sciences Citation Index
UCL	University College London
UK	United Kingdom
UN	United Nations
UNCRC	UN Convention on the Rights of the Child
USA	United States of America
VBE	Verband Bildung und Erziehung (English: German Education Association)
WHO	World Health Organization
WoS	Web of Science

List of Figures

Fig. 1.1	Number of students of medicine and psychology in Germany, 1998–2020 (Statistisches Bundesamt [Destatis], 2022, own calculations)	13
Fig. 3.1	The biopsychosocial welfare state framework	67
Fig. 4.1	OECD (2022), public spending on incapacity as a % of GDP (indicator); DOI: 10.1787/f35b71ed-en (last accessed 10 June 2022), own graph	81
Fig. 4.2	Flowchart of the institutional process through which unemployed individuals who are ill must navigate	85
Fig. 4.3	Share (bars) of medical case reports completed by the medical service agency of the Federal Employment Agency among all unemployed people in Germany (lines). Sources: data on medical assessment services from the Federal Employment Agency, and annual reports on unemployment and minimum income benefits for jobseekers in Germany (2006–2018)	91
Fig. 4.4	Type of sickness over time for the unemployed/sick leave for the unemployed. Source: PASS Waves 2–13, DOI: 10.5164/IAB.PASS-SUF0619.de.en.v3, weighted Federal Employment Agency sample, $N = 20{,}196$	94
Fig. 4.5	Transitions within the German minimum income system. Source: PASS Waves 2–13, DOI: 10.5164/IAB.PASS-SUF0619.de.en.v3, weighted Federal Employment Agency sample, $N = 20{,}196$	95
Fig. 4.6	Comparison of subjective health status over time between the unemployed and those on sick leave for the unemployed (left), and a comparison of subjective health status before and after a transition to sick leave for the unemployed ($T = 0$) between	

gender groups (right). Source: PASS Waves 2–13, DOI: 10.5164/IAB.PASS-SUF0619.de.en.v3, weighted Federal Employment Agency sample, $N = 20{,}196$ 97
Fig. 4.7 Multivariate OLS coefficients and 95% confidence intervals of approval ratings for the question of whether the described unemployed individuals were themselves to blame for (1) their unemployment and (2) not finding a new job based on different reasons for unemployment. Widths of bars indicate the difference in approval ratings on a 7-point Likert scale compared with the reference category (employer bankruptcy). Source: vignette study, Wave 2 (in 2020) ($N = 1843$), own weighted sample calculations 99
Fig. 4.8 Behavior deemed necessary in order to receive the full amount of minimum income benefits for different causes of unemployment. Source: vignette study, Wave 2 (in 2020) ($N = 1843$), own weighted sample calculations 100
Fig. 5.1 Share of health-related and psychological research areas in the Top 50 most-cited articles on poverty 113
Fig. 5.2 Different dimensions of poverty in the Top 50 most-cited articles of all time 114
Fig. 5.3 Bar chart on the share of medical and psychological themes in parliamentary debates 117
Fig. 5.4 Poverty rate before and after taxes and transfers 120
Fig. 6.1 Weighted share of respondents who assessed the various reasons provided as 50/50, likely, or very likely causes of the described child's behavior. Categorization into medical, psychological, social, and moral reasons based on theoretical reasoning. Source: vignette study, Wave 1 (in 2019) ($N = 2093$), own calculations 145
Fig. 6.2 Weighted share of respondents who agreed or strongly agreed with different parental recommendations. Source: vignette study, Wave 1 (in 2019) ($N = 2307$), own calculations 147
Fig. 6.3 Weighted share of respondents who agreed or strongly agreed with entitlements, obligations, and sanctions. Source: vignette study, Wave 1 (in 2019) ($N = 2289$), own calculations 148

List of Tables

Table 1.1	Examples of how health and illness matter across various fields in welfare states (*unemployment* and *poverty* based on Eggs et al. (2014); *work* based on DAK-Gesundheit (2019); *homelessness* based on Schreiter et al. (2017); *families* based on AFET Bundesverband für Erziehungshilfe (2020) and Ravens-Sieberer et al. (2021); *education* based on Rommel et al. (2018) and KMK (2021); *social care* based on GBE Bund (2020))	9
Table 2.1	Comparison of medicalization and psychologization (*attribution of responsibility* based on Brickman et al. (1982))	38
Table 6.1	Medicalization and resistance to medicalization by the German Education Association and the German Professional Association of Pediatricians	143
Table 7.1	Key characteristics of neoliberalism and social investment	182

CHAPTER 1

Introduction

Nadine Reibling

"Maybe you should see a doctor or talk to a therapist about that." Many of us have likely given this advice to someone who has approached us with a personal problem—maybe a colleague with recurring headaches, a friend who feels overburdened at work, or a teenager in our own family who has had continued difficulties at school. Some of us may even have received this advice ourselves. Consulting medical doctors or psychologists has become a primary course of action for dealing with various problems that individuals experience in modern societies. Even in the absence of concrete problems, we draw on knowledge from medicine and psychology and on techniques for guidance regarding how to stay happy, healthy, and productive.

But it is not only individuals who turn to medicine and psychology with their personal problems. Indeed, the welfare state has also resorted to these disciplines. While both medicine and psychology have always played an important role in healthcare, their influence is not limited to this one field of the welfare state alone; rather, they are also relevant for social

N. Reibling (✉)
University of Applied Science Fulda, Fulda, Germany
e-mail: nadine.reibling@pg.hs-fulda.de

N. Reibling, M. Ariaans (eds.), *Toward a Biopsychosocial Welfare State?*, https://doi.org/10.1007/978-3-031-32793-3_1

policy more generally. Welfare states enact social policies as measures to meet human needs and to respond to social problems. These social problems are not necessarily social in their causes or solutions, but the social responsibility that the welfare state takes on for an issue makes the problem a *social* one (Gusfield, 1989).

As scientific studies from medicine and psychology have accumulated evidence suggesting that many social problems (e.g., aging, poverty, unemployment, disability, low educational achievement, homelessness, and problems in childhood or adolescence) have both biological and psychological causes and consequences, the *ideas* from these disciplines influence how such problems are constructed in welfare discourses. For instance, scientific studies and governmental reports have revealed that unemployed, poor, and homeless people across Western countries are much more likely to suffer from physical or mental illness (BMAS, 2021; e.g., Dufford et al., 2020; Fazel et al., 2014; Paul & Moser, 2009; UCL Institute of Health Equity, 2013). These health inequalities are usually the result of disadvantaged material and social situations (UCL Institute of Health Equity, 2013). Nevertheless, in welfare discourses, targeting health through preventive, curative, and rehabilitative measures has repeatedly been presented as a solution to unemployment and poverty:

> **The health status of individuals strongly influences their labour market participation.** For example, early labour market exit is often the result of health-related problems. (European Commission, 2013, p. 11; bold in original)

> It is therefore possible **to boost economic growth by improving the health status of the population and enabling people to remain active and in better health for longer.** Access to quality health care is a constituent part of the maintenance of a productive workforce and an integral part of the flexicurity setup. (European Commission, 2013, p. 12; bold in original)

This example from the European Commission's communication about the Social Investment Package promotes "access to quality healthcare" as a strategy for solving social problems and achieving social and economic goals. While the example references health as a rather general notion, concrete medical and psychological concepts and theories are taken up in the discourse on social problems. Personality traits, resilience, and self-efficacy have become popular concepts for understanding inequalities and social disadvantage from a psychological perspective (Friedli, 2015; Haushofer & Fehr, 2014). Economic Nobel laureate James J. Heckman, for instance, has advocated for early childhood programs as the most effective solution to poverty. Heckman bases his argument on the concept of character skills, which "personality psychologists have studied [...] for the past century" (Heckman & Kautz, 2013, p. 10):

> The foundations for adult success are laid down early in life. Many children raised in disadvantaged environments start behind and stay behind. Poverty has lasting effects on brain development, health, cognition, and character. Gaps in skills emerge early, before formal school begins. Waiting until kindergarten to address these gaps is too late. It creates achievement gaps for disadvantaged children that are costly to close. (Heckman & Kautz, 2013, p. 7)

Over the last five decades, a large body of social science research has investigated how medicine and psychology have become more important in societies (Foster, 2016; Nye, 2003). These processes—which can be described as *medicalization* and *psychologization*—have been identified through the growing role of medical and psychological concepts in the discourses outlined above. However, the processes do not unfold in discourses alone. Indeed, it is also through *actors* as well as their promotion of and increasing use of medical and psychological practices that we can determine medicalization and psychologization. For instance, in Western countries, physicians and psychologists are often easily accessible, and it is thus in their offices that social problems frequently show up or end up. In a survey of general practitioners in one region of Germany, respondents reported that in over half of all consultations, social problems represented at least part of the reason why individuals had come into the doctor's office. However, most medical doctors in this survey had felt forced to give their patients a medical diagnosis and had been willing to give them a sick leave certificate, even if they could not identify a medical problem (Wilfer et al., 2018). This practice has even been acknowledged in the recent version of the International Classification of Disease (ICD), in which Chapter 24 now includes "problems associated with employment or unemployment," "problems associated with education," and "problems associated with social insurance or welfare" for "occasions when circumstances other than a disease, injury or external cause classifiable elsewhere are recorded as 'diagnoses' or 'problems'" (World Health Organization, 2022).

Psychology has developed its own diagnostic tools and techniques—such as personality tests—and instruments for assessing motivation, resilience, and so on, which are regularly applied when profiling unemployed people or when assessing children with social or education problems. Not only are these concepts applied by psychologists themselves, but they have become widely diffused into various social professions, such as education and social work (Ecclestone & Brunila, 2015). Moreover, caseworkers in the welfare administration rely on these tools and techniques, as outlined in a report on youth unemployment by the International Labour Organization:

> Although screening techniques vary from country to country, the degree of risk is usually assessed using psychological models (based predominantly on unobservable characteristics, such as motivation, self-efficiency, personal behaviour and attitudes). [...] Attitudinal diagnostic tools aim to identify jobseekers whose attitudes represent a barrier to finding a job, and design activities to change individuals' behaviour. Examples of attitudinal screening tools can be found in Denmark (*Job Barometer*), France (*Copilote Insertion*), Germany (*Placement Characteristics*) and Portugal (*Forecast Guide to the Difficulties of Insertion*). (International Labour Organization/European Commission, 2017, p. 15)

The influence of medicine and psychology in the welfare state is also tied to *institutions*. The institutional setup of welfare states puts physicians and psychologists in a powerful position that has received little attention in the literature on the welfare state. Indeed, medical doctors' and psychologists' opinions are central to making decisions not only about who should receive medical treatment, but also about who is eligible for long-term care, sick leave, and incapacity benefits (Aurich-Beerheide & Brussig, 2017). Medical doctors and psychologists are involved in assessing *who* is able to work, *when*, and *for how long*. They are consulted when deciding which children are ready for school, require special education, or should be exempted from certain school subjects or from receiving grades in these subjects (Ecclestone & Hayes, 2009; Harwood & Allan, 2016). In particular, the welfare state seeks the expertise of medical doctors and psychologists if claims are controversial or if other efforts fail. Thus, members of these professions are regularly involved in decision-making on social rights and obligations in the welfare state. Their role is so significant because they are called upon to settle conflicts and controversies created by existing institutional structures:

> Since *social security between citizens* (as in labor law) and the *social benefits of the community* (such as social insurance, social assistance etc.) are all too often and to a large extent indispensably linked to treatment processes or illnesses for which the physician is the only competent assessor, the physician becomes the arbitrator in the welfare state. In contrast, employers' human resource departments—as well as social administrations, labor courts, and social courts, to name the most important examples—often perform only an executive function. (Zacher, 1985, p. 223; translated from German, emphasis in original)

1.1 Moving Toward a Biopsychosocial Welfare State?

Why have we chosen to study the influence of the two disciplines of medicine and psychology in the welfare state? It could be argued that science and professions in general have become more important in the organization of the welfare state. While there is convincing evidence for this hypothesis, others have in fact investigated this extensively (e.g., Blom et al., 2017; Brückweh, 2012). We focus in this book on medicalization and psychologization in the welfare state not as an example of a general scientization or professionalization of social policies; rather through our focus we aim to uncover the qualitative changes that stem from including medicine and psychology in our understanding of social problems and social policies as compared with a situation in which *social* ideas and measures guide welfare states.

The cultural narrative in which the welfare state is embedded is one in which the state deals with problems that originate in social relations and solves these problems by providing social rights and services. Our understanding of the medicalization and psychologization of the welfare state does not mean that either of these disciplines (or both together) have taken over the welfare state. However, both disciplines have indeed changed the narrative by adding ideas, techniques, and the voices of the professionals who work within them to what had formerly been considered "social problems," thereby also rendering these problems medical and psychological. Medicine and psychology, however, do not merely make the picture more colorful; rather, their disciplinary backgrounds provide a qualitative change to our understanding of the above-mentioned problems. Since medicine and psychology focus primarily on the individual (the body, genetic makeup, thoughts, emotions, personality, etc.) rather than on the social relations between individuals (which can be economic, political, social, cultural, etc.), the medicalization and psychologization of social issues shifts the perspective to a more individualized notion of the problem.

To highlight the fact that our understanding of the medicalization and psychologization of the welfare state represents a process of growing interdisciplinarity and complexity rather than a takeover of the welfare state by these disciplines, we draw on the concept of the biopsychosocial model as a metaphor for the development we have identified. The biopsychosocial model was developed by George L. Engel in 1977 to illustrate the complex interplay of biological, psychological, and social factors in the genesis of health or illness (Engel, 1977). The model is a widely known framework that illustrates how these three factors are linked and interrelated. We can imagine the changing role of medicine and psychology in the welfare state in a similar way since the influence of these disciplines has been linked to and integrated with existing social ideas, actors, and practices.

This book was written for scholars and students of social policy who are interested in the welfare state. By including the role of medicine and psychology in our concepts and analyses, we can gain a new perspective on the institutional configurations and historical dynamics of the welfare state. This book was also written for students and researchers who are interested in medicalization and psychologization. If our goal is to understand these processes better, we must not merely consider the welfare state an abstract phenomenon, but instead deconstruct it to see how it can be an agent of for (de-)medicalization and (de-)psychologization and the concrete institutional context in which these processes unfold. Therefore, we examine three social problems in this book to see how the welfare state works through specific institutions, ideas, and actors in concrete fields of social policy.

1.2 An Academic Dialogue

As outlined above, examining the role of medicine and psychology in the welfare state should prove interesting to readers from two fields of academic inquiry: *medicalization and psychologization research* on the one hand and *welfare state research* on the other hand. The purpose of this book is to bring these two fields together and to foster a lacking academic dialogue. Such an exchange of ideas can provide both fields with new perspectives on their research objects and their theoretical frameworks and can also uncover novel empirical puzzles and research strategies.

Medicalization and psychologization research is an interdisciplinary research area that is strongly influenced by writers from philosophy, medical sociology, cultural sociology, and critical psychology. The research we review here as medicalization and psychologization research is a large body of work that uses a variety of theoretical concepts, including "medicalization," "biomedicalization," "psychologization," "therapeutization," "therapy culture," and Foucault's concepts of "biopower" and "biopolitics" (e.g., Conrad, 1992, 2007; Nolan, 1998). What all this research includes as either a single element or a focal point is an analysis of how medicine and/or psychology—that is, the ideas, practices, and professions of medicine and psychology—have become central to how modern societies deal with problems and govern life. Some contributions to medicalization and psychologization have been critical of this development and have been concerned, for instance, with the depoliticization of social issues or the transfer of social control to medical and psy-professions. Other scholars have used the abovementioned processes as analytical concepts and aim first and foremost to describe and explain these processes.

From the beginning, the sociopolitical consequences of medicalization and psychologization have formed an integral part of this research area (e.g., Foucault, 1976 [1973]; Szasz, 1960; Zola, 1975). In works that specifically deal with the state, it is clear that medical and psychological ideas, practices, and professions have been considered to legitimize the modern state (Nolan, 1998) or to provide a form governmentality that resonates with the ideational basis of liberal democracies (Rose, 1998). However, in these contributions, the state is treated as an abstract, complex phenomenon, and little interest is paid to its specifics. In contrast, we consider the state to be an actor in medicalization and psychologization processes as well as to provide a context that impacts these processes depending on its specific institutional configuration (Bourgeault, 2017). Adding such an institutional perspective of the state provides a tool for better understanding how and why medicalization and psychologization vary across countries and over time (Olafsdottir & Beckfield, 2011). A specific analysis of the welfare state as the cornerstone of the modern state (Kaufmann, 2012; Rothgang et al., 2006) also highlights how medicalization and psychologization are associated with the social stratification of societies. Moreover, examining medicalization and psychologization in the context of the *social* welfare state allows us to expand the ideas of simultaneity and layering. Our image of the *biopsychosocial welfare state* builds on the idea that medicalization and psychologization do not need to be conceptualized as having successfully dominated a given problem by assuming a single professional perspective; rather, they can also be conceived concurrently with other approaches in a "layering of institutional control and [an] increasing multi-institutional management of social problems" (Medina & McCraine, 2011, p. 139).

Welfare state research is also an interdisciplinary field that receives contributions from political science, sociology, history, and economics but that constitutes a much more coherent research discourse in comparison. The field of welfare state research theorizes, describes, and analyzes the development both of different social policy programs and of the welfare state as a coherent macro-phenomenon. This field is interested in explaining the dynamics of welfare discourses and policies and aims to establish causal relations between the welfare state and various outcomes on both the macro-level (e.g., growth) and the micro-level (e.g., educational attainment). The welfare state is not merely one function of the state; rather, it is what makes a state a modern state—that is, what distinguishes a modern state from earlier forms of statehood (Kaufmann, 2012). Integral to welfare state research is the segmentation of research into various fields, such as pensions, healthcare, unemployment protection, and family policy. As a result, the influence of medicine and psychology has been subsumed into welfare state research under the field of healthcare, where the strong influence of the medical profession has long been acknowledged (Tuohy & O'Reilly, 1992).

For welfare state research, engagement with medicalization and psychologization offers a new perspective on the wide influence of medicine and psychology on the welfare state because the concepts and involvement of medicalization and psychologization cut across various welfare fields (see Table 1.1). The social-constructivist background of medicalization and psychologization research also provides analytical concepts that respond to the cultural turn of welfare state research (Pfau-Effinger, 2005; Sachweh, 2011). Specifically, this background adds an important dimension to the analysis of changing welfare discourses and reforms within both the neoliberal era and the most recent years, which have built on the social investment paradigm.

Table 1.1 Examples of how health and illness matter across various fields in welfare states (*unemployment* and *poverty* based on Eggs et al. (2014); *work* based on DAK-Gesundheit (2019); *homelessness* based on Schreiter et al. (2017); *families* based on AFET Bundesverband für Erziehungshilfe (2020) and Ravens-Sieberer et al. (2021); *education* based on Rommel et al. (2018) and KMK (2021); *social care* based on GBE Bund (2020))

Box 1: Examples of how health and illness matter across various fields in welfare states

- Unemployment and poverty: 40% of minimum-income recipients in Germany report having serious health limitations.
- Work: Sick days for mental illness have tripled over the last twenty years in Germany, with 2.2 million people taking sick leave days in 2019.
- Homelessness: 77% of homeless people in Germany suffer from mental illness.
- Families: About 3 million children (i.e., 1 in 4 children in Germany) grow up with at least one parent with mental illness (including addiction). One in five children (17.5%) is classified as having signs of psychological strain. This rate has increased to one in every three children (30.4%) since the onset of the COVID-19 pandemic.
- Education: In 2020, out of 8.83 million school children, 571,671 received special-needs education, 15% of 3- to 6-year-olds received logotherapy, and 16.7% of 14- to 17-year-olds received physical therapy.
- Social care: In 2019, 4.1 million people in Germany received social care. The need for such care is assessed by medical staff and based on medical and psychological criteria.

1.3 A German Case Study

This book developed within a research group entitled the "Medicalization and Psychologization of Social Problems: Challenges and Chances for Social Policy (MEPYSO)," which was funded by the German Ministry of Labour and Social Affairs. Our research focuses on medicalization and psychologization within the German welfare state. We consider an investigation into the move toward a biopsychosocial welfare state within the German context to be both innovative and theoretically fruitful. Such an investigation is *innovative* because most existing work on medicalization and psychologization has focused on either liberal or social-democratic welfare states, particularly if this work has linked these processes to social policy and to the welfare state (*Scotland*: Allan & Harwood, 2014; *England/Finland*: Ecclestone & Brunila, 2015; *England/Scotland*: Friedli, 2015; *England*: Garthwaite, 2014; *USA*: Hansen et al., 2014; *Sweden*: Holmqvist, 2009; *England*: Macvarish et al., 2015; *Norway*: Madsen, 2014; *USA*: Nolan, 1998; *Canada*: Pulkingham & Fuller, 2012; *England*: Rose, 1985, 1998; *USA*: Schram, 2000; *England/USA*: Wastell

& White, 2012; *USA*: Wong, 2016). There are good reasons for this focus: in social-democratic welfare states, medicalization and psychologization are considered to be forms of well-intentioned "generosity" and serve as an explanation for why standard social services have not yet solved existing social problems (Holmqvist, 2009). In liberal welfare states, medicalization and psychologization are instead portrayed as institutionally created necessities or last resorts, with losing a disability status, for instance, potentially meaning no longer having access to any type of benefits at all (e.g., Hansen et al., 2014; Wong, 2016). These results suggest that medicalization and psychologization can be institutionally linked both to strong conditionality (liberal welfare states) and to the universalist orientation (social-democratic welfare states) of welfare states. Therefore, a study from another world of welfare states is important to understanding whether and how medicalization and psychologization unfold in a system with a welfare orientation that includes a mixture of both elements.

As a conservative welfare state, Germany is a *theoretically interesting* case, because it has specific institutional features that could shed light on other mechanisms that pertain to how the state is involved in processes of medicalization and psychologization. Moreover, the German welfare state has experienced a strong reform dynamic over the last three decades, which allows us to investigate how medicalization and psychologization are incorporated into paradigmatic changes that are associated with ideas of neoliberalism and social investment.

In comparative welfare state research, Germany constitutes the archetype of the conservative welfare state regime (Esping-Andersen, 1990). In Germany, social policy is strongly based on social insurance systems with earnings-related contributions and benefits and with family policies oriented toward a male-breadwinner model. An important aspect of this institutional configuration is a strong demarcation between different welfare programs, which creates problems when different social problems intersect. Social policies are also strongly codified in the 12 books of the German Social Code. Benefits and services are thus institutionalized as social rights. Citizens perceive these benefits and services as individual social rights because contributions for pension, healthcare, unemployment, and social care insurance are taken directly from citizens' monthly employment income, as is visible on each individual paycheck. Another important feature of the German welfare system is corporatism. The self-governance of corporate actors grants physician organizations in Germany direct decision-making power in the public health insurance system.

Over the last few decades, Germany has borne witness to a strong reform dynamic in different sectors of the welfare state. This dynamic was influenced in the 1990s and 2000s by neoliberal thinking, and since the 2000s, it has also been influenced by the social investment paradigm. Neoliberal reforms to unemployment and social assistance programs have strongly increased the conditionality of welfare benefits and imposed work obligations on all non-employed people unless their health status precludes them from working. Social investment ideas have influenced the shift in German family policy. While Germany has long supported a male-breadwinner family model, the introduction of an earnings-related maternity leave and the substantial expansion to childcare facilities have created strong support for mothers' employment participation. Some scholars have argued that the passing of these fundamental reforms "no longer warrants labeling Germany a conservative welfare state" (Seeleib-Kaiser, 2016, p. 235), while others consider "[t]he German social insurance state [to be] alive and kicking" (Blank, 2019, p. 522). In any case, this dynamic provides an empirically interesting case for studying how medical and psychological ideas, practices, and actors have been, respectively, the fuel, catalyst, and outcome of these welfare state reforms.

The focus used in past reforms guided the selection of the social problems or social policy areas that we analyzed in our research. First, because one of the most significant transformations in the German welfare state was the reform of the German unemployment and social assistance system in the early 2000s, we studied the medicalization and psychologization of *unemployment* and *poverty*, thereby adding to an evolving body of international literature on these issues (Buffel et al., 2017; Friedli, 2015; Hansen et al., 2014; Shepherd & Wilson, 2018; Wong, 2016). We extend this work by linking medicine and psychology as two distinct yet strongly interactive disciplines and professions that have changed their role in dealing with poverty and unemployment. Second, family policy reforms—and particularly the reforms that expanded and transformed childcare in Germany—reflect the new level of attention that is paid to early childhood in German social policy. Children in families with difficult circumstances and issues of child protection constitute another area in which new policies have been enacted. Such policies include the National Initiative for Early Childhood Intervention, which was launched in 2006. Viewing difficulties in childhood as a social problem also resonates with the medicalization and psychologization literature, which has long considered the changing role of medicine and psychology in childhood to be an important research topic (e.g., Conrad, 1975; Ramey, 2015; Timimi, 2002).

1.4 Medicine and Psychology in Germany

Medicine and psychology are both popular academic disciplines in Germany. For years, access to the two fields of study has been restricted because demand has exceeded the number of available places at universities (Fehling, 2018). Medicine is clearly the more powerful profession in Germany as it holds a strong position in the self-governing body of the German healthcare system in the form of the Federal Joint Committee. With 4.3 medical doctors per 1000 population, Germany has a high physician density, ranking 6th in a 2018 comparison of 28 OECD nations (OECD average: 3.6) (OECD, 2021). As in many Western countries, the number of physicians in Germany has increased immensely from a historical perspective. There was one medical doctor per roughly 3000 inhabitants in 1885, one per 700 inhabitants in 1952, one per 329 inhabitants in 1991 (Busse & Blümel, 2014), and finally one medical doctor per 233 inhabitants in 2019 (OECD, 2021).

However, psychology has also grown substantially in importance. Table 1.1 illustrates this development quantitatively. Until 2007, there were about twice as many students studying medicine compared with psychology. Between 2007 and 2020, the number of students enrolled in psychology increased by 223%, and the figure fully caught up to medicine despite the simultaneous increase in the number of medical students between 2010 and 2020 (Fig. 1.1).

Psychology also consolidated its professional status in 1999 with its acknowledgment as an independent profession (psychological psychotherapist) and the right for these professionals to establish their own practices (PsychThG, 1998). In 2020, psychological psychotherapists also gained the right to see patients without a physician's referral, thereby increasing their independence from physicians in the outpatient healthcare sector (PsychThG, 2019). In light of these changes, the number of psychological psychotherapists rose from about 30,000 in 2006 to around 50,000 in 2020 (GBE Bund, 2021).

Most physicians and psychologists work in private practices, hospitals, and clinics. In their clinical practice, their diagnoses are often relevant when it comes to sick leave, social security benefits, welfare services, or exemptions from certain social obligations. Thus, many medical doctors and psychologists act as arbitrators for social problems both through their regular practice and as independent reviewers for courts and welfare

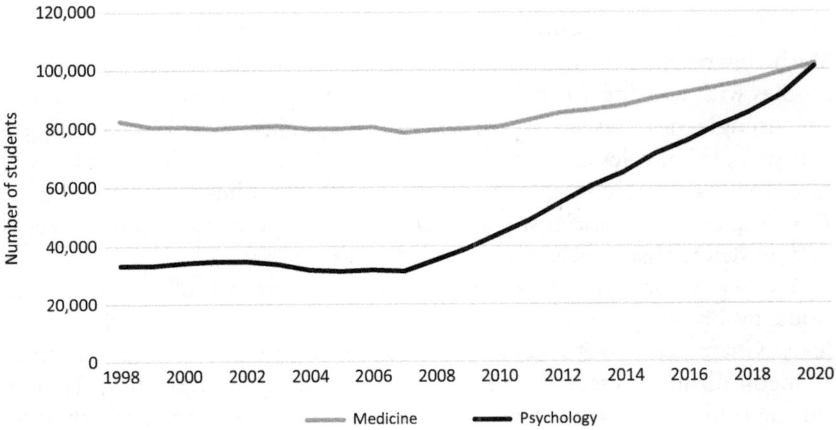

Fig. 1.1 Number of students of medicine and psychology in Germany, 1998–2020 (Statistisches Bundesamt [Destatis], 2022, own calculations)

administrations. Moreover, German statutory health insurance, statutory pensions insurance, and the Federal Employment Agency have individual medical review boards, and the Federal Employment Agency also has a psychological review board. In these boards, employed physicians and psychologists provide socio-medical expertise, which in many cases directly translates to a legal status that either grants or does not grant benefits (e.g., disability pensions), services (e.g., rehabilitative services), and obligations (e.g., active job search). Psychologists and medical doctors are also employed in communities and work in different social settings, such as schools. However, it is not the number of physicians and psychologists who work in a field that determines their influence on the welfare state. Indeed, it may be that the rather small number of physicians and psychologists who work in the welfare administration and in the political system (compared with in clinical practice) are the most influential in the medicalization and psychologization of social problems because their work is influenced by their professional socialization and professional networks. For instance, medical doctors who work in a ministry might be more inclined to support medical explanations or to call upon medical expertise for a given problem than would someone with a different professional background.

1.5 The Book

With this book, we aim to integrate research agendas from welfare state studies with existing work from the field of medicalization as well as with psychologization research. We thereby investigate the following questions: (1) What roles do medicine and psychology play in the welfare state? (2) How have these roles developed? (3) What implications does a move toward a biopsychosocial welfare state have? These broad questions serve as a guideline throughout the chapters of this book.

We begin our investigation into these questions in the first part of this book by bringing the diverse lines of research together on a theoretical level: Chap. 2 lays out the primary concepts and theoretical assumptions of medicalization research on the one hand and psychologization research on the other hand and offers a systematic comparison and currently lacking synthesis of the ideas found in these bodies of research. Chapter 3 then integrates this debate using theories from the welfare state and social policy research. Using the analytical dimensions of *ideas*, *actors*, and *institutions*, we develop a multifaceted theoretical framework that provides guidance on how to trace and understand medicalization and psychologization in the welfare state.

The second part of the book applies this framework to three social problems that are integral to welfare state activity: unemployment, poverty, and childhood problems. The chapters in this part illustrate medicalization and psychologization in the respective welfare fields by combining a multitude of data sources, including analyses of legal categories, qualitative and quantitative discourse analyses, analyses of bibliographic data, and analyses of data from an experimental vignette survey that we fielded in Germany in 2019. Chapter 4 illustrates how medicalization and psychologization have unfolded in the welfare state's response to unemployment. In this highly dynamic field of activating reforms, the boundaries between unemployment and disability and the importance of illness in precluding work obligations are illustrated and discussed in terms of the relevance of these issues to individuals' social rights and obligations, the social legitimacy associated with the status of sickness, and the continuous attempts of the government to "deal with long-term unemployment." Chapter 5 illustrates the medicalization and psychologization of poverty by showing how the two disciplines have gained ground both quantitatively—in the scientific discourse on poverty—and qualitatively—through the elaboration of poverty as a multidimensional concept in which notions of health and psychological concepts are integral. The role of scientists in the medicalization and psychologization of poverty can also be traced in the periodical governmental reports on poverty and wealth, but medical and psychological ideas are of little relevance in parliamentary debates on poverty. In Chap. 6, we turn to a field of welfare state activity that has become increasingly important over the past three decades: policies that address children and children's problems. We investigate the role of interest groups in the medicalization and psychologization of children and study institutional implications in terms of the relevance of diagnostic categories for social rights in the field of education. Finally, we describe the results from our survey, which shows the legitimacy of social rights and the obligations that the general public considers to be adequate for children with emotional and behavioral problems.

Finally, in the third part of the book, Chap. 7 discusses how the move toward the biopsychosocial welfare state can be interpreted partially as a result of how medical and psychological explanations and interventions have resonated with the two dominant social policy paradigms that have guided the transformation of the welfare state over the past decades: neoliberalism and social investment. The concern that the medicalization and psychologization of social problems is accompanied by individualization and depoliticization is visible in parts of our empirical results, particularly during the period of the neoliberal restructuring of welfare policies. However, we can also see how medical and psychological arguments have been used to argue for greater societal responsibility and social solutions, particularly in more recent years. This shift reflects a greater focus on social investment ideas as well as on learning from difficulties that stem from neoliberal policy changes. Finally, in Chap. 8, we summarize the key lessons learned from our research as presented throughout the chapters and look to the future of the biopsychosocial welfare stateWelfare state.

References

AFET Bundesverband für Erziehungshilfe. (2020). *Abschlussbericht: Arbeitsgruppe*. Kinder psychisch- und suchtkranker Eltern. Hannover.

Allan, J., & Harwood, V. (2014). Medicus interruptus in the behaviour of children in disadvantaged contexts in Scotland. *British Journal of Sociology of Education, 35*(3), 413–443. https://doi.org/10.1080/01425692.2013.776933

Aurich-Beerheide, P., & Brussig, M. (2017). Assessment of work ability in competing strands of social insurance: the German case. *Journal of Poverty and Social Justice, 25*(2), 163–176. https://doi.org/10.1332/175982717X14937395831424

Blank, F. (2019). The state of the German social insurance state: Reform and resilience. *Social Policy and Administration, 54*(3), 505–524. https://doi.org/10.1111/spol.12542

Blom, B., Evertsson, L., Perlinski, M., & (Eds.). (2017). *Social and caring professions in European welfare states: Policies, services and professional practices.* Policy Press.

BMAS. (2021). *Lebenslagen in Deutschland: Der 6. Armuts- und Reichtumsbericht der Bundesregierung.* Berlin.

Bourgeault, I. L. (2017). Conceptualizing the Social and Political Context of the Health workforce: Health Professions, the State, and its Gender Dimensions. *Frontiers in Sociology, 2*(16). https://doi.org/10.3389/fsoc.2017.00016.

Brückweh, K. (Ed.). (2012). *Engineering society: The role of the human and social sciences in modern societies, 1880–1980.* Palgrave Macmillan. https://doi.org/10.1057/9781137284501

Buffel, V., Beckfield, J., & Bracke, P. F. (2017). The institutional foundations of medicalization: A cross-national analysis of mental health and unemployment. *Journal of Health and Social Behavior, 58*(3), 272–290. https://doi.org/10.1177/0022146517716232

Busse, R., & Blümel, M. (2014). Germany: Health system review. *Health Systems in Transition, 16*(2), 1–296.

Conrad, P. (1975). The discovery of hyperkinesis: Notes on the medicalization of deviant behavior. *Social Problems, 23*(1), 12–21.

Conrad, P. (1992). Medicalization and social control. *Annual Review of Sociology, 18*(1), 209–232. https://doi.org/10.1146/annurev.so.18.080192.001233

Conrad, P. (2007). *The medicalization of society: On the transformation of human conditions into treatable disorders.* Johns Hopkins University Press.

DAK-Gesundheit. (2019). *Psychoreport 2019: Entwicklung der psychischen Erkrankungen im Job. Langzeitanalyse; 1997–2018.* IGES Insitut GmbH.

Dufford, A. J., Kim, P., & Evans, G. W. (2020). The impact of childhood poverty on brain health: Emerging evidence from neuroimaging across the lifespan. *International Review of Neurobiology, 150*, 77–105. https://doi.org/10.1016/bs.irn.2019.12.001

Ecclestone, K., & Brunila, K. (2015). Governing emotionally vulnerable subjects and 'therapisation' of social justice. *Pedagogy, Culture & Society, 23*(4), 485–506. https://doi.org/10.1080/14681366.2015.1015152

Ecclestone, K., & Hayes, D. (2009). *The dangerous rise of therapeutic education.* Routledge.

Eggs, J., Trappmann, M., & Unger, S. (2014). *Grundsicherungsempfänger und Erwerbstätige im Vergleich: ALG – II – Bezieher schätzen ihre Gesundheit schlechter ein*. IAB Kurzbericht 23/2014.

Engel, G. L. (1977). The need for a new medical model: A challenge for biomedicine. *Science, 196*(4286), 129–136. https://doi.org/10.1126/science.847460

Esping-Andersen, G. (1990). *The three worlds of welfare capitalism*. Wiley. https://books.google.de/books?id=KHdnAgAAQBAJ

European Commission. (2013, February 20). *Communication from the Commission to the European Parliament, the Council, the European Economic and Social Committee and the Committee of the Regions: Towards Social Investment for Growth and Cohesion – including implementing the European Social Fund 2014–2020*. Brussels. European Commission.

Fazel, S., Geddes, J. R., & Kushel, M. (2014). The health of homeless people in high-income countries: Descriptive epidemiology, health consequences, and clinical and policy recommendations. *The Lancet, 384*(9953), 1529–1540. https://doi.org/10.1016/S0140-6736(14)61132-6

Fehling, M. (2018). Die Verteilung des Mangels – Zum neuen Numerus Clausus-Urteil des Bundesverfassungsgerichts. *Recht der Jugend und des Bildungswesens, 66*(1), 100–111. https://doi.org/10.5771/0034-1312-2018-1-100

Foster, R. (2016). Therapeutic culture, authenticity and neo-liberalism. *History of the Human Sciences, 29*(1), 99–116. https://doi.org/10.1177/0952695115617384

Foucault, M. (1976 [1973]). *The birth of the clinic: An archaeology of medical perception*. Tavistock.

Friedli, L. (2015). The politics of tackling inequalities: The rise of psychological fundamentalism in public health and welfare reform. In K. E. Smith, C. Bambra, & S. E. Hill (Eds.), *Health inequalities: Critical perspectives* (pp. 206–221). Oxford University Press.

Garthwaite, K. (2014). Fear of the brown envelope: Exploring welfare reform with long-term sickness benefits recipients. *Social Policy & Administration, 48*(7), 782–798. https://doi.org/10.1111/spol.12049

GBE Bund. (2020). *Pflegestatistik*. https://www.gbe-bund.de/gbe/pkg_isgbe5.prc_menu_olap?p_uid=gast&p_aid=76748832&p_sprache=D&p_help=0&p_indnr=510&p_indsp=138&p_ityp=H&p_fid=

GBE Bund. (2021). *Psychologische Psychotherapeutinnen und -therapeuten und Kinder- und Jugendlichenpsychotherapeutinnen und -therapeuten*. https://www.gbe-bund.de/gbe/pkg_isgbe5.prc_menu_olap?p_uid=gast&p_aid=42524296&p_sprache=D&p_help=3&p_indnr=697&p_indsp=&p_ityp=H&p_fid=

Gesetz über den Beruf der Psychotherapeurin und des Psychotherapeuten, November 15, 2019.

Gesetz über die Berufe des Psychologischen Psychotherapeuten und des Kinder- und Jugendpsychotherapeuten, June 16, 1998.
Gusfield, J. R. (1989). Constructing the ownership of social problems: Fun and profit in the welfare state. *Social Problems, 36*(5), 431–441. https://doi.org/10.2307/3096810 .
Hansen, H., Bourgois, P., & Drucker, E. (2014). Pathologizing poverty: New forms of diagnosis, disability, and structural stigma under welfare reform. *Social Science & Medicine, 103*, 76–83. https://doi.org/10.1016/j.socscimed.2013.06.033
Harwood, V., & Allan, J. (2016). *Psychopathology at school: Theorizing mental disorders in education*. Theorizing education series. Routledge.
Haushofer, J., & Fehr, E. (2014). On the psychology of poverty. *Science, 344*(6186), 862–867. https://doi.org/10.1126/science.1232491
Heckman, J. J., & Kautz, T. (2013). *Fostering and measuring skills: Interventions that improve character and cognition*. National Bureau of Economic Research.
Holmqvist, M. (2009). Medicalization of unemployment: Individualizing social issues as personal problems in the Swedish welfare state. *Work, Employment and Society, 23*(3), 405–421. https://doi.org/10.1177/0950017009337063
International Labour Organization/European Commission. (2017). *Profiling youth labour market disadvantage: A review of approaches in Europe*. International Labour Organization.
Kaufmann, F.-X. (2012). *European foundations of the welfare state*. Berghahn Books. http://site.ebrary.com/lib/uniregensburg/Doc?id=10583759
Macvarish, J., Lee, E., & Lowe, P. (2015). Neuroscience and family policy: What becomes of the parent? *Critical Social Policy, 35*(2), 248–269. https://doi.org/10.1177/0261018315574019
Madsen, O. J. (2014). Psychologisation and critique in modern-day western culture. *Social and Personality Psychology Compass, 8*(5), 193–200. https://doi.org/10.1111/spc3.12103.
Medina, T. R., & McCraine, A. (2011). Layering control: Medicalization, psychopathy, and the increasing multi-institutional management of social problems. In B. A. Pescosolido, J. K. Martin, J. D. Mclead, & A. Rogers (Eds.), *Handbook of the sociology of health, illness, and healing: A Blueprint for the 21st century* (pp. 139–158). Springer.
Nolan, J. L. (1998). *The therapeutic state: Justifying government at century's end*. New York University Press. http://www.loc.gov/catdir/enhancements/fy0808/97021234-b.html
Nye, R. A. (2003). The evolution of the concept of medicalization in the late twentieth century. *Journal of History of the Behavioral Sciences, 39*(2), 115–129.
OECD. (2021). *OECD Health Statistics 2021*. https://stats.oecd.org/Index.aspx?ThemeTreeId=9

Olafsdottir, S., & Beckfield, J. (2011). Health and the social rights of citizenship: Integrating welfare-state theory and medical sociology. In B. A. Pescosolido, J. K. Martin, J. D. Mclead, & A. Rogers (Eds.), *Handbook of the sociology of health, illness, and healing: A Blueprint for the 21st century* (pp. 101–115). Springer.

Paul, K. I., & Moser, K. (2009). Unemployment impairs mental health: Meta-analyses. *Journal of Vocational Behavior, 74*(3), 264–282. https://doi.org/10.1016/j.jvb.2009.01.001

Pfau-Effinger, B. (2005). Culture and welfare state policies: Reflections on a complex interrelation. *Journal of Social Policy, 34*(1), 3–20.

Pulkingham, J., & Fuller, S. (2012). From parent to patient: The medicalization of lone motherhood through welfare reform. *Social Politics: International Studies in Gender, State & Society, 19*(2), 243–268. https://doi.org/10.1093/sp/jxs007

Ramey, D. M. (2015). The social structure of criminalized and medicalized school discipline. *Sociology of Education, 88*(3), 181–201. https://doi.org/10.1177/0038040715587114

Ravens-Sieberer, U., Kaman, A., Erhart, M., Devine, J., Schlack, R., & Otto, C. (2021). Impact of the COVID-19 pandemic on quality of life and mental health in children and adolescents in Germany. *European Child & Adolescent Psychiatry* 31(6): 879-889. https://doi.org/10.1007/s00787-021-01726-5

Rommel, A., Hintzpeter, B., & Urbanski, D. (2018). Inanspruchnahme von Physiotherapie, Logopädie und Ergotherapie bei Kindern und Jugendlichen in Deutschland – Querschnittergebnisse aus KiGGS Welle 2 und Trends. *Journal of Health Monitoring, 3*(4), 22–37. https://doi.org/10.17886/RKI-GBE-2018-090

Rose, N. S. (1985). *The psychological complex: Psychology, politics and society in England; 1869–1939*. Routledge & Paul.

Rose, N. S. (1998). *Inventing ourselves: Psychology, power, and personhood*. Cambridge University Press.

Rothgang, H., Obinger, H., & Leibfried, S. (2006). The state and its welfare state: How do welfare state changes affect the make-up of the nation state? *Social Policy and Administration, 40*(3), 250–266. https://doi.org/10.1111/j.1467-9515.2006.00488.x

Sachweh, P. (2011). Ideen, Werte und Kultur als Erklärungsfaktoren in der Wohlfahrtsstaatsforschung. *Zeitschrift Für Sozialreform, 57*(4), 371–382. https://doi.org/10.1515/zsr-2011-0402

Schram, S. F. (2000). *After welfare: The culture of postindustrial social policy*. New York University Press. http://www.loc.gov/catdir/enhancements/fy0807/99006916-b.html

Schreiter, S., Bermpohl, F., Krausz, M., Leucht, S., Rössler, W., Schouler-Ocak, M., & Gutwinski, S. (2017). The prevalence of mental illness in homeless peo-

ple in Germany – A systematic review and meta-analysis. *Deutsches Ärzteblatt International, 114*, 665–672. https//doi.org/10.3238/arztebl.2017.0665 .
Seeleib-Kaiser, M. (2016). The end of the conservative german welfare state model. *Social Policy & Administration, 50*(2), 219–240. https://doi.org/10.1111/spol.12212
Sekretariat der Ständigen Konferenz der Kultusminister der Länder in der Bundesrepublik Deutschland IVC/Statistik. (2021). *Sonderpädagogische Förderung in allgemeinen Schulen (ohne Förderschulen): 2019/2020.* https://www.kmk.org/fileadmin/Dateien/pdf/Statistik/Dokumentationen/Aus_SoPae_Int_2019.pdf
Shepherd, L., & Wilson, R. F. (2018). Introduction: The medicalization of poverty. *The Journal of Law, Medicine and Ethics, 46*, 563–566. https://doi.org/10.1177/1073110518804197
Statistisches Bundesamt. (2022). *Hochschulstatistik.* www.genesis-destatis.de
Szasz, T. S. (1960). The myth of mental illness. *American Psychologist, 15*(2), 113–118. https://doi.org/10.1037/h0046535
Timimi, S. (2002). *Pathological child psychiatry and the medicalization of childhood.* Routledge.
Tuohy, C., & O'Reilly, P. (1992). Professionalism in the welfare state. *Journal of Canadian Studies, 27*(1), 73–92. https://doi.org/10.3138/jcs.27.1.73
UCL Institute of Health Equity. (2013). *Health Inequalities in the EU – Final Report of the Consortium.* Consortium Lead: Sir Michael Marmot. https://doi.org/10.2772/34426
Wastell, D., & White, S. (2012). Blinded by neuroscience: Social policy, the family and the infant brain. *Families, Relationships and Societies, 1*(3), 397–414. https://doi.org/10.1332/204674312X656301
Wilfer, T., Braungardt, T., & Schneider, W. (2018). Soziale Probleme in der hausärztlichen Praxis. *Zeitschrift für Psychosomatische Medizin und Psychotherapie, 64*(3), 250–261. https://doi.org/10.13109/zptm.2018.64.3.250
Wong, S. (2016). Geographies of medicalized welfare: Spatial analysis of supplemental security income in the U.S., 2000–2010. *Social Science & Medicine, 160*, 9–19. https://doi.org/10.1016/j.socscimed.2016.05.018
World Health Organization. (2022). *ICD-11 for Mortality and Morbidity Statistics* (2nd Version). https://icd.who.int/
Zacher, H. F. (1985). Arzt und Sozialstaat. *Sozialer Fortschritt, 34*(10), 217–224.
Zola, I. K. (1975). In the name of health and illness: On some socio-political consequences of medical influence. *Social Science & Medicine (1967), 9*(2), 83–87. https://doi.org/10.1016/0037-7856(75)90098-0

CHAPTER 2

The Biopsychosocial Welfare State: A Theoretical Framework

Nadine Reibling and Lisa Bleckmann

In this chapter, we discuss concepts and theories that allow us to better understand and explain the prominent role of medicine and psychology in the German welfare state. Although most medical doctors and psychologists are paid by public health insurance and some also work as employees in public organizations, welfare state research has considered both professions—if at all—only in terms of their relevance to healthcare. However, over the last 10–15 years, several scholars have proposed that processes of medicalization and psychologization are linked in a more fundamental way to the welfare state and its institutions (Buffel et al., 2017; Holmqvist, 2012; Olafsdottir, 2011; Pulkingham & Fuller, 2012; Sage & Laurin, 2018; Schram, 2000; Wastell & White, 2012; Wong, 2016).

In fact, medicine and psychology have been relevant to the welfare state since its beginnings in the nineteenth century. Nikolas Rose (1996), for

N. Reibling (✉)
Fulda University of Applied Sciences, Fulda, Germany
e-mail: nadine.reibling@gw.hs-fulda.de

L. Bleckmann
University of Siegen, Siegen, Germany

N. Reibling, M. Ariaans (eds.), *Toward a Biopsychosocial Welfare State?*, https://doi.org/10.1007/978-3-031-32793-3_2

instance, claims that psychology and the welfare state developed not only around the same time (at the end of the nineteenth century), but also as part of an interdependent relationship: "As the human soul became the object of a positive science, human subjectivity and intersubjectivity became possible targets of government intervention" (Rose, 1996, p. 68). Nevertheless, recent contributions suggest that medicalization and psychologization in the welfare state have taken on new significance in parallel to changes to Western welfare states over the last three decades. "Concern with the psychological dimension has always been present in welfare practices but has typically played a subordinate role in political constructions of policy. We raise the idea that we have entered an epoch in which the 'psycho' resonates as surely as the 'social' alongside 'welfare'" (Stenner & Taylor, 2008, p. 415).

Our conceptual framework is based on the concepts of *medicalization* and *psychologization*. This framework contrasts with many recent contributions in the field, which are based on the notions of therapeutization, therapy culture, and/or biopolitics (e.g., Ecclestone & Hayes, 2009; Illouz, 2008; Lupton, 1995; Nolan, 1998; Rose, 2006). While these concepts were developed in order to better grasp a broader phenomenon independent of disciplinary and professional boundaries (Anhorn & Balzereit, 2016), we are explicitly interested in these boundaries as well as in relationships between these disciplines and professions. The processes of medicalization and psychologization certainly share many commonalities, and the boundaries between the two fields can quite often seem blurred, as, for example, with psychiatry. However, important differences also exist between medicalization and psychologization. These differences are evident not only in the professions themselves and in their roles and foundations in the (welfare) state, but also in terms of their consequences for individual subjects and for the welfare state.

In both this and the following chapter, we outline how we can identify, understand, and explain processes of medicalization and psychologization in the welfare state. To that end, in Chap 3, we first discuss medicalization theory, followed by accounts of psychologization, and we conclude with a systematic comparison of both processes. In Chap. 4, we integrate these theoretical approaches to welfare state theory in an analytical framework that specifies how we can (a) understand the role of medicine/psychology on different dimensions (actors, institutions, ideas) and levels (micro, meso, macro) of the welfare state and (b) explain cross-national differences and (c) changes over time.

2.1 Making Things Medical…

is how Peter Conrad (2007)—one of the most prominent American scholars in this field—synthesizes the concept of medicalization. At its core, the concept centers around understanding how and why social problems or conditions move into (and out of) the medical realm.

The significance of medicalization stems from its potential to describe and explain why the number of life problems and social conditions that have *become medical* has grown substantially in recent past decades. What used to be considered *madness* is now understood to be *mental illness*. *Drunkenness* is now acknowledged as *alcohol dependence*, *chronic stress at work* has been re-defined as *burnout syndrome*, and maladjusted child behavior has been classified as various forms of *childhood and adolescent behavioral and emotional disorders*, including *ADHD*. Most notably, this medicalization of society is visible in the rising number of medical diagnoses, for instance, in the International Standard Classification of Disease (ICD), which grew from 14,000 codes in Version 9 (1978) to 375,000 codes in Version 10 (1990) (Winters-Miner et al., 2014).

"Deviant behaviors" were among the first problems to become medicalized. With their seminal contribution, "From Badness to Sickness," Conrad and Schneider (1992) revealed that many phenomena that were once treated by religion or the justice system are now understood to be medical problems. This transfer of the social control of deviance to the field of medicine has accompanied the modernization of societies. While deviant behavior was among the first examples that sparked interest in processes of medicalization, later research has shown that the reach of medicalization goes much further. Two other frequently medicalized phenomena are "natural life processes," such as childbirth, involuntary childlessness, menopause, and impotence, and "everyday problems of living," such as sadness, loneliness, shyness, and fear (Davis, 2016, p. 221).

It was this empirical observation—namely, that more and more things were becoming medically defined and controlled by the medical profession—that sparked the development of medicalization theory from the 1950s to the 1970s. Early work took a predominantly critical perspective on the rising *medicalization* of society (Freidson, 1995; Illich, 1974; Szasz, 1960). On the one hand, researchers highlighted the risks and problems associated with *labeling* individuals as ill. Ironically, these risks and problems included both the concern that individuals would no longer take responsibility for their own problems (i.e., what individuals themselves can do) (Szasz, 1960) and the fear that responsibility would become individualized and that social causes would be ignored (i.e., what society can do for individuals) (Zola, 1972). On the other hand, concern was voiced over the fact that *social control* for many social problems was being transferred to the medical profession. This transfer was considered problematic because medical doctors' actions are generally perceived by the public as objective and scientific despite the fact that medical doctors are also guided by their own values and political objectives (Zola, 1975). As Robert Nye (2003, p. 116) put it, the "medical discourse reinforced a conception of reason as the enlightened self-interest of the rich and powerful and located the domain of unreason among women, the mad, the poor, and the criminal classes."

This early critical perspective of medicalization was attenuated in the further course of medicalization research. Peter Conrad, in particular, maintained that medicalization should first be seen as a descriptive and analytical concept that allows us to measure how the role of medicine has changed both for specific empirical phenomena and for society at large, independent of the consequences of this development. A vibrant body of research by Conrad and many others called a number of the early assumptions of medicalization theory into question.

First, medicalization is not a binary category (i.e., problems are not simply medicalized or not medicalized); instead, medicalization can be assessed "on at least three distinct levels: the conceptual, the institutional, and the interactional levels" (Conrad, 1992, p. 211). Thus, medicalization can mean that a problem is described in medical terms on the *conceptual level*, that it is treated with a medical approach on the *institutional level*, or that it involves the medical profession directly on the *interactional level*. Problems can be medicalized on these levels to varying degrees, such as minimally, partially, or fully.

Using such a differentiated perspective reveals that the hypothesis that medicalization has been continuously expanding—that is, that all aspects of society are becoming more and more medicalized—does not hold. Instead, the definition and treatment of problems is much more dynamic and regularly involves both medicalization *and* de-medicalization, sometimes simultaneously (Halfmann, 2012).

2.1.1 The "Medical" in "Medicalization"

While this differentiated perspective on medicalization is generally agreed upon, controversy exists around the core of the concept: In other words, what exactly should count as *medical*? How can we distinguish *medical* from *non-medical*? What are the necessary conditions for medicalization? Three positions are outlined here:

(1) *Narrow the concept 1: No medicalization without the medical profession*: At one end of the spectrum, Davis (2006) argues that the definition of medicalization has become blurred because the social control of the medical profession is no longer a necessary part of (conceptual) medicalization. Instead, the "medical" framing of a problem suffices in order to consider the problem *medicalized*. Davis warns against relying solely on language when diagnosing processes of medicalization since there is no clear guideline as to what constitutes a medical word, and indeed, many words (e.g., "symptom," "diagnosis") have both a medical and a non-medical meaning: How can a problem be fully medicalized, Davis asks, if no responsibility is transferred to the medical profession? Based on this analysis, Davis suggests that the concept of medicalization be sharpened and refocused on medicine as an institution.

(2) *Narrow the concept 2: No medicalization without a medical label*: Similar to Davis, Williams et al. (2017) argue for a narrower or stricter application of the concept of medicalization, but from a different angle. The authors claim that if medical treatments and technologies are used without defining the underlying problem as a medical problem (i.e., pathology), these medical treatments and technologies should not be considered a form of medicalization. The example the authors provide that they do not consider medicalization is the use of pharmaceuticals for purposes of enhancement (e.g., to sleep or concentrate better, even if no diagnosis has been made that indicates a problem). Thus, from their perspective, *conceptual medicalization* is the essential component of the concept.

(3) *Extend the concept: Medicalization outside of Western biomedicine*: At the other end of the spectrum, Correia (2017) asserts that the concept of medicalization remains overly narrow and overly conflated with both the biomedical model and the Western medical

profession. Correia therefore suggests that anything that has the ontological features of medicine from a philosophical perspective—regardless as to whether it is currently accepted in a medical context—should be included in the concept. According to Correia, "medicine can be defined as the use of discretionary-based skills that are taught to turn abstract principles into concrete situations according to specific truths aimed at health recovery" (Correia, 2017, p. 6). Correia thereby takes the opposite position from Davis and aims to undo the coupling of medicalization with the (Western) medical profession.[1]

This discussion is important because it illustrates how challenging it is to pinpoint the definition of medicalization. It is therefore critical to be clear with what we mean with our use of the term and how we aim to measure it empirically. In this book, we follow Halfmann (2012) in considering three dimensions of medicalization: For our purposes, medicalization includes (1) a rising use of medical *ideas* and concepts, (2) a stronger involvement of medical doctors as *actors*, and (3) an increasing *institution*alization of medicine, for example, through the requirement that a medical opinion be given. All three dimensions capture one aspect of medicalization and highlight the different mechanisms through which medicalization happens in discourses, in practices, and in institutions (see Chap. 3).

2.1.2 What Causes Medicalization?

An obvious first attempt at explaining medicalization involves investigating who benefits from the process. Thus, the power and activities of the *medical profession* are considered a source of medicalization. This notion has led many to believe that the concept of medicalization implies that it is driven by medical doctors who actively extend their jurisdiction and thereby increase their power. Pawluch (2017), for instance, argues that with the improved health of children after World War II and the declining number of children during the 1970s, "the specialty began to suggest that primary care pediatrics could be revitalized if pediatricians addressed themselves to children's unmet needs, particularly those that were not strictly medical" (Pawluch, 2017, p. 222). Thus, strategic actions by the

[1] In this sense, Correia argues for transforming the concept of medicalization into therapeutization since the definition of medicalization is focused on actions aimed at health recovery, which closely resembles the common understanding of the concept of "therapy."

medical profession are considered in this case to be a cause of medicalization. While these actions have certainly played a role in some cases, extreme versions of this argument that consider medicalization to be a form of "medical colonization" or "medical imperialism" are now rejected by most scholars in the field as they are not in line with empirical data (Busfield, 2017). Medical doctors are surely the central gatekeepers of the healthcare system and are therefore generally involved in processes of medicalization (Conrad, 2005), but they are quite often not the initiators. In fact, comparative-historical analyses indicate that whether, how, and when medical doctors engage in medicalization varies substantially across time and contexts, which suggests that the reasons for medicalization are more complex (Halfmann, 2019; Nye, 2003).

A second, important driver of medicalization includes activities by *individuals and social movements* that fight for the recognition of their problems as medical conditions. One example is alcoholism, which was advocated for by a social movement (Alcoholics Anonymous) and was only later accepted by the medical profession (Conrad & Schneider, 1992).

While medical doctors and social movements were seen as the primary drivers of medicalization in the twentieth century, Conrad (2005, p. 10, emphasis added) argues that "the engines of medicalization have proliferated and are now driven more by commercial and *market* interests than by professional claims-makers." This increasing importance of pharmaceutical, biomedical, and biotech companies in expanding the definitions of diseases has been a prominent feature of medicalization research[2] in US sociology due to the system's market orientation. This idea has also been taken up by Adele Clarke et al. (2003) in their concept of biomedicalization, in which they highlight "technoscientific innovations" and the "commodification of health" as fundamental aspects of biomedicalization.

However, not only the market but also the *state* is another important force behind medicalization. Early medicalization theorists highlighted this aspect and warned about the growing link between state power and medical power (Zola, 1972). This early perspective of the state's strategic use of medicalization to oppress groups has lost influence. To some extent, this is the result of the fact that much of the research on medicalization is based in the US, where market forces are comparatively strong and the welfare state's influence is considered to be modest. More importantly, the understanding of the role that the state plays in processes of

[2] Or, more specifically, of biomedicalization and pharmaceuticalization.

medicalization was transformed by the work of Michel Foucault (1991, 1976 [1973]). Both his late work and the research it has inspired consider medicalization to be a form of governance in modern liberal states. These governmentality studies have "abandoned the notion of an essentialized and willful state" (Nye, 2003, p. 118). In other words, medicalization is still linked to processes of knowledge, power, and governance within states. However, the state as an actor in its own right—as well as its specific institutions and their direct legal, material, and coercive power—has received little emphasis in this line of research.

Newer medicalization research, however, has posited that the state in general and the *institutions* of the welfare state in particular need to be reconsidered and seen as having a powerful influence on processes of medicalization (Buffel et al., 2017; Halfmann, 2019; Holmqvist, 2012; Olafsdottir, 2007). This claim is often the result of a comparative perspective that has shown that medicalization works quite differently across nations due to the way the welfare state is organized. The role of the state (i.e., its institutions and bureaucracies) can vary from that of an engine that powers processes of medicalization to that of a break that halts these processes (Reibling, 2019). More importantly, the existing institutions of the welfare state provide the context that shapes *how* medicine and psychology are included in both the discourse and practices around social problems. These institutions can be political and deal with topics ranging from constitutionalism (Halfmann, 2019) to the general welfare state regime (Olafsdottir, 2007), or they can belong to specific fields of government activity, such as unemployment insurance (Buffel et al., 2017).

2.2 Making Things Psychological?

The growing importance of psychology in modern societies has paralleled trends of growing medicalization (Castel, 1979; Gross, 1978; Havemann, 1957; Lasch, 1979; Rieff, 1987). However, while medicalization research has been strongly centered in medical sociology, the debate on psychologization is centered in other (sub-)disciplines, especially cultural sociology (Furedi, 2013; Illouz, 2008; Rieff, 1987), philosophy (Rose, 1996; de Vos, 2013), and critical psychology (Madsen, 2018; Madsen & Brinkmann, 2016). Even though medicine and psychology are used to address similar social problems, have similar consequences, and interact as professions in many social systems, debates on medicalization and psychologization have evolved separately and are only rarely compared or discussed (to some extent; see Madsen & Brinkmann, 2016). One reason for this is that the concept of psychologization has gained less ground than that of medicalization since psychologization has often been theoretically absorbed by the concepts of therapeutization or therapy culture. In these concepts, the focus has traditionally been on the therapeutic approach rather than on the psychological profession or on psychology as a discipline.

Nevertheless, existing definitions of psychologization generally center around the concept of a process that is similar to that of medicalization. For instance, Madsen (2014, p. 171) suggests that psychologization denotes a process in which "increasingly more non-psychological phenomena are understood as something that arises from and thereby has its natural solution in the psyche of the individual, or, even better, in the brain." This definition highlights the conceptual dimension of psychologization. This dimension—which describes the idea that psychologization works by forming knowledge and shaping discourses on social phenomena—has had a very strong focus in the literature. Rose (1985, 1996), however, advocates for another orientation and argues that we should also examine the technologies of psychology, such as diagnostic manuals, assessment tests, and therapeutic techniques. Rose argues that psychology has developed historically not through the scientific growth of psychological knowledge—as is commonly argued in histories of psychology—but rather as due to psychologists' work on solving practical problems in various organizations, such as "the school, the reformatory, the court, the army and the factory" (Rose, 1985, p. 5). Finally, some work has also examined the growing influence of the academic discipline and practical profession of psychology as an indication of psychologization. However, since the visibility and power of the profession is considered comparable to that of other academic professions (and lower than that of older professions, such as medicine), it is unclear whether the growing number of psychologists and psychotherapists represents psychologization or whether it is merely an expression of a general professionalization trend in modern democratic societies.

Numerous social issues reveal trends in psychologization. Such issues include romantic relationships (Illouz, 2008), education (Ecclestone & Hayes, 2009), social work, childhood development, religion, sports (Madsen, 2014), work, poverty (Thomas et al., 2018), and various deviant behaviors. Psychologization has also been studied in terms of the importance of specific psychological concepts and discourses, such as the idea of mental hygiene in the 1920s and 1930s (Rose, 1996), the self-esteem movement in the 1980s and 1990s (Cruikshank, 1993), the stress discourse (Becker, 2013), and the currently popular concept of resilience (Gill & Orgad, 2018). Psychologization has also been attributed to the rising popularity of psychological techniques, such as intelligence tests, assessments of personality traits, psychological experiments, and various therapeutic techniques (e.g., cognitive behavior therapy, transactional analysis). However, psychologization is usually conceived as more than the process of growing popularity of certain psychological concepts or techniques. Indeed, psychologization is considered a fundamental element of modern societies that undergirds the notion of (a good) life: "Psychology not only provides us with a conception of what we are but also offers us an image of what we could be and a toolbox for achieving this image" (Neill, 2013, p. vii). It is this vastness of psychologization that scholars have criticized because it has evolved into a system of meaning without alternatives (Madsen & Brinkmann, 2016). It is therefore no longer possible for modern societies to think outside of the box created by psychological categories and meanings.

Various critical perspectives on the psychologization of modern societies exist. For instance, early "communitarian critique" (Illouz, 2008, p. 2) posited that psychology encourages self-involvement and narcissism, thereby undermining social relations and culture. Social problems become depoliticized, and social solutions based on values such as solidarity are rendered difficult—if not impossible—to achieve (Lasch, 1979; Rieff, 1987). A second line of critique has highlighted the social control aspects of the process of psychologization and argued that people become overly dependent on experts for dealing with their own lives instead of taking responsibility and action themselves (Furedi, 2013). The involvement of therapeutic professions can go hand in hand with paternalistic monitoring and control and the devaluation of individuals' personal values, particularly for marginalized groups of society (Polsky, 2008). More recent work has stepped back from the influence of professions and the notion of social control. Inspired by Foucault's (1991) ideas of systems of knowledge and governmentality, psychology has also been considered a paradigmatic discipline that provides "technologies of the self"—that is, techniques through which individuals govern themselves and transform their subjectivity (Rose, 1996). Psychology provides both the knowledge and the ethical resources for government through self-governance in which societal needs and personal objectives become aligned. For instance, individuals take responsibility for their own health or parenting, but the internalization of these goals and the used techniques are based on the psychological knowledge and psychologized discourses in our society.

The wide concern about the negative consequences of psychologization, however, has itself been reflected upon by various authors. For instance, von Kardorff (1984) argued that to deem psychology to have complete social control would be to overvalue the discipline and to undervalue individuals' critical resources. In a similar vein, Illouz (2008) suggests that we should ask why citizens so happily endorse psychological concepts and techniques and posits that they do so because these concepts and techniques provide meaning and resources for individuals' lives that enable them to understand and lead their lives in our current society. Finally, as Madsen and Brinkmann (2016, p. 197) state, "[c]ertainly, there should be a space for critique and utopian thinking; but rather than being safe from psychologization, shouldn't we be worrying about being saved from global warming, flooding, and hunger?" Thus, psychologization is generally viewed from a critical perspective, but concern exists around the notion that in certain respects, its negative consequences might be exaggerated.

2.2.1 *What Is Psychology, Anyway?*

In order to assess how extensive the phenomenon of psychologization is, it is also necessary to understand its core: In other words, what is psychology, anyway? This question is even more difficult to answer for psychology than for medicine. The simple notion that *psychology is what psychologists do* has been rejected by most of the literature. Indeed, the discipline has gained professional prestige, rights, and resources over the course of the twentieth century, and the number of psychologists has increased tremendously. Nevertheless, the prestige of psychologists is lower than that of the medical profession (Ebner & Rohrbach-Schmidt, 2019), and the political power that psychologists wield is weaker. This power difference is particularly evident in corporatist healthcare systems such as Germany, where medical associations have an institutionalized role and are highly visible in public debates (Klenk, 2018). But why has psychology come to have such a dominant role in modern societies? The argument put forth in the literature is that it is precisely the fact that psychological knowledge and techniques have been shared with other professions as well as with patients and clients (Madsen, 2014; Rose, 1996) that has made psychology so powerful. Thus, unlike medicine, which strongly protects its knowledge and rights, psychology has been rather open with its ideas and inventions. This diffusion of psychology should not be seen as an intentional strategy of the psychological profession, although the profession has clearly advocated for and actively extended its jurisdiction. Instead, this transparency is the result of the history of psychology, which has developed by solving practical problems in various inter-professional organizations (Rose, 1996). Moreover, therapeutic techniques require therapy patients to understand and apply the methods themselves. As a result, psychological concepts have not only been adopted by many other professions, but they have also gained a strong foothold in everyday life and popular culture (e.g., in self-help books) (Illouz, 2008).

Psychology contains a wide variety of subfields, research areas, theories, and methods. Nevertheless, certain aspects are generally put forth as the core of what psychology does: Psychology develops an objective, scientific understanding of what it means to be a person (de Vos, 2013). The psychological concept of a person includes many elements (e.g., perceptions, cognitions, behavior); however, emotions have been highlighted as a specifically important contribution of psychology because they have historically received little attention in society (Furedi, 2013; Nolan, 1998). Finally, psychology provides techniques for differentiating between individuals (e.g., their intelligence, personality, motivation, and capabilities) (Rose, 1996). While psychology does engage with individuals and sets norms and thresholds for when they and their behavior are considered pathological or non-normal, the discipline's focus is broader and includes not only mentally ill individuals. Especially, The turn toward positive psychology in the late 1990s has meant that psychological insights are relevant for everyone because these insights provide knowledge and techniques that can be used to lead a productive, happy, and healthy life.

2.2.2 What Causes Psychologization?

The literature on psychologization has put less emphasis on explaining why psychologization has evolved in comparison with describing it and evaluating its consequences. However, various ideas have been posited as to why psychology has become so important in modern societies. *Actors* have mostly been considered less relevant to psychologization, at least in the sense of strategic actions made by social movements, psychological professions, and so on. Nevertheless, actors are indeed mentioned in works on psychologization. For instance, Rose (1996) argues that psychologists who work in social organizations (e.g., factories, the army) and who aim to solve the practical problems that these organizations face were critical in leading to the development of psychology as a profession. Illouz (2008, p. 20) points to individuals as agents in the process of psychologization and argues that psychology provides "a cultural resource" for individuals and that its techniques would not be adopted if these techniques did not accomplish something for the individuals. Thus, by adopting psychological techniques and embracing their ideas, individuals contribute to psychologization. Finally, Polsky (2008) argues that philanthropists and personnel in welfare services and agencies have been influential to psychologization because they have continuously advocated for a therapeutic approach to dealing with marginal groups. As public employees, social personnel have a vested interest in demonstrating that the continued need for their techniques and services is present. In addition, their jobs allow them to use bureaucratic and street-level strategies to maintain this approach, even if their social organization and political power as a group is limited (Polsky, 2008).

A second, more influential hypothesis for the rising influence of psychology involves the role of *ideas*. Many scholars depict psychologization as a functional solution to the problems and needs of modern societies. Indeed, as Nolan states in *The Therapeutic State*, "[t]he therapeutic ethos is a system of meaning that is right for the time" (1998, p. 18). Bureaucratized modern institutions, flexible and individualized work and private life, and the lack of other forms of authority and legitimization—such as tradition and religion—create a need that is filled by what psychology has to offer. Thus, psychological ideas resonate with the conditions and requirements of modern life. As a transcendent orientation to life is no longer pursued by most citizens, health, happiness, and self-realization have evolved to become life's ultimate goals, and it is psychology that provides the scientific knowledge, techniques, and professional services that can help individuals to reach these goals. The underlying cultural narrative of psychologization depicts the process as a form of liberation—that is, a beneficial force that is good. In other words, the more psychology, the better (Madsen, 2014)—a view not only endorsed by most psychologists, but also held in public. However, critical psychologists such as Madsen have argued that psychologization can no longer be conceived as an alternative to social norms and traditions. Because psychology has become so popular, psychological interpretations of our world have become the norm, and the techniques used in psychology have become the standard for dealing with life's problems.

Finally, *institutions* are also considered a relevant force behind psychologization. Psychology and the welfare state developed around the same time, and there seems to be an interdependency between the two. According to Rose (1996, p. 68), "[a]s the human soul became the object of a positive science, human subjectivity and intersubjectivity became possible targets of government intervention." Psychological knowledge has allowed for a new form of governance that provides a natural fit with the idea of liberal democracies and their citizens as responsible and rational individuals (Madsen, 2014). Individual behavior is aligned with governmental goals through experts and technologies of the self, which have become institutionalized in the welfare state. Thus, throughout the expansion of the welfare state, psychology and its practices have become institutionalized in schools, clinics, companies, and so on (Furedi, 2013). In return, the "therapeutic ethos" has legitimized the broad activities of the state, as shown in Nolan's (1998) historic analyses of fields of state activities in the US. This symbiosis between the welfare state and psychologization should not be interpreted as an intentionally built system of power relations. Indeed, "'[t]he state' is neither the origin nor puppet master of all these programs of government. Innovations in government have usually been made, not in response to grand threats to the state, but in the attempt to manage local, petty, and even marginal problems" (Rose, 1996, p. 76). However, the result is nevertheless that psychology has become an important part of the way that social control is organized in advanced, industrialized democracies. This form of guided self-management is generally less coercive and repressive than other forms of control, but it still represents a form of governance. However, the state has not given up coercive measures altogether. This notion is important in the therapeutic approach to marginal groups, where psychological solutions are often coupled with (the threat of) coercive measures (Polsky, 2008). For instance, in the welfare state, a lack of cooperation or conformity (e.g., school absence) has been tied with a reduction in or cancelation of welfare benefits (e.g., Cantillon & van Lancker, 2012; Friedli, 2016).

2.3 Similarities, Differences, and Suggestions for an Integrated Analysis

> Psychology may be defined as the study of experience and behaviour. Medicine concerns itself with those areas of experience and behavior known as sickness and health (however one wishes to define these words). It might be expected that the two subjects would be inextricably linked through their common interest in human functioning. History has, however, erected barriers between them, leading to a lack of understanding on both sides. (Hunt, 1974, p. 105)

Thus far, we have discussed the fact that one interdisciplinary body of literature has studied how medicine has become more important in societies while another interdisciplinary body of literature has conducted similar research for psychology. As both disciplines share many interests, subject areas, and scientific methods and also often work together professionally, the general lack of debate on how medicalization and psychologization are interlinked is quite striking. We therefore next aim to compare and integrate these two processes. In so doing, we do not mean to suggest that medicalization and psychologization generally co-occur or are interdependent, nor do we view the two processes as mere dimensions of a more abstract societal process, such as scientization (Ziemann et al., 2012) or modernization.

Instead, we argue that analytically combining the two processes allows us to sharpen and reflect on existing concepts and categories in both research areas, including what is considered to be (or ignored as) as their driving forces. This analytical combination also draws attention to the boundaries of the disciplinary and professional ideas, practices, and identities and thereby creates new puzzles and theoretically engaging research questions. Finally, a combined framework wields new analytical leverage in the empirical analysis of issues in which both disciplines are involved. The welfare state is the subject on which we focus in this book because it is in the welfare state that much of the activity around psychology and medicine occurs.

Table 2.1 compares medicalization and psychologization and displays their commonalities and differences. The descriptions of medicalization and psychologization may appear oversimplified, but the idea is to accentuate the differences concisely and illustratively. We thereby highlight the

Table 2.1 Comparison of medicalization and psychologization (*attribution of responsibility* based on Brickman et al. (1982))

	Medicalization	*Medicalization and Psychologization*	*Psychologization*
Discipline/ Profession	• The medical profession is strong and autonomous and possesses monopolized medical knowledge and exclusive jargon. • Illness and pathology are the central focus. • The field is practice-oriented and has a clear job profile.	• Both disciplines share many interests, subject areas, and scientific methods and often work together professionally. • Their members are considered specialized experts who possess scientific knowledge that is grounded in the natural-science paradigm. • Their authority is based on the fact that access to the profession is only possible through an academic education with high barriers (restricted access, long training periods).	• Psychologists have a less effective political organization. • Psychologists' knowledge and techniques are more accessible and are therefore widely diffused in society. • Psychology works on a general understanding of the human psyche and thus on defining what is both "normal" and "pathological."
Techniques	Medical care and pharmaceuticals	Diagnostics and therapy	Coaching, self-help groups, self-help literature, and psychological tests
Institutions	• Medical doctors have their own organizations (i.e., hospitals) and sit at the top of the hierarchy of all other health professionals. • Medical doctors usually work jobs with a traditional, medical profile. • Medical doctors have established roles in the institutions of the welfare state (medical chambers, company physicians, etc.).	• Many medical doctors and psychologists are self-employed health professionals in private practices. • Both disciplines share the role of experts in the welfare state and its institutions. These experts are responsible for making decisions in defined situations.	• Psychologists work in various sectors (companies, schools, etc.) and often in positions that are also open to members of other disciplines.

(*continued*)

Table 2.1 (continued)

	Medicalization	*Medicalization and Psychologization*	*Psychologization*
Attribution of responsibility	*Medical model:* The individual is responsible neither for the problem nor for the solution.	Both disciplines concentrate on the individual. Medicalization is moving toward the compensatory model.	*Compensatory model:* The individual is responsible not for the problem, but for the solution.
Driving forces (Actors, Ideas, Institutions)	• All driving forces apply, but strong focus is placed on actors as a driving force behind medicalization.		• All driving forces apply, but strong focus is placed on cultural ideas as a driving force behind psychologization.

ideal-typical differences between both processes, but the empirical reality is more complex than the model suggests.

2.3.1 Differences Between the Disciplines and Their Institutional Anchoring

Medicine is a large academic discipline that has a long history as a field of study since the foundation of the first medieval universities. Moreover, the medical profession continues to be among the most prestigious and politically influential professions and occupations in advanced, industrialized countries (Ebner & Rohrbach-Schmidt, 2019; Klenk, 2018). However, with the development of psychology in the middle of the nineteenth century, "the boundaries among medicine, psychiatry, and psychology had to be negotiated" (Pickren & Rutherford, 2010, p. 109). Since then, psychology has grown substantially and has become a well-established discipline and profession in its own right. Nevertheless, medicine has remained the more powerful discipline in academia, with entire schools and faculties dedicated to the field, whereas psychology is usually subsumed into the humanities, the social sciences, or the life sciences. In the healthcare system in general and in hospitals in particular, psychologists usually work under the formal supervision of medical doctors, but not vice versa. While both disciplines have become more diverse and interdisciplinary, it is critical to consider their different histories when aiming to understand their different disciplinary and professional identities.

Medicine remains oriented toward *the physical*, *the material*, and *the objective*, whereas psychology—with its focus on cognition, emotion, and motivation–is centered around *the mind* and *the subjective* (Hunt, 1974). Although most topics in medicine are difficult for laypeople to grasp (due in large part to medical jargon), concepts and evidence from psychology are "by and large still at the stage where [they are] comprehensible to most people" (Hunt, 1974, p. 106). Medical knowledge is therefore strongly monopolized by the medical profession, which means that medical doctors have special and exclusive rights over many processes. For instance, only medical doctors (can) practice medicine. In contrast, psychological knowledge is widely diffused in other fields (including social work, pedagogy, educational science, and economics) (Rose, 1996) and is also deeply ingrained in everyday life. For example, many psychological concepts (e.g., self-esteem) have become widespread in everyday language. Eva Illouz therefore talks about the "dual status of psychology" as both a profession and an aspect of popular culture (2008, p. 7). While general knowledge about psychology may be very influential in society at large, it weakens the professional power that psychology wields.

Another significant difference between medicine and psychology is that medicine remains much more strongly oriented toward the pathological. Indeed, "[t]he business of medicine is the diagnosis and treatment of illness" (Zola, 1975, p. 83). Therefore, medicine has a clear purpose to its research—namely to identify pathologies and to find solutions to them. While the prevention of illness and the improvement of public health have certainly been strengthened throughout the history of medicine, pathology has remained the major focus of the curriculum and of the process of the professionalization of medicine.

Moreover, research and practice are strongly coupled. Medical doctors are professionalized to be able to make life-and-death decisions when facing uncertainty. Their professional training and motivation are therefore strongly practical and are less concerned with expressing uncertainty or with the scientific process per se (Hunt, 1974). Even though many psychologists later also work with patients, their academic discipline is focused on understanding human behavior, cognitions, and emotions more broadly: Like most natural and social sciences, psychology is oriented at the development of general scientific laws (basic science), while medical research has a strong applied focus and aims to develop evidence and techniques that can be used in medical practice (Hunt, 1974). Thus, psychological research contributes at least as much to what makes people smart, productive, happy, and healthy as it does to understanding and helping people with (mental) illness. Psychology has become important in gaining newer understandings of health, which is now no longer defined as the absence of disease, but as the ability to assume social roles (Anhorn & Balzereit, 2016). This concept of health—famously introduced by the World Health Organization's Ottawa Charter—sets the course for nearly infinite possibilities for individuals to work on themselves. As a result, self-optimization via psychological methods and self-enhancement via pharmaceuticals are considered important aspects of psychologization and medicalization, respectively. Moreover, both disciplines also engage in the general discourse on public health and health promotion, which focuses on health rather than on illness (Lupton, 1995). While this example reveals that the two disciplines have been coalescing over the past decades in many ways, it is important to bear in mind that the historic differences between them remain potent in terms of the disciplines' identities, practices, and interactions with each other.

2.3.2 Driving Forces Behind Medicalization and Psychologization

Despite the notable differences between medicine and psychology, the influence of both disciplines on society has expanded substantially since the nineteenth century (Nye, 2003; Rose, 1985). Thus, one of the most important questions involves finding an explanation for the rising role of medicine and psychology in modern societies.

Medicalization theory is rooted in a social constructionist perspective and is strongly interested in the role of *actors* as driving forces behind medicalization. The notion that "some active agents are necessary for most problems to become medicalized" (Conrad, 2007, p. 6) has been a primary assumption in the literature. The explicit aim is to identify the causal factors and processes that underlie medicalization (Brown, 1995) using a perspective of social causation that assumes that social action is the basis of change. Thus, it is actors who discover, diagnose, claim, fight, and decide what is considered a disease and what is dealt with by medicine. In its initial work, the medical profession was considered the primary agent. In the 1980s and 1990s, however, social movements were acknowledged as important actors in campaigning for the medicalization of social problems (Ballard & Elston, 2005; Davis, 2016). More recently, Peter Conrad outlined the myriad "engines of medicalization" (Conrad, 2005, p. 5) and argued that their relative importance has changed over time. While actors have been considered the major driving force behind medicalization, cultural context—such as the role of rationality and modernity—has also been suggested to have played a role in shaping medicalization (Ballard & Elston, 2005):

> It is likely that the very idea of a consciously driven process needs to be rethought. Institutions like the medical profession in the past or the pharmaceutical industry in the present may reap some of the benefits of medicalisation but the process itself is an outcome of a cultural dynamic rather than the intentional behaviour of individuals. (Furedi, 2008, p. 101)

More recent accounts have pointed toward the role that institutions play in shaping processes of medicalization (Halfmann, 2019; Olafsdottir, 2011), such as characteristics of the political system or of welfare state institutions. These accounts have thereby broadened the scope of the driving forces that are considered in current research.

In contrast to the social constructionist medicalization research, research on psychologization has a different theoretical and epistemological stance. For many scholars, Foucault's work serves as a central reference point and with this a methodology that aims to deconstruct discourses and practices rejecting the concept of social causation (e.g., Rose, 1996).

Psychologization either is presented as the result of cultural transformations (e.g., modernization) or points to the role of psychological knowledge and practice in the current political-historic regime of (neo-) liberalism. Actors are less prominent, though they are also important in the literature. However, rather than collective actors, it is individuals who are discussed as being able to create their own subjectivity through technologies of the self that are based on psychological knowledge and practices. In this sense, psychologization—much more than medicalization—could be argued to be the result of individuals' search (even in the absence of manifest problems) for health, happiness, and self-realization, for which modern psychology provides concrete techniques and strategies (Illouz, 2008).

2.3.3 Concept of the Individual

While both disciplines can be distinguished by many elements, they also share the key feature of placing focus on the individual (Bunge, 1990). Whether through dealing with genes, biology, behavior, emotions, or cognitions, both psychological and medical theories and practices work with the individual. While the two disciplines are well aware of the influence of the social context, this influence is allocated to specific subfields (e.g., social psychology or social medicine) and does not constitute the core of medicine or psychology.

However, the concept of the individual differs between medicine and psychology, and the processes of medicalization and psychologization therefore have different implications both for individuals and for society at large. The typical difference can be illustrated using Brickman et al.'s (1982) four models of helping and coping (i.e., a *moral model*, a *enlightenment model*, a *compensatory model*, and a *medical model*), which are based on two dimensions: (1) attributing responsibility for problems to the self and (2) attributing responsibility for solutions to the self. In the medical model, the individual bears responsibility neither for the problem nor for the solution. For the individual, the model has the benefit of relieving them from blame and justifying their acceptance of help, their state of being weak, and their decision to not participate in social obligations. The downside is the dependency associated with the medical model, which can make the individual passive and transfers power and social control to medical doctors. Psychology, on the other hand, builds on the compensatory model, in which the individual is also not considered responsible for the problem, but for its solution. The compensatory model is considered empowering since it considers the individual to be both good and competent. However, the compensatory model also has downsides. As Brinkmann and colleagues put it, "[t]he potential deficiency of the compensatory model lies in the fact that those who see themselves as continually having to solve problems that they did not create are likely to feel a great deal of pressure in their lives and to wind up with a rather negative or even paranoid view of the world" (Brickman et al., 1982, p. 372).

These different attributions of responsibility are relevant for the welfare state, in which the perceived legitimacy of benefits and services is crucial and continuously debated (van Oorschot et al., 2017). Medicalization and psychologization are therefore intertwined with changing welfare policies that also adjust their institutions based on cultural concepts of responsibility that are based inter alia on ideas and expertise from medicine and psychology.

While even today, medicine is more strongly associated with the medical model and psychology with the compensatory model, compensatory logic has gained importance in medicine over the last decades (Furedi, 2008). Indeed, with increasing knowledge about lifestyle risks as causes of diseases, the (perceived) responsibility that individuals have for becoming ill has grown. At the same time, patients have additionally become more responsible for dealing with their illnesses, for example, through chronic-disease-management programs.

2.3.4 *The Consequences of Medicalization and Psychologization*

What are the consequences of medicalization and psychologization? While many authors warn against viewing the contribution of these processes as representative of a case for or against medicine/psychology, the implications of the processes nevertheless motivate a significant proportion of the research. The consequences that we can theoretically consider are numerous: What are the implications for how individuals view themselves and conduct their lives? How do medicalization and psychologization affect social relationships? What are the consequences of medicalization and psychologization for social problems? How do medicalization and psychologization relate to the development of society more broadly and to the state more specifically?

A first approach to these questions stems from the observation that medicalization and psychologization would not be successful if they did not "work" in some way. For individuals, medicine and psychology offer concepts that provide meaning to their experiences as well as guidelines for their actions (Illouz, 2008). Thus, medical and psychological professions can be approached with problems of daily life (Conrad, 2007). The same is true for organizations and for the state. Medicine and psychology offer strategies and tools that help individuals in governing their behavior and in aligning it with their own goals (Rose, 1996). Due to their objective-scientific grounding and to the professional ethics of working in the interest of their clients, medical and psychological professionals legitimize the actions of organizations and of the state (Rose, 1985). This "positive" perspective on the consequences of medicalization and psychologization becomes particularly clear when considering the historical alternatives to these fields, such as the religious moral judgment of deviant behavior or legal punitive measures. In comparison, medical and psychological approaches are generally considered more humane (Conrad & Schneider, 1992). The medical model provides benefits for individuals with diagnosed diseases by offering accepted explanations that de-stigmatize personal problems and enable access to treatment (Broom & Woodward, 1996). As Parsons suggests, medical doctors continue to maintain an important role in assigning individuals to the sick role, thereby relieving these individuals of their social obligations—particularly the obligation to work. Psychology's influence is simultaneously more subtle and more extensive. As it provides explanations as to how an individual is, thinks, feels, and acts, the effects of psychology are visible in everyday life. Statements such as "that was a traumatic experience" and "I am so stressed right now" represent interpretations of everyday experiences. While medical expertise guides political decisions on health and illness (as has been borne out during the COVID-19 pandemic), the influence of psychology is nevertheless more encompassing because psychology provides expertise on so many issues, including child development, relationships, and work and productivity. The influence of psychology in these various social problems has many benefits for the affected groups (e.g., children, families, employees) because members of these groups receive access to benefits and services. Moreover, psychology and other social professions often advocate for these groups, thereby bringing the groups' needs both public and political attention. For instance, using the example of inquiries into institutional child abuse, Wright (2018, p. 189) revealed that a therapeutic framing can promote "processes of democratization in which people who have traditionally not had a public voice now have new avenues to assert claims for justice."

Despite the myriad positive consequences of the increasing influence of medicine and psychology in modern societies, the early literature on medicalization and psychologization between the 1950s and 1970s began from a critical perspective. Since then, much of what has been written on medicalization and psychologization has been a critique of the idealistic view of medicine and psychology in society and of the low level self-reflection in both disciplines (e.g., Madsen, 2018; Szasz, 1960; Zola, 1975). Similar critiques have been levied against medicalization and psychologization. First, even if medicine and psychology can be considered to provide more "humane" ways of dealing with social problems, the processes still constitute forms of social control. For medicalization, in particular, the major concern has been the power that is given to the medical profession when diagnosing and making decisions about the pathological nature of human life. Processes of de-medicalization—as has been the case for homosexuality—have revealed that such diagnoses are strongly interwoven with social and ethical ideas. Even evidence-based medicine must be perceived as being socially constructed when the selection of research questions and research designs is guided by ideas such as specific concepts of gender. Moreover, because the role of medical doctors remains institutionally strongly tied to sickness (or to the lack thereof), medicalization is often associated with the pathologization of social phenomena. Thus, medicine usually includes a diagnosis and thus gives individuals the message that they are sick, which commonly results in the development of a (chronic) illness identity (Schneider, 2013). This implication of medicalization is related to the institutional configuration of the medical practice: Physicians in hospitals and private practices have a limited set of medical practices, which include diagnosing, deciding on a medical treatment, referring to a healthcare professional, and granting an individual sick leave. Thus, even if the source of a problem originates in a social context (e.g., work, an abusive relationship), medical doctors may use options such as pharmaceuticals or sick-leave certificates because they have no jurisdiction to intervene further.

The concept of social control is also important in relation to the rising influence of psychology. Psychologists are considered to represent a "new elite" who have a wide-ranging influence in society (Madsen, 2018). Their social control mechanism is based on technologies that rely on self-governance; thus, individuals control themselves through certain forms of thinking, techniques of emotional control, and so on. These technologies of the self—which are part of why psychology is perceived as helpful—can also have oppressive implications. While both medicine and psychology have been criticized for their tendency to individualize social problems, the assumption of psychology—namely, that individuals are responsible for finding solutions to their own problems by changing their own cognitions, emotions, and behavior—means that not only is the problem associated with the individual, but the responsibility for the problem is also attributed to them. Since the focus of psychology lies in competences, resources, and capabilities, such as resilience and self-efficacy, the field of psychology suggests that strengthening individuals' resources and developing adequate coping mechanisms are key to solving problems. The concept of taking charge of one's own problems, however, is more than a mere suggestion by psychologists. Instead, the concept has evolved into a moral imperative that is reproduced in popular culture and that has become institutionalized in organizations. For example, educational institutions are considered a suitable setting for psychological interventions, regardless as to whether a problem has already occurred (Ecclestone & Brunila, 2015; Ecclestone & Hayes, 2009). For instance, while children were expected to be God-fearing and well-behaved in nineteenth and early twentieth centuries (Nolan, 1998), they are now evaluated in terms of their emotional intelligence and character skills (Heckman & Kautz, 2013). Thus, not only is psychological therapy a targeted strategy for dealing with children who are considered to fall outside of the norm, but psychological assessments and techniques have also become part of the general curriculum. While these techniques are frequently considered meaningful or helpful, problems occur when they do not do the trick and particularly when individuals are unwilling or incapable of engaging with this way of thinking. Not living up to the expectation of taking charge of one's own life or to the imperative of self-optimization leads to new problems for the self, such as feelings of guilt and social stigma. Moreover, in the context of social institutions and welfare programs, not accepting or complying with psychological strategies is often coupled with material consequences or coercive measures (Polsky, 2008). Since socially disadvantaged groups often find it more difficult to adopt this psychologized way of life, psychologization often reproduces existing inequalities (Friedli, 2016).

What unites both processes is that their general approach is focused on the individual, be it on the individual's body, psyche, or both. The growing role played by medicine and psychology over time is therefore associated with attributing more and more problems and solutions to the individual. Thus, medicalization and psychologization have also been criticized for undermining the impetus for finding social and political solutions to problems (e.g., Zola, 1972; Conrad, 1975; Conrad & Schneider, 1992, for medicalization; Madsen & Brinkmann, 2016; de Vos, 2012, for psychologization).

> [D]efining a condition as an illness and adopting a medical approach can have major social consequences and close off alternatives. While it is clear that in some instances medicalisation can lead to important gains for individuals, in others the issue becomes one of the individual and the task to treat what is judged as their pathology, depoliticising the problem and largely ignoring the wider social and institutional context of individuals' physical and mental states and behaviour and the deficiencies of the society in which we live. (Busfield, 2017, p. 771)

As medicine and psychology become increasingly institutionalized, their practice contributes to a consolidation of existing power structures and social systems. The classical medical model remains primarily oriented around the old idea of the welfare state and acts as a gatekeeper to the benefits and services that are solitarily financed. However, reformed medical practice and psychologization align strongly with neoliberalism and with the social investment paradigm, both of which advocate for equality of opportunity and individual accountability. In the long run, this narrative can undermine support for both the political system and the welfare state. Indeed, according to Foster, "[t]he new form of managed freedom poses a threat to democratic self-organization through its evisceration of the notions of public welfare, collective responsibility and social solidarity" (Foster, 2016, p. 109).

In this chapter, we described medicalization and psychologization as two processes that have exerted growing influence in modern societies. These processes share many features, but they are also distinct and sometimes have subtle yet important differences. Their concepts, techniques, and expertise have been readily adopted and integrated by the welfare state in advanced, industrialized countries. In the following chapter, we describe in greater detail the important connection between the two processes and explain how they can be linked to theoretical ideas on the welfare state from the social policy literature.

References

Anhorn, R., & Balzereit, M. (Eds.). (2016). *Handbuch Therapeutisierung und Soziale Arbeit*. Springer Fachmedien Wiesbaden.

Ballard, K., & Elston, M. A. (2005). Medicalisation: A multi-dimensional concept. *Social Theory & Health, 3*(3), 228–241. https://doi.org/10.1057/palgrave.sth.8700053

Becker, D. (2013). *One nation under stress: The trouble with stress as an idea*. Oxford University Press.

Brickman, P., Rabinowitz, V. C., Karuza, J., Coates, D., Cohn, E., & Kidder, L. (1982). Models of helping and coping. *American Psychologist, 37*(4), 368–384. https://doi.org/10.1037/0003-066x.37.4.368

Broom, D. H., & Woodward, R. V. (1996). Medicalisation reconsidered: Toward a collaborative approach to care. *Sociology of Health and Illness, 18*(3), 357–378. https://doi.org/10.1111/1467-9566.ep10934730

Brown, P. (1995). Naming and framing: The social construction of diagnosis and illness. *Journal of Health and Social Behavior, Extra Issue*, 34–52. https://doi.org/10.2307/2626956

Buffel, V., Beckfield, J., & Bracke, P. (2017). The institutional foundations of medicalization: A cross-national analysis of mental health and unemployment. *Journal of Health and Social Behavior, 58*(3), 272–290. https://doi.org/10.1177/0022146517716232

Bunge, M. (1990). What kind of discipline is psychology: Autonomous or dependent, humanistic or scientific, biological or sociological? *New Ideas in Psychology, 8*(2), 121–137. https://doi.org/10.1016/0732-118X(90)90002-J

Busfield, J. (2017). The concept of medicalisation reassessed. *Sociology of Health & Illness, 39*(5), 759–774. https://doi.org/10.1111/1467-9566.12538

Cantillon, B., & van Lancker, W. (2012). Solidarity and reciprocity in the social investment state: What can be learned from the case of Flemish school allowances and truancy? *Journal of Social Policy, 41*(4), 657–675. https://doi.org/10.1017/S0047279412000359

Castel, R. (1979). *Die psychiatrische Ordnung: Das goldene Zeitalter des Irrenwesens.* Suhrkamp.

Clarke, A. E., Mamo, L., Fishman, J. R., Shim, J. K., & Fosket, J. R. (2003). Biomedicalization: Technoscientific transformations of health, illness, and U.S. biomedicine. *American Sociological Review, 68*(2), 161. https://doi.org/10.2307/1519765

Conrad, P. (1975). The discovery of hyperkinesis: Notes on the medicalization of deviant behavior. *Social Problems, 23*(1), 12–21. https://doi.org/10.2307/799624

Conrad, P. (1992). Medicalization and social control. *Annual Review of Sociology, 18*(1), 209–232. https://doi.org/10.1146/annurev.so.18.080192.001233

Conrad, P. (2005). The shifting engines of medicalization. *Journal of Health and SocialBehavior,46*(1),3–14. https://doi.org/10.1177/002214650504600102

Conrad, P. (2007). *The medicalization of society: On the transformation of human conditions into treatable disorders.* Johns Hopkins University Press.

Conrad, P., & Schneider, J. W. (1992). *Deviance and medicalization.* Temple University Press.

Correia, T. (2017). Revisiting medicalization: A critique of the assumptions of what counts as medical knowledge. *Frontiers in Sociology, 2*, Article 14, 603. https://doi.org/10.3389/fsoc.2017.00014

Cruikshank, B. (1993). Revolutions within: Self-government and self-esteem. *Economy and Society, 22*(3), 327–344. https://doi.org/10.1080/03085149300000022

Davis, J. E. (2006). How medicalization lost its way. *Society, 43*(6), 51–56. https://doi.org/10.1007/BF02698486

Davis, J. E. (2016). Medicalization, social control, and the relief of suffering. In W. C. Cockerham (Ed.), *Wiley-Blackwell companions to sociology. The new Blackwell companion to medical sociology* (pp. 211–241). Wiley Blackwell.
de Vos, J. (2012). The deadlock of Husserl's life-world: From a critique of psychologism to psychologization. *Theory & Psychology, 22*(3), 324–341.
de Vos, J. (2013). *Psychologization and the subject of late modernity.* Palgrave Macmillan.
Ebner, C., & Rohrbach-Schmidt, D. (2019). *Berufliches Ansehen in Deutschland für die Klassifikation der Berufe 2010: Beschreibung der methodischen Vorgehensweise, erste deskriptive Ergebnisse und Güte der Messung.* BIBB Preprint. https://bibb-dspace.bibb.de/rest/bitstreams/73a1b9ca-84c6-442a-a940-6fe5a5a7de25/retrieve
Ecclestone, K., & Brunila, K. (2015). Governing emotionally vulnerable subjects and 'therapisation' of social justice. *Pedagogy, Culture & Society, 23*(4), 485–506. https://doi.org/10.1080/14681366.2015.1015152
Ecclestone, K., & Hayes, D. (2009). *The dangerous rise of therapeutic education.* Routledge.
Foster, R. (2016). Therapeutic culture, authenticity and neo-liberalism. *History of the Human Sciences, 29*(1), 99–116. https://doi.org/10.1177/0952695115617384
Foucault, M. (1976). *The birth of the clinic: An archaeology of medical perception.* World of man. Tavistock. (Original work published 1973).
Foucault, M. (1991). Governmentality. In B. Burchell, C. Gordon & P. Miller (Eds.), *The Foucault effect: Studies in governmentality* (pp. 87-104). The University of Chicago Press.
Freidson, E. (1995). *Profession of medicine: A study of the sociology of applied knowledge.* University of Chicago Press (Original work published in 1970).
Friedli, L. (2016). The politics of tackling inequalities: The rise of psychological fundamentalism in public health and welfare reform. In K. E. Smith, S. Hill, & C. Bambra (Eds.), *Health inequalities: Critical perspectives* (pp. 206–221). Oxford University Press.
Furedi, F. (2008). Medicalisation in a therapy culture. In D. Wainwright (Ed.), *A sociology of health* (pp. 97–114). SAGE.
Furedi, F. (2013). *Therapy culture: Cultivating vulnerability in an uncertain age.* Routledge. https://doi.org/10.4324/9780203098684
Gill, R., & Orgad, S. (2018). The amazing bounce-backable woman: Resilience and the psychological turn in neoliberalism. *Sociological Research Online, 23*(2), 477–495. https://doi.org/10.1177/1360780418769673
Gross, M. L. (1978). *The psychological society: A critical analysis of psychiatry, psychotherapy, psychoanalysis and the psychological revolution.* Random House.

Halfmann, D. (2012). Recognizing medicalization and demedicalization: Discourses, practices, and identities. *Health (London, England: 1997), 16*(2), 186–207. https://doi.org/10.1177/1363459311403947

Halfmann, D. (2019). Political institutions and the comparative medicalization of abortion. *Journal of Health and Social Behavior*, 22146519843935. https://doi.org/10.1177/0022146519843935

Havemann, E. (1957). *The age of psychology*. Simon and Schuster.

Heckman, J. J., & Kautz, T. (2013). Fostering and measuring skills: Interventions that improve character and cognition. *National Bureau of Economic Research*. https://www.nber.org/papers/w19656.pdf

Holmqvist, M. (2012). *The institutionalization of social welfare: A study of medicalizing management*. Taylor & Francis.

Hunt, S. M. (1974). The relationship between psychology and medicine. *Social Science & Medicine (1967), 8*(2), 105–109. https://doi.org/10.1016/0037-7856(74)90040-7

Illich, I. (1974). Medical nemesis. *The Lancet, 303*(7863), 918–921. https://doi.org/10.1016/S0140-6736(74)90361-4

Illouz, E. (2008). *Saving the modern soul: Therapy, emotions, and the culture of self-help*. University of California Press.

Klenk, T. (2018). Interessenlagen und Interessenpolitik im Gesundheitssektor. In T. Spier & C. Strünck (Eds.), *Studien der Bonner Akademie für Forschung und Lehre praktischer Politik. Ärzteverbände und ihre Mitglieder: Zwischen Einfluss- und Mitgliederlogik* (1st ed., pp. 19–46). Springer.

Lasch, C. (1979). *The culture of narcissism: American life in an age of diminishing expectations*. Norton.

Lupton, D. (1995). *The imperative of health: Public health and the regulated body*. SAGE.

Madsen, O. J. (2014). *The therapeutic turn: How psychology altered Western culture. Concepts for critical psychology*. Taylor and Francis.

Madsen, O. J. (2018). *The psychologisation of society: On the unfolding of the therapeutic in Norway. Therapeutic cultures ser.* Routledge.

Madsen, O. J., & Brinkmann, S. (2016). The disappearance of psychologisation? *Annual Review of Critical Psychology, 8*, 179–199.

Neill, C. (2013). Foreword. In J. de Vos (Ed.), *Psychologization and the subject of late modernity* (pp. vi–x). Palgrave Macmillan.

Nolan, J. L. (1998). *The therapeutic state: Justifying government at century's end*. New York University Press.

Nye, R. A. (2003). The evolution of the concept of medicalization in the late twentieth century. *Journal of History of the Behavioral Sciences, 39*(2), 115–129. https://doi.org/10.1002/jhbs.10108

Olafsdottir, S. (2007). *Medicalizing mental health: A comparative view of the public, private, and professional construction of mental illness* [Dissertation]. Indiana University, Bloomington, IN.

Olafsdottir, S. (2011). Medicalization and mental health: The critique of medical expansion, and a consideration of how markets, national states, and citizens matter. In A. Pilgrim David, Rogers, & B. A. Pescosolido (Eds.), *The SAGE handbook of mental health and illness* (pp. 239–260). SAGE.

Pawluch, D. (2017). Medicalizing childhood. In D. R. Loseke & J. Best (Eds.), *Social problems:: Constructionist readings* (pp. 219–225). Routledge.

Pickren, W. E., & Rutherford, A. (2010). *A history of modern psychology in context*. Wiley.

Polsky, A. J. (2008). *The rise of the therapeutic state*. Princeton University Press.

Pulkingham, J., & Fuller, S. (2012). From parent to patient: The medicalization of lone motherhood through welfare reform. *Social Politics: International Studies in Gender, State & Society, 19*(2), 243–268. https://doi.org/10.1093/sp/jxs007

Reibling, N. (2019). Engine and brakes: European welfare states and the medicalization of social problems. *Europe Now*. https://www.europenowjournal.org/2019/06/10/engine-and-brakes-european-welfare-states-and-the-medicalization-of-social-problems/

Rieff, P. (1987). *The triumph of the therapeutic*. University of Chicago Press.

Rose, N. S. (1985). *The psychological complex: Psychology, politics and society in England; 1869–1939*. Routledge & Paul.

Rose, N. S. (1996). *Inventing our selves: Psychology, power, and personhood. Cambridge studies in the history of psychology*. Cambridge University Press. https://doi.org/10.1017/CBO9780511752179

Rose, N. S. (2006). *The politics of life itself: Biomedicine, power, and subjectivity in the twenty-first century*. Princeton University Press.

Sage, W. M., & Laurin, J. E. (2018). If you would not criminalize poverty, do not medicalize it. *The Journal of Law, Medicine & Ethics: A Journal of the American Society of Law, Medicine & Ethics, 46*(3), 573–581. https://doi.org/10.1177/1073110518804199

Schneider, W. (2013). Medikalisierung sozialer Prozesse. *Psychotherapeut, 58*(3), 219–236. https://doi.org/10.1007/s00278-013-0977-5

Schram, S. F. (2000). *After welfare: The culture of postindustrial social policy*. New York University Press.

Stenner, P., & Taylor, D. (2008). Psychosocial welfare: Reflections on an emerging field. *Critical Social Policy, 28*(4), 415–437. https://doi.org/10.1177/0261018308095278

Szasz, T. S. (1960). The myth of mental illness. *American Psychologist, 15*(2), 113–118. https://doi.org/10.1037/h0046535

Thomas, F., Hansford, L., Ford, J., Wyatt, K., McCabe, R., & Byng, R. (2018). Moral narratives and mental health: Rethinking understandings of distress and healthcare support in contexts of austerity and welfare reform. *Palgrave Communications, 4*(39), 1–8. https://doi.org/10.1057/s41599-018-0091-y

van Oorschot, W., Roosma, F., & Reeskens, T. (2017). *The social legitimacy of targeted welfare: Attitudes to welfare deservingness.* Edward Elgar Publishing.

von Kardorff, E. (1984). Soziale Kontrolle durch Psychologie und Psychologen: Einige Vorüberlegungen. *Psychologie und Gesellschaftskritik, 8*(3), 87–105.

Wastell, D., & White, S. (2012). Blinded by neuroscience: Social policy, the family and the infant brain. *Families, Relationships and Societies, 1*(3), 397–414. https://doi.org/10.1332/204674312X656301

Williams, S. J., Coveney, C., & Gabe, J. (2017). The concept of medicalisation reassessed: A response to Joan Busfield. *Sociology of Health & Illness, 39*(5), 775–780. https://doi.org/10.1111/1467-9566.12576

Winters-Miner, L. A., Bolding, P. S., Hilbe, J. M., Goldstein, M., Hill, T., Nisbet, R., Walton, N., & Miner, G. D. (2014). Chapter 8 – ICD-10. In L. Miner, P. Bolding, J. Hilbe, M. Goldstein, T. Hill, R. Nisbet, N. Walton, & G. Miner (Eds.), *Practical predictive analytics and decisioning systems for medicine: Informatics accuracy and cost-effectiveness for healthcare administration and delivery including medical research* (pp. 106–115). Elsevier Science. https://doi.org/10.1016/B978-0-12-411643-6.00008-9

Wong, S. (2016). Geographies of medicalized welfare: Spatial analysis of supplemental security income in the U.S., 2000–2010. *Social Science & Medicine, 160*, 9–19. https://doi.org/10.1016/j.socscimed.2016.05.018

Wright, K. (2018). Challenging institutional denial: Psychological discourse, therapeutic culture and public inquiries. *Journal of Australian Studies, 42*(2), 177–190. https://doi.org/10.1080/14443058.2018.1462237

Ziemann, B., Wetzell, R. F., Schumann, D., & Brückweh, K. (2012). Introduction: The scientization of the social in comparative perspective. In K. Brückweh (Ed.), *Engineering society: The role of the human and social sciences in modern societies, 1880–1980* (pp. 1–40). Palgrave Macmillan.

Zola, I. K. (1972). Medicine as an institution of social control. *The Sociological Review, 20*(4), 487–504. https://doi.org/10.1111/j.1467-954X.1972.tb00220.x

Zola, I. K. (1975). In the name of health and illness: On some socio-political consequences of medical influence. *Social Science & Medicine (1967), 9*(2), 83–87. https://doi.org/10.1016/0037-7856(75)90098-0

CHAPTER 3

Medicine, Psychology, and the Welfare State

Mareike Ariaans, Nadine Reibling, and Lisa Bleckmann

While the previous chapter defined medicalization and psychologization and provided a detailed description of the similarities and differences between the two concepts, the present chapter draws on these theoretical considerations and links both concepts to the welfare state. Although the disciplines of medicine and psychology have always been discussed as a part of the healthcare system of welfare states, the link between the two disciplines and other areas of the welfare state remains unclear, and an overall theoretical idea of how processes of medicalization and psychologization are embedded in the welfare state remains missing. Hence, the present chapter links medicalization and psychologization theory to theories of the welfare state. We first briefly recapitulate our understanding of the two concepts and then examine how they are connected to welfare state theory. We subsequently examine how medicalization and psychologization have been part of the welfare state restructuring that has been underway in all Western nations since the end of the 1970s. Finally, we

M. Ariaans (✉) • L. Bleckmann
University of Siegen, Siegen, Germany
e-mail: ariaans@soziologie.uni-siegen.de

N. Reibling
Fulda University of Applied Sciences, Fulda, Germany
e-mail: nadine.reibling@gw.hs-fulda.de

N. Reibling, M. Ariaans (eds.), *Toward a Biopsychosocial Welfare State?*, https://doi.org/10.1007/978-3-031-32793-3_3

present an integrated model of medicalization and psychologization within the welfare state. The categories of this model are illustrated with examples from our research in order to demonstrate how the model can be applied as an analytical tool in empirical research.

3.1 Medicalization and Psychologization as Processes in the Welfare State

As described in the previous chapter, the simple definition of medicalization is "to make something medical" (Conrad, 2007). Medicalization has been analyzed in relation to various processes, including deviant behavior, everyday-life problems (e.g., sadness, loneliness, shyness, fear), and natural life processes (e.g., childbirth, involuntary childlessness, menopause, impotence) (Davis, 2016). However, there has recently been a growing interest in the medicalization of the *social problems* that are considered central to the welfare state, such as unemployment, poverty, disability, aging, and problems in childhood and youth (Friedli, 2016; Schram, 2000; Stenner & Taylor, 2008). A second line of literature has discussed the growing role that psychology plays in social problems in Western societies (Madsen, 2014). Although medicalization and psychologization have been described for social problems, these problems are not subsumed by either medicine or psychology. Instead, medicalization and psychologization should be considered processes of the growing influence of medicine and psychology. These processes can be analytically assessed on different levels, in different dimensions, and to varying degrees. Halfmann (2012) organized processes of medicalization in a typology that differentiates between three levels (micro, meso, and macro) and three dimensions, which he calls discourses, practices, and identities.[1] He defines medicalization in these three dimensions, which can be described as (1) the increasing use of medical ideas and concepts, (2) the stronger involvement of medical practices and of medical doctors as actors, and (3) the expanding institutionalization of medicine, for example, through requirements of medical assessments. All three dimensions capture an aspect of medicalization and highlight the different mechanisms through which medicalization can occur. We build on his framework but consider three concepts

[1] Both Halfmann's dimensions and our framework are also based on earlier categorizations by Conrad (1992) of medicalization on the conceptual, the institutional, and the interactional level.

that are commonly used to differentiate strands of welfare state theory—that is, ideas, actors, and institutions.

In the welfare state, medicine and psychology have an important place in the healthcare system, where their knowledge systems guide services and both medical doctors and psychologists are acknowledged as high-status health professionals (Marshall, 1939; Webster, 2020). However, outside of healthcare, the welfare state literature has taken little interest in the role of these two disciplines in other fields of social policy. Apart from healthcare, the role that medical and psychological professions and categories play in social problems has only recently been established, for example, for dealing with poverty and unemployment (Holmqvist, 2009; Schneider, 2013; Thomas et al., 2018; Wong, 2016) or homelessness (Mathieu, 1993). This body of literature reveals how important medicine and psychology are to defining social problems and social policies in specific fields of the welfare state. However, if there is evidence that medicine and psychology are important in many social policy areas, should we not go further and investigate the role that the two fields play in the welfare state overall? To do this, we first examine welfare state theories and investigate how the processes of medicalization and psychologization can be linked to these ideas.

3.2 The Welfare State and Its Relation to Medicine and Psychology

The welfare state is ubiquitous in the lives of individuals in advanced, industrialized countries and influences these individuals' life chances from the cradle to the grave. This welfare state is the way in which modern societies acknowledge and act on social problems. What the state does about a social condition or situation becomes the defining feature of whether or not the issue is considered a social problem (Gusfield, 1989). Once a social problem has been acknowledged, it is necessary for the state to act on it in some way. As social policies represent the majority of the activities that are undertaken by modern states, the welfare state is central to the legitimacy of the government and of state bureaucracies in modern democracies.

With its onset of welfare state activity at the end of the nineteenth century, the state assumed increasing responsibility for social security in various areas of social life, thereby leading to the foundation of welfare states across Western nations. In the post-war era, which is commonly called the "golden age of the welfare state," Western nations expanded their welfare programs both by including more and more parts of the population in existing schemes and by addressing the increasing number of social problems and risks through new programs and policies (Nullmeier & Kaufmann, 2021). While this process can be observed in most advanced, industrialized countries, welfare states look very different across countries. Describing and explaining this wide variation in welfare discourses, practices, and institutions across countries (Verhoest & Mattei, 2010) has been the central interest of comparative welfare state research for decades, with Esping-Andersen's (1990) typology of the three worlds of welfare capitalism representing a landmark study in the field. In his work, Esping-Andersen argues that there are three distinct welfare state regimes, which are characterized by specific forms of social rights, stratification, and relationships between the state, the market, and the family: (1) Liberal welfare states provide modest benefits that are mainly targeted at the poor and that are subjected to means testing, with market-based solutions to social problems being preferred. (2) Conservative welfare states are based on the male breadwinner model, in which social security is organized through earnings-related contributions to social insurance schemes. Benefits from social insurances are usually related to prior income, with spouses and children enjoying derived rights. (3) The social democratic—often also called the Nordic or Scandinavian—welfare state rests on the principle of equality, provides high levels of benefits, and places a strong emphasis on public social services, such as public childcare.

While Esping-Andersen's typology of welfare states has been criticized, revised, expanded, and replaced by newer typologies, it remains a central reference point in many debates because it has led to important insights for welfare state research. While a significant amount of research in the 1970s and 1980s aimed to find the common cause as to why welfare states had developed and expanded across Western nations, interest has since shifted to the question of why countries have established such different arrangements of welfare state provision and what these differences mean for welfare outcomes. This line of research is also crucial to determining how we can theorize medicalization and psychologization processes within the welfare state. We can view the issue in quantitative terms, meaning that certain welfare state arrangements enable medicalization and psychologization while others impede these processes (Reibling, 2019). Moreover, the *rationales* behind and the *mechanisms* through which medicalization and psychologization might work in different welfare state regimes could look different depending on the respective discourses, actors, and institutions. Finally, the specific medicalization and psychologization process could vary across welfare regimes, for example, across levels and dimensions, as suggested by Halfmann (2012).

3.3 Welfare State Theories and Dimensions of Medicalization and Psychologization

Welfare state theory has aimed to explain why the welfare state has developed as a new historical phenomenon, how and why it varies across nations, and what the consequences of this variation are. Multiple theories and concepts have been suggested to answer these questions and can be subsumed into four strands of theoretical accounts: (1) *functions*, (2) *actors* along with their interests and power resources, (3) *institutions*, and (4) *ideas* (Lessenich, 2016).

To begin, *functionalist approaches* were the first theoretical accounts that developed in an effort to explain why the welfare state had developed in Western countries as a new social phenomenon. Their focus lies on economic developments and in particular on the challenges and problems that arise from capitalist economic systems. The rise of the welfare state was thus a "necessary" political reaction to changing socio-economic conditions at the end of the nineteenth and beginning of the twentieth century. Functionalist approaches view welfare state change as a response to (new) social risks that emanated from processes such as industrialization, modernization, and capitalism. For instance, in the development of societies from pre-industrial to industrial, many new social problems arose (e.g., the expansion of cities, unsafe working conditions in factories, miserable living conditions in cities), thereby creating a need for the state to replace the weakened and overburdened traditional safety nets of the family and the community (Wilensky & Lebeaux, 1958). In essence, functionalist accounts argue that the welfare state developed because there was a need for it. This line of reasoning has also been used to explain medicalization and psychologization by arguing that these processes occur as a reaction to the declining role of traditions and religion (e.g., Rieff, 1987). While functionalist accounts are still considered in welfare state theory and new variants have evolved (e.g., globalization theory), these theories are limited since the assumption that the welfare state (or any form of it) fulfills a function is never sufficient to explain its development. Actor-centered approaches thus developed in an attempt to address this limitation.

Second, these *actor-centered approaches* stem from the argument that politics matters. Thus, in these approaches, the expansion of the welfare state is attributed to the power resources of population groups and parties that have an interest in welfare policies in modern democratic systems. Labor unions and social democratic parties have been considered a central force that led to the development of universalistic welfare states, particularly in Scandinavia (Korpi, 1989), whereas conservative parties and churches have contributed to the development of social capitalism in conservative welfare states (van Kersbergen, 1995). These actor- and policy-centered approaches argue that even if there had once been a need for a welfare state, its implementation required political decisions based on majorities in a democratic system. The medical profession has been considered a relevant actor in the development of public healthcare systems; however, the specific role of these medical professionals has been considered controversial, particularly because they had quite often been opposed to public healthcare (Webster, 2020). Nevertheless, actor-centered approaches have been popular in earlier medicalization research, which reveals that the medical profession has at times actively campaigned for or indirectly supported the medicalization of social conditions (Conrad, 2005). As outlined in the previous chapter, psychologists have always had less political power than their colleagues in the medical profession, but psychologists' practice in various organizations (e.g., hospitals, companies, prisons, schools, etc.) is considered central to psychologization (Rose, 1985, 1996). Thus, actor-centered approaches represent a fruitful perspective for better understanding the role of medicine and psychology in the welfare state. If we expect to find a move toward a biopsychosocial welfare state, we should look for actors who have supported such a development both because it serves their interests *and* because they have sufficient power to accomplish such a change. Clearly, the medical and psychological profession as well as bio-pharma-tech companies and social movements are likely candidates (Clarke et al., 2003; Conrad, 2005) for pushing medicine and psychology (likely bundled together in the concept of "health") onto welfare state agendas. Nevertheless, medical and psychological explanations and solutions are also often endorsed by other actors—such as employers, policymakers, teachers, or street-level bureaucrats—when these solutions serve the actors' interests. For instance, employers have endorsed health-promotion initiatives that medicalize and psychologize experiences of workplace stress through individualized solutions (e.g., counseling, stress trainings) so that they would not have to re-evaluate working conditions (Foster, 2018). Labor market officers support the medicalization of unemployment if an individual's labor market integration is unlikely (Holmqvist, 2009), or they employ psychologized training measures as solutions to joblessness (Friedli, 2016). Teachers are considered crucial actors in the practice of medicalizing children and young adults because they promote medical and psychological examinations (Rafalovich, 2005). Finally, scientists and the media should be considered important actors in the medicalization and psychologization of social problems because they provide and circulate new evidence on the medical and psychological causes of social problems (Clarke et al., 2003; Harwood et al., 2017; Ross Arguedas, 2020). Science journalism, for instance, has favored medical news in the last few decades over findings from other disciplines (Bauer, 1998).

Third, *institutionalist accounts* in welfare state theory have argued that what actors want to do, are able to do, and actually do depends on the institutional context in which they act (Immergut, 1998). Thus, social action is always institutionally embedded. Institutions are reproduced or changed through social actions, but even in the case of change, existing institutions remain the reference point for transformation. Institutionalist accounts consider the state to be central to providing the institutions that shape action, as is the case when political institutions shape electoral rules or federalism. Moreover, the welfare state comprises a myriad of institutions through its bureaucratized and professionalized system of welfare financing, provision, and regulation, including social laws, public agencies, bureaucracies, insurance schemes, and professional organizations.

As the institutional setup of the welfare state varies across nations, these setups provide different opportunities to (dis)integrate medical and psychological ideas into welfare state policies. This notion goes hand in hand with institutionalist accounts, which have highlighted the idea that decisions at a certain point in time create path dependencies. Such path dependencies arise because the established institutions produce vested interests and cultural narratives that support the maintenance and expansion of existing institutional solutions (Pierson, 2000). Despite the centrality of institutions, most of the medicalization and psychologization literature has paid scant attention to how these institutions shape the role that medicine and psychology play in a given society (Reibling, 2019). Nevertheless, newer studies have shown that it is important to pay attention to institutions if we want to understand medicalization and psychologization processes. For example, the medical profession can perceive medicalization as an opportunity in one institutional system and as a threat in another system (Halfmann, 2019; Olafsdottir, 2007).

In order to provide greater clarity, we outline two examples (which are elaborated in the thematic chapters of this book) of how institutions in the conservative welfare state of Germany shape medicalization and psychologization processes. By focusing on unemployment (see Chap. 4), we see how paradigmatic change in Germany in terms of both how unemployment is defined and consequently what is required from the unemployed has opened an institutional space for medicalization and psychologization. Today, illness serves as one of the few reasons as to why strict rules for receiving minimum income benefits do not apply. Another example of how institutions matter for medicalization and psychologization is given in the chapter on children (see Chap. 6). The federalist organization of the educational system has resulted in variation in the treatment of children with learning difficulties. While state laws and lawsuits have resulted in the medicalization and psychologization of children with learning difficulties in certain states, other federal states have created regulations that emphasize educational rather than medical or psychological solutions for the same group of children.

Finally, most recently, welfare state theory has become interested in the central role of *culture* and *ideas* in understanding welfare states and social policy. While comparative welfare state research has often referenced the underlying cultural narratives of different welfare state regimes, such as liberalism, conservatism, and socialism, the significance of ideas and the elaboration of welfare culture have only been developed in the last two decades. This new strand of literature argues that welfare culture involves knowledge, values, norms, and narratives that legitimize specific social policies and the welfare state overall (Pfau-Effinger, 2005). This perspective has also paid attention to discourses and to how these discourses contribute both to the development of policies and to the enactment of policies by street-level bureaucrats (Kaufman, 2020; Suavierol, 2015). The central role of ideas and discourses in this strand of literature aligns with arguments put forward in many psychologization or therapeutization accounts that consider the growing role of medicine and psychology to be a cultural narrative that resonates with modern societies. Nolan (1998), for instance, has even argued that the therapeutic narrative has become a new vein of legitimization for the American (welfare) state:

> "Because of the strength of the therapeutic consciousness in American culture, and because of the apparent need for alternative sources of state legitimation, I argue that we should find evidence of the therapeutic ethos beginning to institutionalize itself in the American state." (Nolan, 1998, p. 45)

Although ideas and discourses are analyzed and evaluated as being important to the development both of social policies *and* of process of medicalization and psychologization, hardly any studies on welfare discourses from non-medical areas (e.g., poverty, unemployment, pensions) that focus on how medical and psychological ideas are implemented and promoted have been conducted (exceptions include the recently published work by Ariaans & Reibling, 2021; Krayter & Reibling, 2020).

We have thus far outlined how welfare state theories have employed functions, actors, institutions, and ideas to explain welfare state development and variation. While functionalist accounts are limited in their explanatory values, the other three theoretical accounts continue to hold prominent places in welfare state research. We have additionally shown how the concepts of actors, institutions, and ideas correspond to thinking in medicalization and psychologization research. Therefore, we propose using these concepts as categories through which we can also analytically understand medicalization and psychologization in the welfare state. Using these established concepts from welfare state research links our framework to existing welfare state theory. Moreover, these categories can be conceived as a more abstract take on Halfmann's dimensions of medicalization and de-medicalization—namely discourses, practices, and identities (and actors). Before we discuss our analytical framework in greater detail, we need to introduce another important part of welfare state research: research on welfare state change and restructuring. While the welfare state has long been considered a prime example of a durable social institution that has little opportunity for institutional reform, many countries have transformed their welfare states quite substantially over the past three decades. Not only have neo-liberal reforms and the rise of the social investment paradigm changed welfare states in Western nations, but they can also be considered an important reason as to why medicalization and psychologization in the welfare state have grown and taken on new forms.

3.4 Welfare State Restructuring as a Catalyst for Processes of Medicalization and Psychologization

The dominant cultural narrative of the welfare state during its golden age was that of an institution that provided social security against natural life risks (e.g., aging, illness, motherhood) and protection against the drawbacks of capitalism (e.g., unemployment, poverty) (Nullmeier & Kaufmann, 2021). While welfare regimes differed quite substantially in terms of how and to what extent they both provided social security and employed measures of redistribution (Esping-Andersen, 1990), this general narrative was shared. Social security was in many ways what the welfare state stood for (Kaufmann, 2003). Beginning at the end of the 1970s, this narrative—along with the resulting institutional structure—began to be increasingly criticized: In light of declining economic growth and population aging, the financial sustainability of the welfare state was considered problematic and in need of reform (Pierson, 2000). This view was strongly driven by neo-liberal thinking, which argued that the state—primarily through its welfare programs—was inhibiting macro-economic growth as well as individuals' potential for self-realization and happiness, particularly for individuals who were "stuck" receiving welfare benefits (Banerjee et al., 2017). Beginning in the 1980s in the UK and the US, this view began to lead to neo-liberal welfare reforms, which served as a path toward welfare state restructuring that was followed by all advanced, industrialized nations. While this welfare state restructuring has been moderate in some nations, the period since the 1980s has borne witness to fundamental changes in other countries. In Germany, for instance, Seeleib-Kaiser (2016) has argued that the neo-liberal reforms have transformed the German welfare state from the paradigmatic example of a conservative welfare state to a liberal welfare state.

Overall, neo-liberal reforms have included cutbacks to and privatization of parts of the welfare state (Nullmeier & Kaufmann, 2021). These reforms have also led to an increase in welfare conditionality, which means that the conditions that must be met in order to access benefits have been substantially tightened (Watts & Fitzpatrick, 2018). An important aspect of these conditions is that behavioral expectations must be met in order to access benefits and services. Not only has this neo-liberal transformation changed Western welfare states, but it has also created a context that encourages the medicalization (Barbee et al., 2018) and psychologization of social problems (Madsen, 2018). On the one hand, a number of studies have shown that because many individuals have not been able to either find a job or meet other behavioral expectations, there has been an increase in claims or the actual receipt of health- and disability-related benefits, such as sick leave and disability pensions (Hansen et al., 2014; Holmqvist, 2009; Wong, 2016). Thus, the medicalization of unemployment and poverty has been a paradoxical effect of neo-liberal cutbacks in the welfare state (see Chap. 7). On the other hand, neo-liberal governmentality includes an increasing reliance on psychology in order to enable individuals to act as rational, motivated subjects, as is intended by the neo-liberal agenda. This reliance on psychology can be seen in the use of psychometric testing (International Labour Organization, 2017), in the rise of psychological ideas such as resilience in welfare discourses (Michael Garrett, 2016), in the use of psychological techniques such as nudging in social policies (Peeters, 2019), and in the role of psychotherapy in (re-)producing neo-liberal subjects (LaMarre et al., 2019).

In recent years, the limitations of neo-liberal reforms have been discussed intensively, with international organizations, the EU, and many nations having come to consider the social investment paradigm to be a remedy for neo-liberal thinking (Jane Jenson, 2012). While social investment also considers traditional social security to be unsustainable and potentially detrimental, the concept acknowledges that the state must provide a context in which individuals can develop human capital that helps them avoid risks and the need for social protection (Hemerijck, 2015). Thus, the state needs to strategically invest in areas of human capital formation that strengthen labor force participation and productivity. While the original development of the paradigm strongly focused on education and family policies, the significance of health as a resource for a productive life has been substantially highlighted in recent years (European Commission, 2013b; Goijaerts et al., 2022; Kvist, 2015). The social investment paradigm has opened new routes for the medicalization and psychologization of the welfare state and has resulted in the expansion of medical and psychological ideas, practices, and actors in welfare institutions. Examples of the medicalization and psychologization of the welfare state can be found in initiatives on *active aging*, in the orientation of *early childhood education* toward health and the development of personal and social skills, in *health promotion and rehabilitation* for unemployed people and individuals who receive disability pensions, in the evolution of *parenting initiatives*, in *health promotion in the workplace*, and in the increased attention paid to *mental health and illness* across all areas (European Commission, 2013a, b).

The transformation of the welfare state can thus be divided into three phases: (1) the traditional welfare state, (2) neo-liberalism, and (3) social investment. Using this division enables us to demonstrate the varying potential for medicalization and psychologization within the welfare state. While these models developed in the suggested sequence, no one paradigm has yet fully replaced another. Thus, in reality, today's welfare states are hybrid institutional arrangements; this means that traditional social security, neo-liberal welfare, and social investment policies co-exist. How these institutional complementarities shape medicalization and psychologization processes is illustrated in detail in the following chapters on empirical social issues. However, first, we summarize how medicalization and psychologization can be empirically investigated by outlining our analytical model.

3.5 The Model of the Biopsychosocial Welfare State

Figure 3.1 presents our conceptual model, which we employ throughout this book. With this model, we map changes in the welfare state from the theoretical angles that can be found in the theory of both the welfare state and medicalization—namely the perspectives of *actors*, *institutions*, and *ideas*. Our goal is to capture the processes both within and between these three dimensions, which have thus far been primarily situated and analyzed in "the social realm" (capital–labor conflicts, economic and social inequalities, social rights and services) but have increasingly also been used to address the biological and the psychological realm. In addition to these different dimensions (i.e., actors, institutions, ideas), changes can occur on different levels of the welfare state: (1) on national and international levels of politics and policy = macro, (2) on the level of organizations and bureaucratic procedures = meso, and (3) in individual interactions, such as between clients and street-level bureaucrats or in doctor–patient interactions = micro.

We theorize how medicalization and psychologization processes and thus the move from the welfare state to a biopsychosocial welfare state may unfold by explaining how dimensions and levels interact. We outline

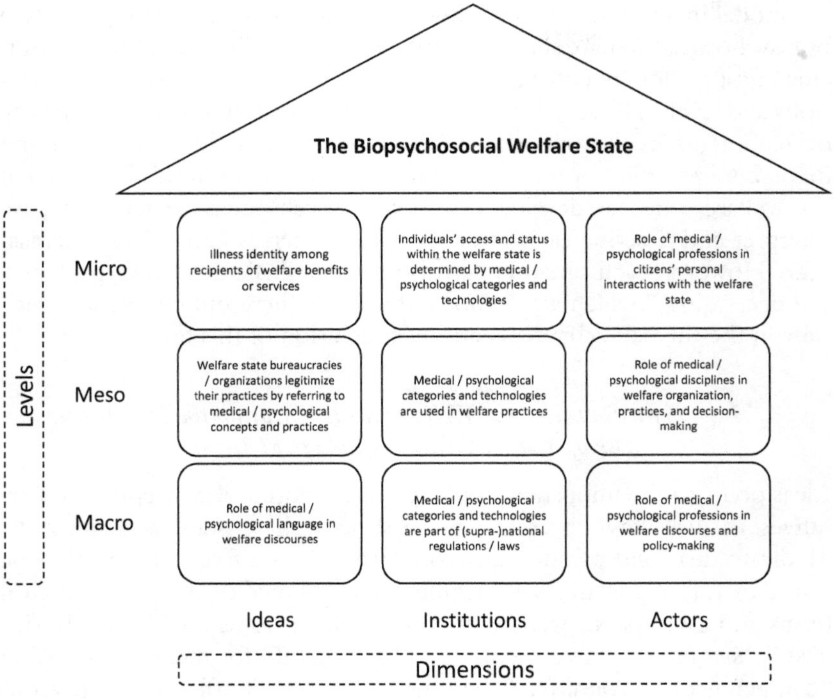

Fig. 3.1 The biopsychosocial welfare state framework

how such processes can materialize when medical and psychological *actors* play a different role within the welfare state. Medicalization and psychologization, can also mean that *institutions* increasingly rely on medical and psychological categories or technologies. Finally, these processes may take place against the background of the changing importance of medical and psychological *ideas* and bodies of knowledge in welfare discourses. Our model should be considered an ideal-typical model that developed from the theoretical considerations in both this and the previous chapter and with contributions from the empirical case studies that are presented in the following chapters. Furthermore, our analytical distinction between dimensions and levels (boxes in Fig. 3.1) aims to illustrate and operationalize the multiplicity and complexity with which processes of medicalization and psychologization unfold. In reality, there are many overlaps and interrelations that are not represented in the model. Finally, we interpret the model in a way that shows how the welfare state has developed into a biopsychosocial welfare state and thus also in a way that reveals how medicine and psychology enter or increase their scope in the different dimensions and levels. However, the model can also be used to label and analyze developments in the opposite direction—that is, de-medicalization and de-psychologization processes. As our main argument in this book is that the welfare state has developed into a biopsychosocial welfare state, we interpret and describe each category with the terms "more" or "increasing." However, each category can also be described with the terms "less" or "decreasing," which we do not elaborate on here but consider empirically in the thematic chapters and the conclusion of this book.

3.5.1 Transforming the Welfare State Through the Increasing Use of Medical and Psychological Ideas

Ideas point to the importance of language, theoretical concepts, and narratives in justifying or criticizing existing welfare state arrangements. Medicalization and psychologization within the welfare state can thus be traced by tracking changes in the importance of medical and psychological terms and concepts in welfare discourses. Such terms could include "illness," "symptom," "treatment," and "biological" for medical issues and "competences," "cognitive," "emotions," and "self-efficacy" for psychological issues. Moreover, there are concepts shared by both disciplines, such as "diagnosis," "therapy," and "health." On the *macro-level*, the development toward a biopsychosocial welfare state could be visible through the increased role of medical and psychological ideas in national discourses, which can be assessed, for instance, through (supra-)national policy documents, debates, court rulings, and media documents. This changing language can spur process on the *meso-level* and enable administrations of welfare state programs to legitimize their practices by referring to medical and psychological concepts in internal documents. Furthermore, organizations that act within the welfare state,—such as companies, unions, professional associations, foundations, and non-governmental associations—may influence discourses by using medical and psychological terms and concepts in external presentations (e.g., press releases, speeches). In the end, medicalization and psychologization can also take place on the *micro-level*, for example, when medical or psychological ideas (e.g., diagnoses, self-regulation skills) are used in interactions (e.g., between teachers and parents) or by individuals in the construction of their identities (e.g., the identity of being disabled).

3.5.2 *Transforming the Welfare State by Incorporating Medicine and Psychology in Welfare Institutions*

The stability of the welfare state is based on the institutionalization of welfare programs as social rights, including the development of public organizations that are responsible for the funding, organization, and regulation of welfare provision. Thus, medicalization and psychologization occur on the institutional level if medical and psychological knowledge and practices have become incorporated in terms of the way that welfare benefits and services are distributed. On the *macro-level*, medicalization and psychologization mean that medicine and psychology have become incorporated into legislation and policies, for example, through the use of medical and psychological categories and technologies. On the *meso-level*, medicalization and psychologization unfold by applying these categories and technologies in order to determine access to benefits and services (e.g., health questions that must be filled in on administrative forms) in welfare state agencies. Moreover, medicalization and psychologization do not necessarily mean that the medical or psychological profession is involved. For instance, in benefit assessments and the provision of services, medical and psychological concepts and technologies could be used by other professionals, such as teachers, social workers, and street-level bureaucrats. Finally, the institutionalization of medical and psychological categories shapes how individuals interact with the welfare state, how and for what benefits and services these individuals (can) apply, and how these individuals are categorized and treated by the system.

3.5.3 *Transforming the Welfare State by Involving Medical Doctors and Psychologists*

Finally, welfare states are reproduced and changed through actors; therefore, another important dimension of medicalization and psychologization in the welfare state is the involvement of medical doctors and psychologists. On the *macro-level*, the development toward a biopsychosocial welfare state can manifest in the growing influence of the professions and bio-medical companies that are involved in social-policy-reform processes. This growing influence might also be evident in the increased presence of representatives from these professions in the media or in political discourses. On the *meso-level*, medicalization and psychologization are visible when members of the two professions are involved in decision-making processes (e.g., as experts) or in service provision (e.g., by offering specialized medical or psychological services to students, unemployed people, families, etc.). At the *micro-level*, the role of the professions can be identified, for example, in the rising number of individuals who (have to) utilize medical or psychological services or who are assessed by these professions.

As defined and described above, the categories in which a move toward a biopsychosocial welfare state should be evident are not separate; rather, they overlap and are interrelated. For example, changing ideas on the macro-level shape whether and how medical definitions and categories become engrained in social law (institutions on the meso-level). These medical definitions have consequences for individuals when medicalized and psychologized categories and technologies are utilized and institutionalized within welfare organizations (institutions on the meso-level). Hence, the categories help us to disentangle certain aspects of a move toward a biopsychosocial welfare state and to pinpoint changes to certain levels and dimensions of the welfare state. The categories also facilitate the empirical measurement of medicalization and psychologization in the welfare state. However, it is important to stress that the interrelated view (i.e., evaluating all developments together) is most important when providing an overall assessment of the development toward a biopsychosocial welfare state.

3.6 An Integrated Model of Medicalization and Psychologization in the Welfare State

In this chapter, we revealed that it is useful and fruitful to analyze medicalization and psychologization within the welfare state. Despite empirical studies on medicalization and psychologization in specific welfare state programs, the different entries from the theoretical literature on medicalization and psychologization and on the welfare state have rarely been brought together. Thus, a theoretical model of how medicalization and psychologization unfold in the welfare state is missing. This issue is surprising because theoretical research angles and categories display similarities and complement one another. Furthermore, developments of and reforms to welfare states after their "golden age" have both intentionally and unintentionally paved the way for medicalized and psychologized welfare.

We developed an ideal-typical model of how welfare states evolve into biopsychosocial welfare states. Our model indicates that this transformation can occur on different levels (i.e., macro, meso, micro) and in different dimensions (i.e., ideas, institutions, and actors) of the welfare state. Hence, the model reveals the complexity of the change toward a biopsychosocial welfare state. As the examples indicate, medicine and psychology are added to and integrated with existing ideas, institutions, and actors of the welfare state. Thus, the welfare state is not fully taken over by medicine or psychology. Indeed, most social problems are neither completely defined by medicine or psychology nor completely transferred into their jurisdiction; however, these social problems are increasingly woven into the fabric of the "social" welfare state.

In the following chapters, we apply this model to three groups of welfare state recipients: the poor, the unemployed, and disadvantaged children. We focus on these groups because they have no direct lobby that stands up for their rights, and only advocates such as social welfare organizations and teachers defend them in welfare state arenas. Furthermore, as these groups have no direct lobby, medical professionals, in particular, might step in as advocates and add medical and psychological ideas to these discourses through the back door. Moreover, these groups are in many ways dependent on the state (i.e., through welfare benefits) and are regulated by it. Thus, they can hardly refuse or resist medicalized or psychologized access to welfare benefits because they depend on these benefits. In this context, processes of medicalization and psychologization are linked with the state monopoly of power. While technologies of the self may have become more important, they are tied to a system of force, rewards, and sanctions in the welfare state. Most importantly, they are also tied to resources and life chances.

References

Ariaans, M., & Reibling, N. (2021). Die Rolle von Gesundheit und Krankheit im deutschen Armutsdiskurs: Eine Inhaltsanalyse der Armuts- und Reichtumsberichte. *Zeitschrift Für Sozialreform, 67*(2), 123–152. https://doi.org/10.1515/zsr-2021-0005

Banerjee, A. V., Hanna, R., Kreindler, G. E., & Olken, B. A. (2017). Debunking the stereotype of the lazy welfare recipient: Evidence from cash transfer programs. *The World Bank Research Observer, 32*(2), 155–184. https://doi.org/10.1093/wbro/lkx002

Barbee, H., Moloney, M. E., & Konrad, T. R. (2018). Selling slumber: American neoliberalism and the medicalization of sleeplessness. *Sociology Compass, 12*(10), e12622. https://doi.org/10.1111/soc4.12622

Bauer, M. (1998). The medicalization of science news – from the "rocket-scalpel" to the "gene-meteorite" complex. *Social Science Information, 37*(4), 731–751. https://doi.org/10.1177/053901898037004009

Clarke, A. E., Mamo, L., Fishman, J. R., Shim, J. K., & Fosket, J. R. (2003). Biomedicalization: Technoscientific transformations of health, illness, and U.S. biomedicine. *American Sociological Review, 68*(2), 161. https://doi.org/10.2307/1519765

Conrad, P. (1992). Medicalization and social control. *Annual Review of Sociology, 18*(1), 209–232. https://doi.org/10.1146/annurev.so.18.080192.001233

Conrad, P. (2005). The shifting engines of medicalization. *Journal of Health and Social Behavior, 46*(1), 3–14. https://doi.org/10.1177/002214650504600102

Conrad, P. (2007). *The medicalization of society: On the transformation of human conditions into treatable disorders.* Johns Hopkins University Press. http://www.loc.gov/catdir/enhancements/fy0703/2006033235-b.html

Davis, J. E. (2016). Medicalization, social control, and the relief of suffering. In W. C. Cockerham (Ed.), *Wiley-Blackwell companions to sociology. The new Blackwell companion to medical sociology* (pp. 211–241). Wiley Blackwell.

Esping-Andersen, G. (1990). *The three worlds of welfare capitalism.* Wiley. https://books.google.de/books?id=KHdnAgAAQBAJ

European Commission. (2013a). *Investing in children: Breaking the cycle of disadvantage.* (Commission Recommendation of 20 February 2013–2013/112/EU). https://eur-lex.europa.eu/legal-content/EN/ALL/?uri=CELEX%3A32013H0112

European Commission. (2013b). *Investing in health: Commission Staff Working Document (SWD(2013)43final.* Brussels. http://ec.europa.eu/health/strategy/docs/swd_investing_in_health.pdf

Foster, D. (2018). The health and well-being at work agenda: Good news for (disabled) workers or just a capital idea? *Work, Employment and Society, 32*(1), 186–197. https://doi.org/10.1177/0950017016682458

Friedli, L. (2016). The politics of tackling inequalities: The rise of psychological fundamentalism in public health and welfare reform. In K. E. Smith, S. Hill, & C. Bambra (Eds.), *Health inequalities: Critical perspectives* (pp. 206–221). Oxford University Press.

Goijaerts, J., van der Zwan, N., & Bussemaker, J. (2022). Health and the social investment state. *Journal of European Public Policy, 1–21.* https://doi.org/10.1080/13501763.2022.2038239

Gusfield, J. R. (1989). Constructing the ownership of social problems: Fun and profit in the welfare state. *Social Problems, 36*(5), 431–441.

Halfmann, D. (2012). Recognizing medicalization and demedicalization: Discourses, practices, and identities. *Health (London, England: 1997), 16*(2), 186–207. https://doi.org/10.1177/1363459311403947

Halfmann, D. (2019). Political institutions and the comparative medicalization of abortion. *Journal of Health and Social Behavior*, 22146519843935. https://doi.org/10.1177/0022146519843935.

Hansen, H., Bourgois, P., & Drucker, E. (2014). Pathologizing poverty: New forms of diagnosis, disability, and structural stigma under welfare reform. *Social Science & Medicine, 1982*(103), 76–83. https://doi.org/10.1016/j.socscimed.2013.06.033

Harwood, V., Jones, S., Bonney, A., & McMahon, S. (2017). Heroic struggles, criminals and scientific breakthroughs: Adhd and the medicalization of child behaviour in Australian newsprint media 1999–2009. *International Journal of Qualitative Studies on Health and Well-Being, 12*(supl), 1298262. https://doi.org/10.1080/17482631.2017.1298262

Hemerijck, A. (2015). The quiet paradigm revolution of social investment. *Social Politics: International Studies in Gender, State & Society, 22*(2), 242–256. https://doi.org/10.1093/sp/jxv009

Holmqvist, M. (2009). Medicalization of unemployment: Individualizing social issues as personal problems in the Swedish welfare state. *Work, Employment and Society, 23*(3), 405–421. https://doi.org/10.1177/0950017009337063

Immergut, E. M. (1998). The theoretical core of the new institutionalism. *Politics and Society, 26*(1), 5–34. https://doi.org/10.1177/0032329298026001002

International Labour Organization. (2017). *Profiling youth labour market disadvantage: A review of approaches in Europe*. International Labour Organization.

Jane Jenson. (2012). Redesigning citizenship regimes after neoliberalism: Moving towards social investment. In B. Palier, J. Palme, & N. Morel (Eds.), *Towards a social investment welfare state? Ideas, policies and challenges* (pp. 61–88). Policy Press. https://bristoluniversitypressdigital.com/view/book/9781847429261/ch003.xml

Kaufman, J. (2020). Intensity, moderation, and the pressures of expectation: Calculation and coercion in the street-level practice of welfare conditionality. *Social Policy & Administration, 54*(2), 205–218. https://doi.org/10.1111/spol.12559

Kaufmann, F.-X. (Ed.). (2003). Vorträge/Nordrhein-Westfälische Akademie der Wissenschaften, Geisteswissenschaften: Vol. 387. *Die Entstehung sozialer Grundrechte und die wohlfahrtsstaatliche Entwicklung: 456.* Sitzung am 16. April 2003 in Düsseldorf. Schöningh.

Korpi, W. (1989). Power, politics, and state autonomy in the development of social citizenship: Social rights during sickness in eighteen OECD countries since 1930. *American Sociological Review, 54*(3), 309. https://doi.org/10.2307/2095608

Krayter, S., & Reibling, N. (2020). Medicalisation and psychologisation of poverty? An analysis of the scientific poverty discourse from 1956 to 2017. *Journal of Poverty and Social Justice, 28*(3), 361–381. https://doi.org/10.1332/175982720X15979441697421

Kvist, J. (2015). A framework for social investment strategies: Integrating generational, life course and gender perspectives in the EU social investment strategy. *Comparative European Politics, 13*(1), 131–149. https://doi.org/10.1057/cep.2014.45

LaMarre, A., Smoliak, O., Cool, C., Kinavey, H., & Hardt, L. (2019). The normal, improving, and productive self: Unpacking neoliberal governmentality in therapeutic interactions. *Journal of Constructivist Psychology, 32*(3), 236–253. https://doi.org/10.1080/10720537.2018.1477080

Lessenich, S. (2016). *Theorien des Sozialstaats zur Einführung* (E-Book-Ausgabe, 1. Aufl.). Junius.

Madsen, O. J. (2014). Psychologisation and critique in modern-day western culture. *Social and Personality Psychology Compass, 8*(5), 193–200.

Madsen, O. J. (2018). *The psychologisation of society: On the unfolding of the therapeutic in Norway*. Routledge. https://ebookcentral.proquest.com/lib/gbv/detail.action?docID=5437564

Marshall, T. H. (1939). The recent history of professionalism in relation to social structure and social policy. *The Canadian Journal of Economics and Political Science, 5*(3), 325. https://doi.org/10.2307/137036

Mathieu, A. (1993). The medicalization of homelessness and the theater of repression. *Medical Anthropology Quarterly, 7*(2), 170–184. https://doi.org/10.1525/maq.1993.7.2.02a00030

Michael Garrett, P. (2016). Questioning tales of 'ordinary magic': 'Resilience' and neo-liberal reasoning. *British Journal of Social Work, 46*(7), 1909–1925. https://doi.org/10.1093/bjsw/bcv017

Nolan, J. L. (1998). *The therapeutic state: Justifying government at century's end*. New York University Press. http://www.loc.gov/catdir/enhancements/fy0808/97021234-b.html.

Nullmeier, F., & Kaufmann, F.-X. (2021). Post-war welfare state development. In D. Béland, S. Leibfried, K. J. Morgan, H. Obinger, C. Pierson, F. Nullmeier, & F.-X. Kaufmann (Eds.), *The Oxford Handbook of the Welfare State* (pp. 92–111). Oxford University Press. https://doi.org/10.1093/oxfordhb/9780198828389.013.6

Olafsdottir, S. (2007). *Medicalizing mental health: A comparative view of the public, private, and professional construction of mental illness* [Dissertation]. Indiana University, Bloomington, IN.

Peeters, R. (2019). Manufacturing responsibility: The governmentality of behavioural power in social policies. *Social Policy and Society, 18*(1), 51–65. https://doi.org/10.1017/S147474641700046X

Pfau-Effinger, B. (2005). Culture and welfare state policies: Reflections on a complex interrelation. *Journal of Social Policy, 34*(1), 3–20. https://doi.org/10.1017/S0047279404008232

Pierson, P. (2000). Increasing returns, path dependence, and the study of politics. *American Political Science Review, 94*(2), 251–267. https://doi.org/10.2307/2586011

Rafalovich, A. (2005). Relational troubles and semiofficial suspicion: Educators and the medicalization of "unruly" children. *Symbolic Interaction, 28*(1), 25–46. https://doi.org/10.1525/si.2005.28.1.25

Reibling, N. (2019). Engine and brakes: European welfare states and the medicalization of social problems. *Europe Now*. https://www.europenowjournal.org/2019/06/10/engine-and-brakes-european-welfare-states-and-the-medicalization-of-social-problems/.

Rieff, P. (1987). *The Triumph of the therapeutic*. University of Chicago Press.

Rose, N. S. (1985). *The psychological complex: Psychology, politics and society in England; 1869–1939*. Routledge & Paul.

Rose, N. S. (1996). *Inventing our selves: Psychology, power, and personhood. Cambridge studies in the history of psychology*. Cambridge University Press. https://doi.org/10.1017/CBO9780511752179

Ross Arguedas, A. A. (2020). Medicalization in the media: News coverage of a new and uncertain diagnosis. *Journalism Practice, 14*(9), 1087–1105. https://doi.org/10.1080/17512786.2019.1684832

Schneider, W. (2013). Medikalisierung sozialer Prozesse. *Psychotherapeut, 58*(3), 219–236. https://doi.org/10.1007/s00278-013-0977-5

Schram, S. F. (2000). *After welfare: The culture of postindustrial social policy*. New York University Press. http://www.loc.gov/catdir/enhancements/fy0807/99006916-b.html.

Seeleib-Kaiser, M. (2016). The end of the conservative german welfare state model. *Social Policy & Administration, 50*(2), 219–240. https://doi.org/10.1111/spol.12212

Stenner, P., & Taylor, D. (2008). Psychosocial welfare: Reflections on an emerging field. *Critical Social Policy, 28*(4), 415–437. https://doi.org/10.1177/0261018308095278

Suavierol, S. (2015). Creating citizen-workers through civic integration. *Journal of Social Policy, 44*(4), 707–727. https://doi.org/10.1017/S0047279415000203

Thomas, F., Hansford, L., Ford, J., Wyatt, K., McCabe, R., & Byng, R. (2018). Moral narratives and mental health: Rethinking understandings of distress and healthcare support in contexts of austerity and welfare reform. *Palgrave Communications, 4*(39), 1–8. https://doi.org/10.1057/s41599-018-0091-y

van Kersbergen, K. (1995). *Social capitalism: A study of Christian democracy and the welfare state*. Routledge.

Verhoest, K., & Mattei, P. (2010). Special Issue on 'Welfare governance reforms and effects in the Post-Golden Age'. *Public Management Review, 12*(2), 163–171. https://doi.org/10.1080/14719031003616024

Watts, B., & Fitzpatrick, S. (2018). *Welfare conditionality* (1st ed.). Key ideas. Routledge.

Webster, C. (2020). Medicine and the welfare state 1930–1970. In R. Cooter & J. V. Pickstone (Eds.), *Medicine in the twentieth century* (pp. 125–140). Taylor & Francis. https://doi.org/10.4324/9781003078456-9

Wilensky, H. L., & Lebeaux, C. N. (1958). *Industrial society and social welfare: The impact of industrialization on the supply and organization of social welfare services in the United States.* Russell SAGE Foundation.

Wong, S. (2016). Geographies of medicalized welfare: Spatial analysis of supplemental security income in the U.S., 2000–2010. *Social Science & Medicine, 160*, 9–19. https://doi.org/10.1016/j.socscimed.2016.05.018

CHAPTER 4

Unemployment: A Case for Medicine and Psychology?

Philipp Linden and Nadine Reibling

Work is more than merely an existential necessity in many nations; indeed, it represents an ethical value and serves as an important source of individuals' identity and social status. Due to the importance attached to work, unemployment is considered a major social problem in most societies (Allmendinger & Ludwig-Mayerhofer, 2007). Providing social security for individuals who do not work is regarded as one of the key functions of the traditional welfare state. For instance, Esping-Andersen's (1990, p. 37) typology of welfare regimes is built on the level of decommodification—that is, "the degree to which individuals, or families, can uphold a socially acceptable standard of living independently of market participation"—that different welfare states provide. In order to deal with unemployment, many welfare states provide unemployment- and/or minimum income benefits, but more benefit schemes—including old-age pensions and

P. Linden (✉)
Fulda University of Applied Sciences, Fulda, Germany
e-mail: philipp.linden@gw.hs-fulda.de

N. Reibling
Fulda University of Applied Sciences, Fulda, Germany
e-mail: nadine.reibling@gw.hs-fulda.de

N. Reibling, M. Ariaans (eds.), *Toward a Biopsychosocial Welfare State?*, https://doi.org/10.1007/978-3-031-32793-3_4

parental-leave benefits—also exist that cover individuals who do not work for specific reasons. Notably, two (usually comparatively generous) programs tie benefits to sickness and involve the medical profession in determining eligibility: *sickness benefits* and *incapacity pensions*.[1] These benefit programs constitute a form of the medicalization of unemployment because they rely on medical ideas, practices, and actors to provide income replacement for an individual's inability to work. Since these programs were among the first to be established in welfare states (e.g., in Germany, invalidity pension insurance was introduced in 1891), the medicalization of unemployment in the welfare state has a long history. Thus, the general notion of the medicalization of unemployment can even be found in some early contributions, such as Parson's (1951) work on medical practice and the sick role and Stone's (1984) book *The Disabled State*. Nevertheless, the medicalization of unemployment has never been an important research topic in the medicalization literature or in social policy research.

However, this neglect of the medicalization of unemployment has changed in the last 20 years as both researchers and the policy community have become interested in the issue. This new concern with the medicalization of unemployment is linked to changes in welfare discourses and policies. While sickness benefits and incapacity pensions were viewed as clear achievements during the golden age of the welfare state, their appraisal changed with the rise of economic recessions and mass unemployment in the 1980s and 1990s. At first, these programs were considered solutions to mass unemployment, and individuals were deliberately channeled toward incapacity pension schemes (Lindsay & Houston, 2011). However, with the turn to neoliberalism and social investment discourses, the medicalization of unemployment came to be increasingly identified as a problem. This change resulted to some extent in the demedicalization of unemployment as access to—and the generosity of—these sickness-related programs became substantially reduced (McVicar et al., 2016) and the use of sickness as a justification for inactivity came to be challenged: "Many people with health problems can work and indeed want to work in ways compatible with their health condition, so any policy based on the assumption that they cannot work is fundamentally flawed" (OECD, 2010, p. 3). Within this new discourse and policy context, not

[1] In the US as well as in some of the research on this issue, the term "disability pensions" is used. We rely on the term "incapacity pensions" because it is closer to the term used by German schemes.

only were unemployed individuals with health problems pushed into labor market participation, but their ill health became increasingly considered a key point of intervention for the welfare state (Friedli, 2016). Considering the central role of medicine in these prevention, disease management, and rehabilitation programs, this time period also bore witness to a new form of medicalization along with both the growing role of mental illness in unemployment and the psychologization of unemployment.

In this context, a number of new social science contributions engaged with the medicalization of unemployment from various theoretical and empirical perspectives. Scholars have discussed the role that general practices (Ford et al., 2000; Wilfer et al., 2018), employment agencies (Holmqvist, 2009), the institutional characteristics of the welfare state (Buffel et al., 2017), and neoliberal policy reforms (Pulkingham & Fuller, 2012) have played in the medicalization of unemployment. Moreover, the medicalization of unemployment has developed from a theoretical concept into a measurable phenomenon. Studies have empirically operationalized the medicalization of unemployment through the use of mental healthcare among the unemployed (Buffel et al., 2015, 2017), through employability assessments of applicants for incapacity pensions (Schneider et al., 2016), through discourses in policy documents (Juberg & Skjefstad, 2019), and through changes in recipiency rates of disability- and non-disability-related benefits (Pulkingham & Fuller, 2012; Wong, 2016).

In this chapter, we synthesize this new line of research using our theoretical framework that conceptualizes the medicalization and psychologization of unemployment as a multi-level and multi-dimensional process (see Chap. 3). Moreover, we add new evidence from several types of data that we have collected to (a) illustrate the many forms in which we can investigate and empirically measure the medicalization and psychologization of unemployment and to (b) elaborate how the context of the German welfare state affects the extent and nature of the medicalization and psychologization of unemployment in comparison with liberal and social democratic welfare states, which have been the focus of the existing research in this area. The chapter proceeds as follows: First, we examine in greater detail how the existing literature views the concept the medicalization of unemployment and how we situate the concept within our own theoretical framework. Next, we turn to the German case and investigate how the institutional context of the welfare state affects medicalization processes. In so doing, we outline both medicalization and de-medicalization trends and highlight how in the case of Germany, the turn to activation has created new institutional categories and processes for medicalizing minimum income beneficiaries. In the following section, we reflect on the implications of these medicalization processes and present results regarding how medicalizing unemployed individuals affects labor market reintegration, health status, and public opinion within the context of the German minimum income system.

4.1 Medicalization and Psychologization of Unemployment: A Closer Look at the Phenomena

Applying Conrad's definition of medicalization (i.e., "to make something medical") to unemployment suggests that unemployment is *made* medical; thus, it is *transformed* into a medical problem. But what exactly does that mean? While many examples can be found in this research where medialization research has resulted in a new diagnosis of a social phenomenon (e.g., alcoholism, ADHD), the situation in the case of unemployment is more complex, and the medicalization of unemployment thus needs to be traced by following less apparent—but nevertheless powerful—changes in the way welfare states address unemployment. Using our conceptual framework, these changes can mean that medical *ideas* play a more important role in how we think and talk about unemployment in the welfare state, that medical categories and technologies are critical to the welfare state's *institutional* apparatus for dealing with unemployment, or that medical doctors become increasingly involved as *actors* in policymaking, welfare organizations, or personal interactions. In this chapter, we address all three dimensions by underlining the notion that the welfare state is integral to this process: Indeed, without its programs, organization, and regulations, there would be no medicalization of unemployment. The literature has also discussed and demonstrated the psychologization of unemployment, for instance, in terms of psychological profiling and psychological training programs, which have expanded with activating reforms (Friedli, 2016; International Labour Organization/European Commission, 2017; Peeters, 2019). However, the data sources that we rely on for Germany provide little evidence of the psychologization of unemployment, which is why this chapter is primarily focused on the medicalization of unemployment.

4.2 Medicalization of Unemployment in the German Welfare State: How Institutions Shape the Form and Dynamics of the (De-)medicalization of Unemployment

As a conservative welfare state, Germany relies heavily on contribution-based social insurance schemes to cover social risks. Much of the interest in and scholarship on the medicalization of unemployment has focused on incapacity pensions since they are costly and usually lead to permanent dependency. Figure 4.1 illustrates public spending on in-cash incapacity benefits as a percent of GDP in OECD countries, which can be taken as an indicator of the prominence of the program in different countries over time. The amount that OECD countries spend on incapacity benefits varies widely. While some countries do not have an established incapacity

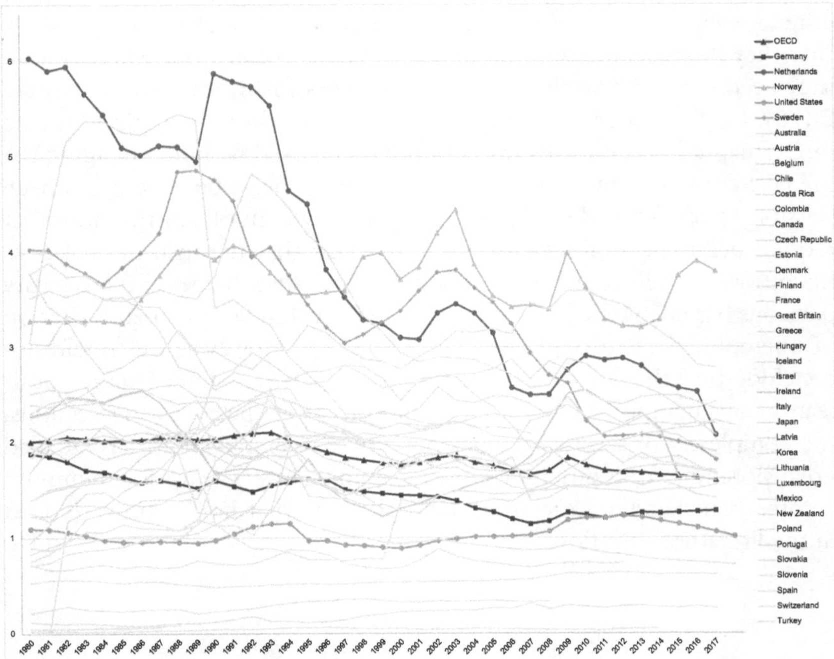

Fig. 4.1 OECD (2022), public spending on incapacity as a % of GDP (indicator); DOI: 10.1787/f35b71ed-en (last accessed 10 June 2022), own graph

pension, other countries sometimes spend up to 6% of their GDP on this scheme. The figure also reveals that between 1980 and 2018, many countries bore witness to a dynamic that looks in part like a convergence on the steadily declining OECD average.

Germany already had a comparatively low spending rate in 1980 that further declined in the following decades. The primary reason for this low spending rate is that in Germany, access to incapacity pensions has been limited due to an early reform that aimed to address the rising recipiency rates over the 1970s (McVicar et al., 2016). Only individuals who have paid social insurance contributions in three of the five years before their application and who have additionally accumulated five years of contributions overall are eligible to receive incapacity pensions. This eligibility criteria excludes young individuals, long-term unemployed individuals, and people—particularly women—who have not worked enough years or who work in so-called mini jobs, for which social insurance contributions are not paid. In 2001, a second reform took place that tightened the eligibility criteria even further. Before the reform, applicants had needed to show that they were unable to work in their trained occupation, whereas now, they need to show that they are unable to work in any job (McVicar et al., 2016). In effect, access to incapacity pensions has been strongly restricted in Germany. However, this restriction has occurred without changing the medical criteria or the underlying assessment process because it has been possible to constrain eligibility based on the payment of contributions that require previous employment. Thus, it seems that the institutional configuration of contribution-based social insurance schemes for incapacity pensions has enabled Germany to achieve a low level of the medicalization of unemployment through incapacity pensions. However, we should not conclude that the conservative welfare state generally limits the medicalization of unemployment. As we demonstrate in the following sections, the complexity of several schemes that cover unemployment has entailed great potential for a different form of temporary sick leave for minimum income beneficiaries—a form of medicalization that has been overlooked in the literature thus far.

4.3 Institutional Complexity and Competing Organizational Actors as Mechanisms of Medicalization

In Germany, benefits for individuals who are unemployed *and* ill do not come from a single welfare scheme; rather, several schemes are involved. This fragmented benefit structure is based on the historical creation of different social insurance schemes and social assistance systems, namely, (1) public *health insurance*, which provides sickness benefits of up to 78 weeks; (2) *unemployment insurance*, which provides unemployment benefits of up to 18 months; (3) means-tested minimum income benefits, which are provided as *social assistance*; and (4) incapacity pensions, which are paid via *pension insurance* to individuals who have limited working capacity. In 2004/5, Germany passed several neoliberal reforms that rearranged the unemployment insurance and social assistance system. In essence, the duration of unemployment insurance benefits was shortened so that now, individuals are transferred to minimum income benefits relatively quickly (after one year) and lose access to benefits if they have savings or a partner who provides sufficient working income. Following other countries, Germany also introduced a new system of unemployment activation measures (Bonoli, 2010) that reinforce work incentives through the increased conditionality of benefits (Clasen & Clegg, 2007; Dwyer, 2008; Watts & Fitzpatrick, 2018). Importantly, the conditionality of benefits is now extended to individuals on minimum income benefits.

As a basis for benefit receipt, individuals on unemployment or minimum income benefits are obligated to sign an integration agreement that specifies the requirements for receiving their benefits. Unemployed individuals must always be available for their Federal Employment Agency officers, attend appointments with them, and participate in suggested training measures. These individuals are additionally required to seek and accept any reasonable job, even if (depending on their personal situation) this requires a change of residence. If they do not comply with these obligations, the Federal Employment Agency can impose sanctions. For instance, minimum income benefits could be reduced by between 10% and 30% for three months if appointments at the Federal Employment Agency are not met.[2]

The underlying idea of these reforms was to create work incentives not only for those who are formally considered unemployed (i.e., those who receive unemployment insurance benefits and who are actively looking for work), but for all inactive individuals. While medical and psychological ideas played hardly any role in the political discourse that preceded the reforms (see Chap. 5), it is clear from this discourse that the general intention of the reforms was to limit the possibilities of being able to justify the receipt of long-term or permanent benefits for most individuals. Thus, activation policies were explicitly extended to vulnerable populations (including sick individuals). This issue was controversial in the reform discussions, as the following quote demonstrates: "The mobilization of the unemployed and of minimum income beneficiaries is particularly difficult for single mothers and fathers, for the elderly, and for the sick. What, then, should be done with those who—despite the strongest will—can no longer be made fit? Are benefit cuts really all that comes to the government's mind?" (Deutscher Bundestag, 2002, p. 417). Despite this protest, the extension of activation to all minimum income beneficiaries was kept in the legislation.

However, the reform set the capability of working as the central legal basis for activation decisions. In §8 (1) of Social Code Book II, the capability of working is defined as follows:

> Someone is considered able to work if they are not incapable of working at least three hours per day for the foreseeable future due to illness or disability under the usual conditions of the general labor market.

Since this definition highlights the fact that sickness and disability are the only accepted reasons that preclude labor market integration, the reform

[2] A recent ruling by the Federal Constitutional Court in 2019 significantly restricted the sanction regulations and called on the legislature to introduce new regulations. According to this ruling, sanctions above 30% of minimum income benefits are generally unconstitutional and must be abolished. Currently, the so-called sanction moratorium applies until the new regulation—that suspends sanctions for breaches of duty (e.g., the rejection of work)—takes effect. However, sanctions for failure to report (e.g., failure to keep appointments) are still possible.

upgraded the legal status of sickness/disability in the context of unemployment. Thus, although it was not the intention of the reform, its implementation resulted in the medicalization of unemployment within the minimum income system.

Aside from this promotion of medicalization through the abovementioned reform, the historically developed coverage system in Germany—with its high degree of *institutional complexity* and *competing organizational actors*—also fosters the medicalization of unemployment. In order to understand how institutional complexity and organizational competition are associated with medicalization, we next walk step by step through the institutional process through which every unemployed person in Germany who becomes ill must navigate. Figure 4.2 outlines the involved organizations and regulations that structure this process.

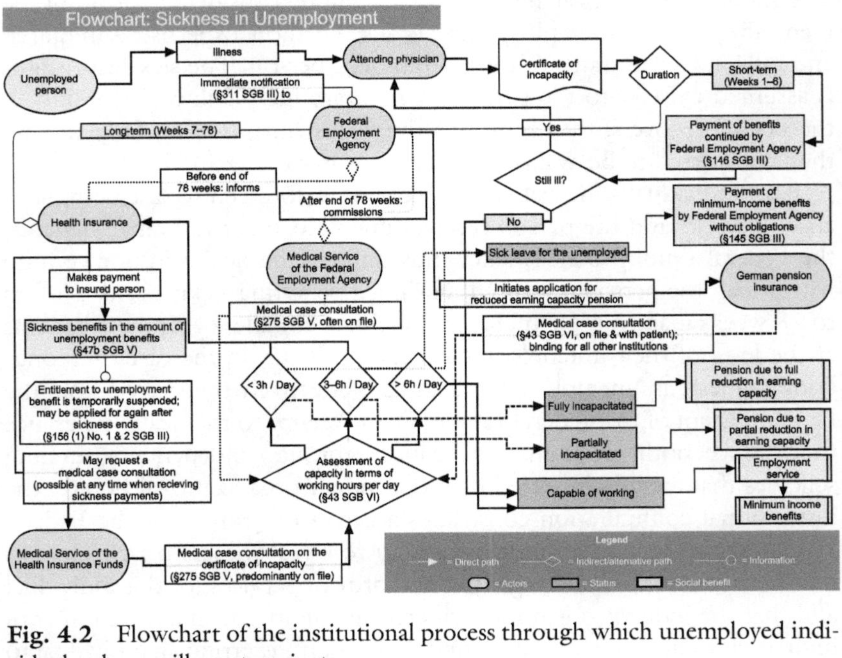

Fig. 4.2 Flowchart of the institutional process through which unemployed individuals who are ill must navigate

4.3.1 Temporarily Incapable of Working: The Transition to Health Insurance Schemes

The process begins with an unemployed person, who—depending on the duration of their unemployment—receives either unemployment insurance or minimum income benefits. If this person becomes ill, they are obligated to promptly report their incapacity to work to the responsible advisor of the Federal Employment Agency. For this purpose, a certificate of the individual's incapacity to work that is issued by a personal physician must be submitted no later than the third day of illness. This certificate must include the expected duration of the illness as noted by the physician. For up to six weeks, the beneficiary receives their usual benefits. The sick-leave certificate is used to justify the individual's incapacity to meet their obligations (e.g., looking for work, participating in training measures) and to safeguard their benefits against sanctions as a result of this incapacity. The status of being incapable of working can be considered a form of the medicalization of unemployment because medical expertise is required and influences the status of the unemployed person. The sick-leave status is assumed to refer to the person's temporary incapability of working. If the person recovers, they return to the status *capable of working* and are then considered to be available to the labor market again.

If an individual's incapability of working is foreseen to last between 7 and 78 weeks and the person receives unemployment insurance benefits, the Federal Employment Agency must inform the health insurance fund with which the person is insured. Having a persisting sickness status of up to 78 weeks makes an unemployed individual eligible for sickness benefits at the level of their unemployment benefits. Thus, in the case of a long-lasting illness, an unemployed individual is effectively transferred from the benefit system of the Federal Employment Agency to the health insurance fund. Since both programs are financed through independent funding schemes that are administered by independent organizational bodies, the institutional configuration constitutes a zero-sum game. For the Federal Employment Agency, an individual who receives sickness benefits means that the agency must no longer pay and provide services for this individual and that the individual is not considered unemployed. In a situation with high levels of unemployment or limited funds, transferring an individual to the health insurance system can constitute temporary relief for an employment agency. The sick unemployed person can receive sickness benefits as long as their personal physician provides a certificate of their incapacity to work for a maximum of 78 weeks. However, the health insurance fund can commission a medical report at any time during this period that reviews the case and provides an assessment of the likelihood that a given treatment will restore the individual's capability of working. These reports are conducted by a health insurance fund's medical service—an agency that is funded and organized by all regional health insurance funds[3]: "The purpose of the expert opinion is to support the therapeutic efforts of the treating physicians with the aim of achieving reintegration into the work process and preventing permanent exclusion from working life" (Pfeiffer & Pick, 2011).

This assessment focuses on evaluating a person's ability to work and their overall health. However, assessing work capability cannot be done with illness symptoms or medical diagnoses alone (Meershoek, 2012); thus, even though medical doctors are responsible for these reports, the decision is considered to be socio-medical and additionally takes into consideration, for example, the individual's work requirements. Health insurance funds commission these assessments in order to review the individual's sick-leave status because these funds have an incentive to terminate the payment of sickness benefits. If the assessment concludes that the person is capable of working, the case is re-transferred to the Federal Employment Agency and the minimum income-benefit system. If the assessment indicates that the person could be partially or fully incapacitated for a longer period, the health insurance fund can inform the pension fund of a potential case for incapacity pensions. Nevertheless, the health insurance fund is still required to exhaust the 78 weeks of sickness benefits before a referral to the pension system may be made.

4.3.2 *Sickness Benefits Exhausted: The Transition Back to the Federal Employment Agency*

Before sickness benefits expire after 78 weeks, an individual's health insurance fund informs the Federal Employment Agency of the individual's status. If the individual is still sick, the Federal Employment Agency usually commissions its own medical service agency to make an assessment. The medical service agency consists of approximately 350 nationally

[3] The legal structure of the medical service has recently been changed, thereby making this service independent from sickness funds and created a nationwide organization with coherent assessment regulations.

operating full-time physicians as well as contracted physicians (about 20–40%, depending on the social security institution). In the case of a mental illness, employed and contracted psychologists are also consulted (Allert, 2021). The medical service agency provides consultancy services that include support and medical/psychological advice for Federal Employment Agency officers regarding both how to proceed as well as arranging meetings with individuals who have health restrictions. Before an individual's health insurance scheme terminates their sickness benefits, employment officers may initiate an assessment by the medical service of the Federal Employment Agency in order to clarify the further course of action. The unemployed person is then required to fill out a health questionnaire and must release any previous treating medical doctors from confidentiality. At this point, the sick-leave status is exclusively assessed and granted by the medical service of the Federal Employment Agency and no longer by the individual's treating medical doctors.

The requested assessment is mostly carried out based on the information ascertained from the health questionnaire and the existing medical documentation (in about 70–80% of cases) and rarely includes a personal examination (in about 20–30% of cases). Personal appearances are especially indicated for addictive disorders, mental illness, or an evaluation for educational or retraining eligibility (Hotz, 2022). Based on this documentation, the medical service provides an assessment of how many hours per day the person is capable of working (in any job). If this assessment establishes that the person is still unable to work more than six hours per day for more than six months, the individual's ability to work is assumed to be incapable of being restored in the foreseeable future. In this case, the employment officer can suggest that the unemployed person apply for an incapacity pension. However, this is only possible for individuals who fulfill the eligibility criteria (i.e., contributions must have been paid to the pension insurance fund for five years in total and in three of the preceding five years). Both during the pension insurance scheme's decision-making process and in the event that the individual does not meet the eligibility criteria, they receive the status of "sick leave for unemployment," which means that they continue to receive minimum income benefits but do not have to meet any work obligations. Moreover, they do not have to fear sanctions for non-compliance, such as a cancelation of their benefits.

4.3.3 (Temporary/Partial) Incapacity Pensions: The Transition to Pension Insurance

Before a final decision has been made as to whether an individual is to receive an incapacity pension, benefit recipients have the option (just like employed individuals who are ill) to apply for occupational rehabilitation in order to restore (partial) work capacity. For this purpose, a transitional rehabilitation allowance for the duration of the medical rehabilitation service is paid. The application is filed with the pension insurance scheme, and the applicant must have paid at least six months of compulsory contributions in the two preceding years. The amount of the benefit is then equal to the amount of the unemployment benefit or the minimum income benefit. Moreover, during occupational rehabilitation, the individual receives an additional benefit of 35% of the general standard benefit on top of their minimum income benefits.

If all other options (including rehabilitation) have been exhausted, an unemployed individual who is ill can apply for an incapacity pension. This application must also be submitted to the pension insurance fund, which itself may use the existing reports by the medical service of the health insurance fund or the medical service of the Federal Employment Agency but can—and often does—prepare its own socio-medical assessment of the individual's capability of working. Similar to the assessment by the medical service of the Federal Employment Agency, these socio-medical case assessments are often carried out on the basis of records as well as—albeit to a lesser extent—via direct interactions with the person concerned. Depending on the number of hours that this assessment determines that the individual is capable of working, this individual may be eligible for a partial or full incapacity pension. The incapacity pension is earnings-related and thus depends on previous earnings and the age of the applicant. In 2020, the average pension was 415 euros for a partial incapacity benefit and 830 euros for a full incapacity pension. This means that the average partial incapacity benefit levels are roughly the same as those of minimum income benefits (which were 432 euros in 2020). The pension insurance fund alone decides on the individual's respective entitlement to incapacity pension benefits. This decision is binding for all other social benefit providers. If an application is rejected by the pension insurance fund, the person remains within the jurisdiction of the Federal Employment Agency and receives minimum income benefits.

4.3.4 *Summary: Medicalization Within the Institutional Process*

The flow chart in Fig. 4.2 illustrates the complexity of the process that we outlined in detail above. This complexity derives from the parallel existence of multiple schemes that provide benefits based on different logics and eligibility criteria. The focus of this institutional process is not on the individual or on the question of how best to support an individual who is unemployed and apparently also has poor health; instead, the process is oriented toward institutions and actors as well as toward the question of who is responsible for this person and who must pay the benefits.

The current system fosters medicalization via several processes. First, organizational actors—particularly the Federal Employment Agency—use medical definitions of employability and accredited illnesses in order to transfer an individual to another benefit system. Thus, the current legal rules incentivize to some extent the provision of sickness-related benefits and thus also medicalization in the *institutional* dimension (see theoretical framework in Chap. 3). Moreover, several medical doctors assess the case throughout the entire process, which is itself indicative of medicalization in the *actor* dimension. These medical assessments are based on medical diagnostic criteria as well as on instructions and regulations from the specific benefit system. Thus, in his comparison of assessments made by the medical service of the Federal Employment Agency and the pension insurance scheme, Brussig (2018) notes that it is not uncommon for performance assessments to differ significantly.

There is some indication that this system may have increased the degree of the medicalization of unemployment in Germany over time. First, between 2009 and 2017, the number of assessments made by the medical service of the Federal Employment Agency varied between 500,000 and 550,000 cases. However, the number of unemployed people steadily decreased from 3.4 million to 2.5 million in the same period (Fig. 4.3). Thus, the share of unemployed individuals who were reviewed by medical services increased over this period from 16% to 22%.

Second, data from a representative survey of minimum income recipients (Linden & Reibling, 2023) indicate that the share of respondents in the survey who were receiving sick leave for unemployment—that is, minimum income benefits without work obligations—had tripled over time.

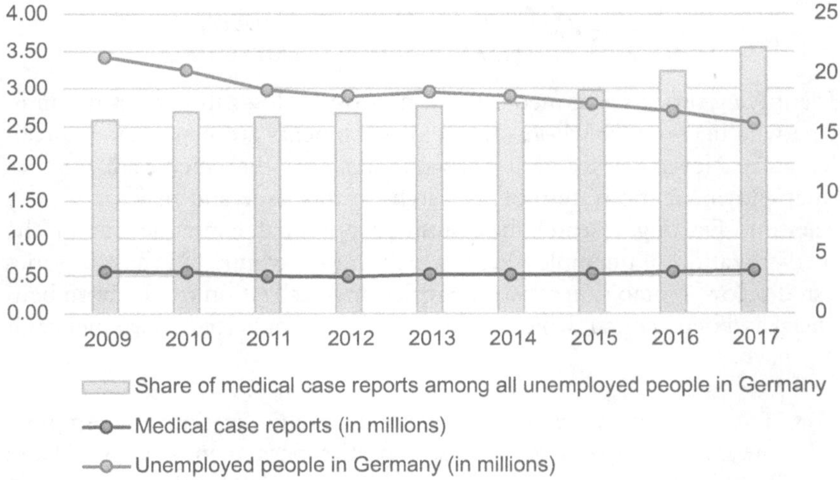

Fig. 4.3 Share (bars) of medical case reports completed by the medical service agency of the Federal Employment Agency among all unemployed people in Germany (lines). Sources: data on medical assessment services from the Federal Employment Agency, and annual reports on unemployment and minimum income benefits for jobseekers in Germany (2006–2018)

While this may also be the result of the poorer health status of the remaining unemployed individuals in the sample (and in the system), the fact that on average 18% of unemployed individuals in the study reported receiving sick leave indicates the importance of this sickness-related category for unemployed individuals in Germany (Linden & Reibling, 2023). Thus, the neoliberal labor market reforms that aimed to include all inactive individuals in the activation regime has led to the inclusion of many individuals with health problems in the minimum income scheme. Despite the ambitious aims and expectations of the reforms, the challenge of integrating this vulnerable group into the labor market has often failed. While this failure likely has many reasons (e.g., locally difficult labor markets, missing instruments for health promotion, and rehabilitation), one result has been a new form of medicalization of unemployment through the category of sick leave for the unemployed.

4.4 What Are the Consequences of the Medicalization of Unemployment?

Identifying processes of medicalization or psychologization does not indicate whether—or for whom—these developments are beneficial or problematic. Nevertheless, the consequences of the medicalization of unemployment motivate most research on this issue and make it socially relevant. Existing research has outlined potential consequences of the medicalization of unemployment, which can be grouped in the categories listed below. Notably, in most categories, medicalization can be both beneficial and detrimental, which highlights the contradictory consequences it can have.

- *Economic consequences*: For society, the medicalization of unemployment is expensive (e.g., medical expertise, permanent sickness-related benefits) and reduces the available human capital for the labor market (Lindsay & Houston, 2011). For individuals, the medicalization of unemployment can mean income security but also increased poverty risk if re-employment opportunities are lower in the long term (Hansen et al., 2014; Holmqvist, 2009).
- *Health consequences*: Tying benefits to sickness and requiring the repeated demonstration of an individual's sickness/incapacity leads to the development of a chronic-illness identity, the acceptance of (potentially harmful) medical/psychological treatment, and an impeded recovery (Hansen et al., 2014; Schneider, 2013). In contrast, the medicalization of unemployment has brought attention to the health consequences of unemployment, has created access to specialized programs, and—in the case of long-term incapacity—may improve health compared with being employed in harmful working conditions (Burgard & Lin, 2013) or living in poverty without access to benefits (Hansen et al., 2014).
- *Individualization and stigmatization*: A central claim of medicalization theory is the inherent risk of individualizing social problems (Conrad, 1992; Zola, 1972). Medicalizing unemployment means that the reason for unemployment—and consequently, also its solution—is attributed to the individual (Holmqvist, 2009). This means that the medicalization of unemployment runs the risk of leading to the further social exclusion of individuals who are not only unemployed, but also sick (Lindsay & Houston, 2011). While being sick

used to be an accepted justification for unemployment and potentially reduced the stigma surrounding illness, the current welfare discourse on activation may induce additional stigma for individuals because it often characterizes these individuals as failing to manage their health or considers them potential "benefit scroungers" (Garthwaite, 2014; Hansen et al., 2014).

While existing studies have used these consequences as a source of motivation or have pointed to the consequences of medicalization in their conclusions, there is limited evidence on the actual consequences of this medicalization of unemployment. Existing evidence comes mostly from qualitative studies, which indicate the difficulties that individuals experience and the strategies that they use to navigate their given situations (Garthwaite, 2014; Hansen et al., 2014; Kupka et al., 2017). In the following two sections, we present the evidence that we have gathered on the consequences of medicalization in Germany. The first of these two sections examines the implications of being on sick leave for the unemployed who do not (yet) have access to incapacity benefits in the minimum income system. The second of the two sections presents data on how the medicalization of unemployment has influenced public attitudes toward the unemployed based on a nationwide vignette survey that we launched in 2020.

4.4.1 *Being on Sick Leave: Consequences Regarding Re-employment Opportunities and Health*

In order to better understand the consequences of the status of "sick leave for the unemployed" in the German minimum income system, we examined data from a representative survey on minimum income beneficiaries: namely, the German Panel Study Labour Market and Social Security (PASS).[4] In this study, 3910 individuals—or 21% of the sample—reported being on sick leave for the unemployed. Of these cases, a transition from unemployment to sick leave can be seen in 1585 cases or 8% of the sample. As outlined above, the number of individuals with this status in the survey tripled over time (observation period: 2008–2019). Moreover, we detect that certain groups who have less favorable labor market outlooks—that is, older people and people with lower levels of education—are more likely to be on sick leave, which serves as a strong indication that this category is

[4] For a description of the study, please refer to Bethmann et al. (2013).

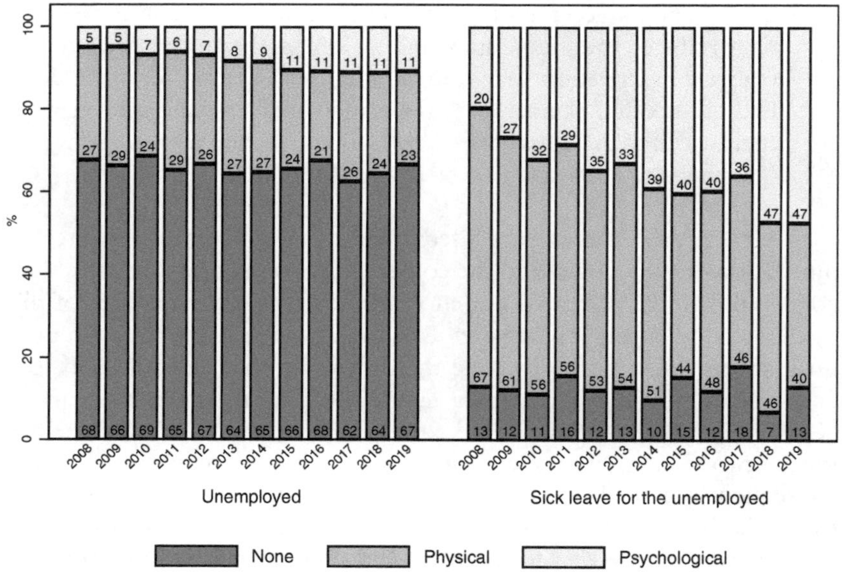

Fig. 4.4 Type of sickness over time for the unemployed/sick leave for the unemployed. Source: PASS Waves 2–13, DOI: 10.5164/IAB.PASS-SUF0619.de.en.v3, weighted Federal Employment Agency sample, $N = 20{,}196$

also used to dealing with the problems of labor market integration (Linden & Reibling, 2023). In line with the literature, there is little indication that this category is abused to cover individuals who are actually in good health (Lindsay & Houston, 2011). Indeed, as can be seen in Fig. 4.4, around 85% of individuals on sick leave report having a long-standing, limiting illness, while only around 35% of the minimum income recipients who are not on sick leave report the same.

Moreover, we see a striking trend in the increasing number of individuals who reported a psychological condition (Fig. 4.4). This trend toward the psychologization of unemployment that we find here for sick-leave status has also been found for sickness benefits and incapacity pensions in many countries. This finding indicates that although this chapter has thus far told the story of the medicalization of unemployment (which is also what we primarily see in the benefit systems), a psychologization of unemployment is also taking place. While our data cannot reveal much more

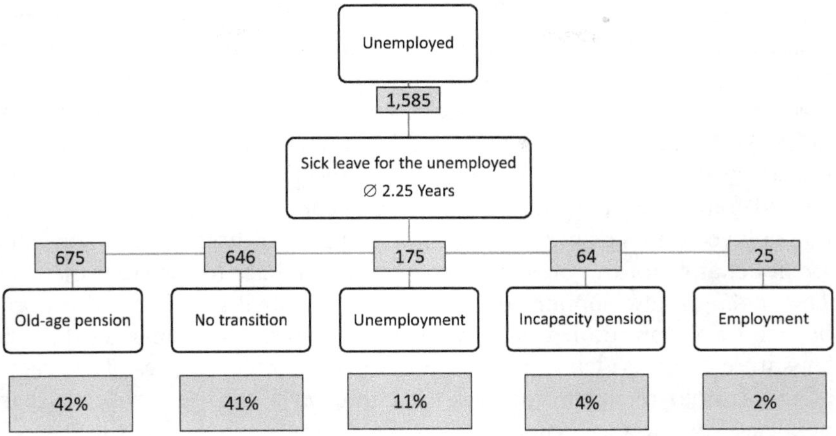

Fig. 4.5 Transitions within the German minimum income system. Source: PASS Waves 2–13, DOI: 10.5164/IAB.PASS-SUF0619.de.en.v3, weighted Federal Employment Agency sample, $N = 20{,}196$

about the latter process, it seems that it is has become a topical issue in both scientific and public debates (Buffel et al., 2017; Friedli, 2016).

Now that we have characterized both the category of sick leave and the individuals who receive these benefits, we can next turn to the consequences of being in this medicalized category in terms of employment/income opportunities and further health development. As outlined above, the medicalization of unemployment has been hypothesized to have ambiguous consequences: On the one hand, medicalization may provide economic stability, lower the pressure caused by being exempt from activation, and provide time for health recovery. On the other hand, this category could cause people to become stuck in the benefit system and increase their levels of social exclusion. Figure 4.5 reveals what happened to individuals who at some point during their participation in the survey were granted the status of sick leave for the unemployed ($N = 1585$). On average, these individuals kept this status for 2.25 years, which indicates that the status often has a long duration.

Forty-two percent of those on sick leave transitioned from this status to old-age pensions, which indicates that sick leave for the unemployed is quite often used for older minimum income beneficiaries in the years before their retirement. Another 41% of those in our sample remained in the sick-leave category for as long as we could observe them. Eleven percent transitioned back to unemployment, which suggests that their health status had improved so much that they were considered capable of working again. Only 4% of those on sick leave transitioned to incapacity pensions, which indicates that sick leave for the unemployed is not primarily a transitory status on the way to receiving incapacity benefits and that it instead compensates for the problem that occurs when individuals who are unemployed and sick but who are not considered incapacitated (or who are not eligible for this benefit) do not transition back to the labor market. This finding is also supported by the fact that only 2% of those who were on sick leave transitioned directly to employment. These analyses do not constitute causal evidence of the re-employment opportunities of medicalizing unemployment through sick leave[5]; however, we can clearly see that sick leave for the vast majority of people means remaining in the benefit system and either staying on sick leave or transitioning to other benefit schemes.

Being on sick leave could also impact the development of an individual's health status, as is illustrated in Fig. 4.6. On the left-hand side, we see that respondents who were on sick leave had a poorer health status on average than did regular minimum income beneficiaries. The health status of both groups remained constant over time. However, if we look at individual transitions, such as how individual health developed before and after the transition to sickness, we see the following pattern: In the three years prior to moving to sick leave, the health status of individuals deteriorated, but after being on sick leave, their health status stabilized at the level of the transition.

In sum, our analyses of the impact of the medicalization of unemployment on re-employment and health suggest that being on sick leave in Germany might simultaneously foster better health and social exclusion. While these results are only first attempts at shedding light on the consequences of the medicalization of unemployment, they illustrate that medicalization often goes hand in hand with ambiguity for the welfare state as well as for the life chances of affected individuals.

[5] Due to endogeneity, this would be difficult to establish with observational data.

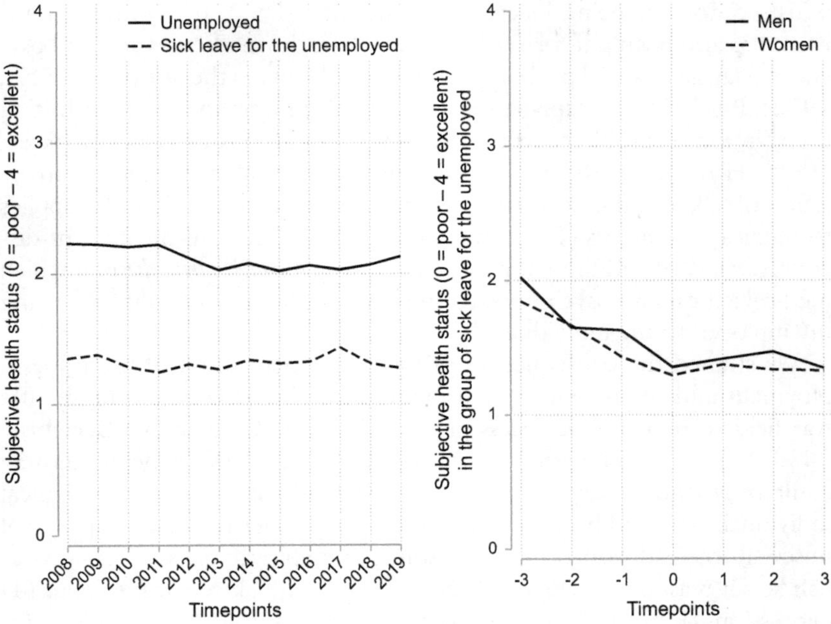

Fig. 4.6 Comparison of subjective health status over time between the unemployed and those on sick leave for the unemployed (left), and a comparison of subjective health status before and after a transition to sick leave for the unemployed ($T = 0$) between gender groups (right). Source: PASS Waves 2–13, DOI: 10.5164/IAB.PASS-SUF0619.de.en.v3, weighted Federal Employment Agency sample, $N = 20,196$

4.4.2 Medicalization and Public Attitudes Toward Unemployed Individuals

Evaluating the implications of medicalization for an individual's life chances is important, but there is another key aspect that should be considered: namely, how the perception of unemployment and unemployed individuals changes through medicalization and psychologization. This aspect has been central to the theoretical literature on medicalization and psychologization and has been shrouded in controversy. On the one hand, some scholars have argued that medicalization and psychologization go hand in hand with the benefit of being relieved from blame and stigma, particularly in comparison with a moral or penal interpretation of a social problem (Conrad & Schneider, 1992; Parsons, 1951). This *relief hypothesis* could also apply in the case of unemployment, where sickness can work as a justification for being inactive. On the other hand, the contrary argument has also been put forward. Nevertheless, the medicalization and psychologization of social problems tie these problems to the individual (Zola, 1972). Psychological explanations in particular always focus on attributing the solution to problems in an individual's cognitions or behavior (Rose, 1998). However, in the current neoliberal and social investment interpretation of sickness, the view that the individual is self-responsible also applies to medical conditions (Holmqvist et al., 2013). Thus, in the current discourse, we could additionally formulate a ***responsibility hypothesis*** in which medicalization and psychologization attribute the responsibility for being unemployed to the individual.

We studied the consequences of the public perception of both unemployment and the unemployed using a self-designed factorial survey that was fielded in an online access panel of YouGov Germany in December 2020/January 2021 with a quota-based sample of the general German adult population. Respondents were given descriptions of hypothetical individuals who had become unemployed for various reasons: (1) personal misconduct—individual; moral reason; (2) employer bankruptcy—external; social reason; (3) chronic back pain—individual; medical reason; (4) depression—individual; psychological reason; and (5) risk group for COVID-19—individual; medical reason. Respondents were asked different questions about this hypothetical vignette person. By comparing answers between groups that had received different vignettes as part of the experimental variation, we can assess how the medicalization or psychologization of unemployment compares with a moral or social explanation of unemployment.

We asked respondents about the extent to which they agreed with the statement that the described person was to blame for (1) losing their job and (2) not having found a new job after 12 months. Respondents provided answers on a 7-point Likert scale ranging from 0 = "not at all" to 6 = "entirely." Figure 4.7 reveals the effects of the multivariate regression model. We can see that compared with individuals who had become unemployed due to the bankruptcy of their employer, individuals who had become unemployed due to chronic back pain or depression were blamed significantly more for their unemployment. At the same time, these individuals were blamed substantially less than if a moral explanation (e.g., personal misconduct) had been given. In terms of blame for not finding a new job, there was no difference between the psychologization of unemployment and employer bankruptcy, whereas the medicalization of

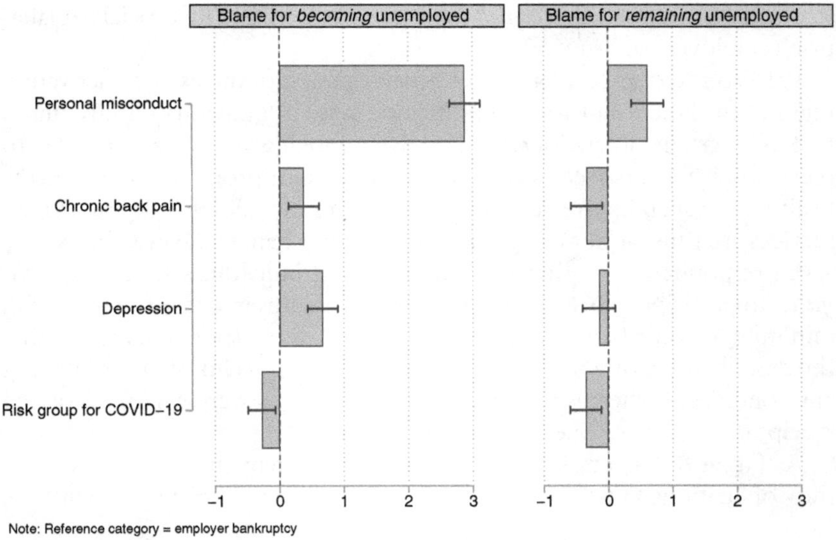

Fig. 4.7 Multivariate OLS coefficients and 95% confidence intervals of approval ratings for the question of whether the described unemployed individuals were themselves to blame for (1) their unemployment and (2) not finding a new job based on different reasons for unemployment. Widths of bars indicate the difference in approval ratings on a 7-point Likert scale compared with the reference category (employer bankruptcy). Source: vignette study, Wave 2 (in 2020) (N = 1843), own weighted sample calculations

unemployment went hand in hand with slightly less blame. Individuals who had lost their job due to personal misconduct were again blamed significantly more, whereas individuals who had lost their job because they belonged to a risk group for COVID-19 were blamed significantly less for both becoming and remaining unemployed. This latter finding could point on the one hand to the respondents' high sensitivity to this issue at the time of data collection (i.e., during the second wave of COVID-19 in Germany). On the other hand, respondents might have attributed less control to the reasoning risk group for COVID-19 than they would have if unemployment had been justified by chronic back pain or depression. In sum, while our results suggest that the medicalization or psychologization of unemployment indeed results in some *relief* compared with the moralization of unemployment (personal misconduct), they also suggest a stronger attribution of ***responsibility*** when compared with a social explanation (employer bankruptcy).

We also asked respondents about their opinion of the existing activation regime. In the current minimum income system, individuals are required to fulfill certain obligations (e.g., actively looking for work) in order to receive full benefits (see Sect. 4.3). While certain programs offer specific health and rehabilitative services to minimum income beneficiaries, these services are thus far not obligatory for receiving benefits. Nevertheless, we asked respondents whether they thought that individuals should be ***obligated*** to participate in such health-related measures in order to receive full minimum income benefits. Overall, two out of ten respondents stated that the described hypothetical person should receive benefits without fulfilling any conditions, whereas the remaining respondents were willing to tie the receipt of benefits to one or more obligations.

As Fig. 4.8 illustrates, the reason for unemployment is associated with the obligations that respondents consider appropriate. When the

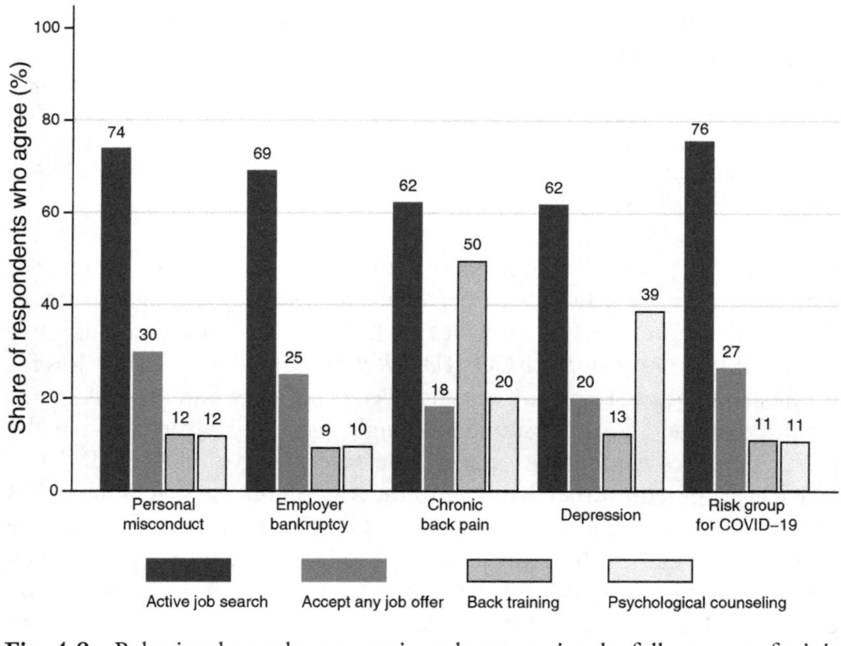

Fig. 4.8 Behavior deemed necessary in order to receive the full amount of minimum income benefits for different causes of unemployment. Source: vignette study, Wave 2 (in 2020) ($N = 1843$), own weighted sample calculations

hypothetical person was described as being ill (i.e., with chronic back pain or depression), fewer respondents supported normal work obligations—such as an active job search or accepting any job offer—compared with all other options. However, most respondents still supported an active job search for this group. Moreover, 50% of respondents supported the notion that the benefits for an individual with chronic back pain could be tied to participating in back therapy, and 39% of respondents supported the notion that psychological counseling could be an obligatory condition for receiving full benefits in the case of depression. Unlike for the question of blame, attitudes regarding obligations for the three health-related groups (i.e., chronic back pain, depression, risk group for COVID-19) were relatively similar and indicated that in this case, actually being sick mattered. Thus, while the medicalization and psychologization of unemployment partially increased respondents' leniency toward this group, which can be seen as an indication of the *relief hypothesis*, the respondents supported obligating these individuals to work on their health in order to restore their employability. All previously described effects remain stable when single obligations are included in a multivariate logistic regression model that controls for respondents' age, gender, and education.

The medicalization and psychologization of unemployment have measurable implications for public opinion. Again, our findings are mixed: There are some signs that medicalization and psychologization are still accepted as a justification both for being inactive and for being treated with greater leniency (*relief hypothesis*); however, we also find that sick unemployed individuals are blamed more if their unemployment is attributed to their sickness and that a segment of the population supports forcing these individuals to improve their health (*responsibility hypothesis*).

4.5 Conclusion

In this chapter, we have taken a tour through the medicalization—and to some extent, also the psychologization—of unemployment. While there is no such thing as "unemployment syndrome," medicine and psychology do have a significant influence on how the welfare state deals with unemployment. On the *institutional* level, we have shown how the definition of sickness- and disability-related benefit schemes and categories as well as the use of medical concepts and assessment tools shapes social rights in the case of unemployment in Germany. Analyzing the pathway through the system also reveals medicalization on the *actor* level because medical doctors are crucial gatekeepers at multiple points in the system. However, medical doctors and psychologists provide their expertise in the unemployment-related benefits systems based on medical, psychological, and even social criteria. This is an example of how different accounts are integrated in a biopsychosocial approach to dealing with unemployment. We have paid less attention to medicalization and psychologization on the *idea* level; indeed, for once, our analyses of parliamentary debates indicated that there has been little influence from high-level political discourses (see Chap. 5 for more details). However, we found that medicalization and psychologization do impact attitudes in terms of the ideas that individuals hold about unemployment.

The medicalization of unemployment is not a new phenomenon, but it has garnered a new level of interest over the past two decades. Similarly, some of the mechanisms that promote medicalization that we have outlined have been used for a long time and are based on the historically developed setup of the German welfare system. Nevertheless, current neoliberal reforms are also important. Ironically, attempts to activate and push individuals toward participating in the labor market have led to an increase in—and the development of—new forms of medicalizing unemployment. This development has also been discussed for other welfare states, including Sweden (Holmqvist et al., 2013), the US (Hansen et al., 2014; Wong, 2016), and Canada (Pulkingham & Fuller, 2012).

Finally, the controversy surrounding the consequences of unemployment in medicalization and psychologization theory points to the ambiguity that these processes entail in real life. Our analyses—which assessed some consequences empirically—revealed that there are in fact contradictory effects caused by the medicalization and psychologization of unemployment. Medicine and psychology are neither a form of salvation nor nemesis (Illich, 1976); nevertheless, they fundamentally shape how the welfare state engages with unemployment—an insight that should receive greater attention in welfare state research.

References

Allert, R. (2021, March 17). *Begutachtung für die Arbeitsvermittlung: Der Ärztliche Dienst der Bundesagentur für Arbeit.* Weiterbildung Sozialmedizin Aufbaukurs E/F. Retrieved from https://www.saluscon.de/wp-content/uploads/2021/03/20210316_Allert_Begutachtung_Arbeitsverwaltung.pdf

Allmendinger, J., & Ludwig-Mayerhofer, W. (2007). Unemployment as a social problem. In G. Ritzer (Ed.), *The Blackwell encyclopedia of sociology.* Blackwell. https://doi.org/10.1002/9781405165518.wbeosu003

Bethmann, A., Fuchs, B., & Wurdack, A. (07/2013). *User guide "Panel Study Labour Market and Social Security" (PASS): FDZ-Datenreport.*

Bonoli, G. (2010). The political economy of active labor-market policy. *Politics and Society, 38*(4), 435–457. https://doi.org/10.1177/0032329210381235

Brussig, M. (2018, June 8). *Zur Organisation sozialmedizinischer Gutachten im Erwerbsminderungsrentenverfahren: Fachbeitrag C4–2018.* Retrieved from https://www.reha-recht.de/fileadmin/user_upload/RehaRecht/Diskussionsforen/Forum_C/2018/C4-2018_Zur_Organisation_sozialmedizinischer_Gutachten.pdf

Buffel, V., Beckfield, J., & Bracke, P. (2017). The institutional foundations of medicalization: A cross-national analysis of mental health and unemployment. *Journal of Health and Social Behavior, 58*(3), 272–290. https://doi.org/10.1177/0022146517716232

Buffel, V., Dereuddre, R., & Bracke, P. (2015). Medicalization of the uncertainty? An empirical study of the relationships between unemployment or job insecurity, professional care seeking, and the consumption of antidepressants. *European Sociological Review, 31*(4), 446–459. https://doi.org/10.1093/esr/jcv004

Burgard, S. A., & Lin, K. Y. (2013). Bad jobs, bad health? How work and working conditions contribute to health disparities. *The American Behavioral Scientist, 57*(8), 1105–1127. https://doi.org/10.1177/0002764213487347

Clasen, J., & Clegg, D. (2007). Levels and levers of conditionality: Measuring change within welfare states. *Investigating welfare state change. The'dependent variable problem'in comparative analysis. Cheltenham/Northampton. Edward Elgar*, 166–197.

Conrad, P. (1992). Medicalization and social control. *Annual Review of Sociology, 18*(1), 209–232. https://doi.org/10.1146/annurev.so.18.080192.001233

Conrad, P., & Schneider, J. W. (1992). *Deviance and medicalization: From badness to sickness.* Philadelphia (PA): Temple University Press.

Deutscher Bundestag. (2002). *Stenografischer Bericht 8.Sitzung/Plenarprotokoll 15/8.*

Dwyer, P. (2008). The conditional welfare state. In M. A. Powell (Ed.), *Modernising the welfare state: The Blair legacy* (pp. 199–218). Policy Press. https://doi.org/10.1332/policypress/9781847420404.003.0012

Esping-Andersen, G. (1990). *The three worlds of welfare capitalism*. Wiley.
Ford, F. M., Ford, J., & Dowrick, C. (2000). Welfare to work: The role of general practice. *The British Journal of General Practice: The Journal of the Royal College of General Practitioners, 50*(455), 497–500.
Friedli, L. (2016). The politics of tackling inequalities: The rise of psychological fundamentalism in public health and welfare reform. In K. E. Smith, S. Hill, & C. Bambra (Eds.), *Health inequalities: Critical perspectives*. Oxford University Press.
Garthwaite, K. (2014). Fear of the brown envelope: Exploring welfare reform with long-term sickness benefits recipients. *Social Policy & Administration, 48*(7), 782–798. https://doi.org/10.1111/spol.12049
Hansen, H., Bourgois, P., & Drucker, E. (2014). Pathologizing poverty: New forms of diagnosis, disability, and structural stigma under welfare reform. *Social Science & Medicine, 1982*(103), 76–83. https://doi.org/10.1016/j.socscimed.2013.06.033
Holmqvist, M. (2009). Medicalization of unemployment: Individualizing social issues as personal problems in the Swedish welfare state. *Work, Employment and Society, 23*(3), 405–421. https://doi.org/10.1177/0950017009337063
Holmqvist, M., Maravelias, C., & Skålén, P. (2013). Identity regulation in neo-liberal societies: Constructing the 'occupationally disabled' individual. *Organization, 20*(2), 193–211. https://doi.org/10.1177/1350508412438704
Hotz, H. G. (2022, September 8). *Beratungs- und Begutachtungsauftrag für den Ärtzlichen Dienst der Bundesagentur für Arbeit: Was machen Ärzte bei der Arbeitsagentur?* Duetsche Gesellschaft für Sozialmedizin und Prävention (DGSMP) & Deutsche Gesellschaft für medizinische Soziologie (DGMS). Gemeinsame Jahrestagung – Soziale Gesundheit neu denken: Herausforderungen für Sozialmedizin & medizinische Soziologie in der digitalen Spätmoderne, Magdeburg.
Illich, I. (1976). *Medical nemesis. The expropriation of health*. Pantheon Books.
International Labour Organization/European Commission. (2017). *Profiling youth labour market disadvantage: A review of approaches in Europe*. Turin.
Juberg, A., & Skjefstad, N. S. (2019). 'NEET' to work? – Substance use disorder and youth unemployment in Norwegian public documents. *European Journal of Social Work, 22*(2), 252–263. https://doi.org/10.1080/13691457.2018.1531829
Kupka, P., Oschmiansky, F., & Popp, S. (2017). Wahl- und Handlungsmöglichkeiten psychisch kranker Menschen im SGB II. *Zeitschrift Für Sozialreform, 63*(3), 415–446. https://doi.org/10.1515/zsr-2017-0019
Linden, P., & Reibling, N. (2023). Medicalization of unemployment within the German minimum income system: An analysis of sick leave for unemployed using a three-level multilevel model (Working paper).
Lindsay, C., & Houston, D. (2011). Fit for purpose? Welfare reform and challenges for health and labour market policy in the UK. *Environment and Planning a: Economy and Space, 43*(3), 703–721. https://doi.org/10.1068/a43442

McVicar, D., Wilkins, R., & Ziebarth, N. (2016). *Four decades of disability benefit policies and the rise and fall of disability recipiency rates in five OECD countries: Unpublished pre-print*. Retrieved from https://www.human.cornell.edu/sites/default/files/pam/people/nrz2/the-rise-and-fall-of-disability-recipiency-rates-in-five-oecd-countries_v11-clean.pdf

Meershoek, A. (2012). Controlling access to sick leave programmes: Practices of physicians in the Netherlands. *Social Policy & Administration, 46*(5), 544–561. https://doi.org/10.1111/j.1467-9515.2011.00825.x

OECD. (2010). *Sickness, disability and work: Breaking the barriers. A Synthesis of Findings across OECD Countries*. Retrieved from https://doi.org/10.1787/9789264088856-en

Parsons, T. (1951). *The social system*. Routledge.

Peeters, R. (2019). Manufacturing responsibility: The governmentality of behavioural power in social policies. *Social Policy and Society, 18*(1), 51–65. https://doi.org/10.1017/s147474641700046x

Pfeiffer, D., & Pick, P. (2011). *Guidelines of the GKV-Spitzenverband to ensure uniform assessment in accordance with § 282, Paragraph 2, Sentence 3 SGB V: Assessment guide for incapacity for work*. Essen.

Pulkingham, J., & Fuller, S. (2012). From parent to patient: The medicalization of lone motherhood through welfare reform. *Social Politics: International Studies in Gender, State & Society, 19*(2), 243–268. https://doi.org/10.1093/sp/jxs007

Rose, N. (1998). *Inventing our selves: Psychology, power, and personhood*. Cambridge University Press.

Schneider, W. (2013). Medikalisierung sozialer Prozesse. *Psychotherapeut, 58*(3), 219–236. https://doi.org/10.1007/s00278-013-0977-5

Schneider, W., Schmiedeberg, J., & Braungardt, T. (2016). Sind die Antragsstellungen auf Renten wegen verminderter Erwerbsfähigkeit von Langzeitarbeitslosen vor allem auch durch soziale Motive begründet? *Zeitschrift für Psychiatrie, Psychologie und Psychotherapie, 64*(3), 153–161. https://doi.org/10.1024/1661-4747/a000274

Stone, D. A. (1984). *The disabled state. Health, society, and policy*. Temple University Press.

Watts, B., & Fitzpatrick, S. (2018). *Welfare conditionality*. Routledge.

Wilfer, T., Braungardt, T., & Schneider, W. (2018). Soziale Probleme in der hausärztlichen Praxis. *Zeitschrift für Psychosomatische Medizin und Psychotherapie, 64*(3), 250–261.

Wong, S. (2016). Geographies of medicalized welfare: Spatial analysis of supplemental security income in the U.S., 2000–2010. *Social Science & Medicine, 160*, 9–19. https://doi.org/10.1016/j.socscimed.2016.05.018

Zola, I. K. (1972). Medicine as an institution of social control. *The Sociological Review, 20*(4), 487–504. https://doi.org/10.1111/j.1467-954X.1972.tb00220.x

CHAPTER 5

Poverty: More Than Just a Lack of Material Resources?

Stephan Krayter and Mareike Ariaans

Poverty is a complex phenomenon. Despite having once only encompassed financial and economic elements, the concept has since become multidimensional and now also includes the facets of health and psychology. The scientific literature has established a mutual relationship between health and psychology on the one hand and poverty trajectories on the other hand. However, exactly how important medical and psychological ideas, institutions, and actors are today and how their importance has developed are rarely researched. Therefore, this chapter focuses on the question of how medicine and psychology have developed and manifested in the scientific and political discourse and in welfare state institutions in the field of poverty. The discovery of an increase of—and a shifting meaning in—medical and psychological ideas, institutions, and actors would provide evidence of the medicalization and psychologization of poverty. This chapter proceeds as follows: First, poverty is placed in its historical context, and the changing definitions of the concept in recent decades are discussed. The second section follows up on the scientific discussion of poverty and examines whether and how scientific actors have increasingly

S. Krayter (✉) • M. Ariaans
University of Siegen, Siegen, Germany
e-mail: stephan.krayter@uni-siegen.de

N. Reibling, M. Ariaans (eds.), *Toward a Biopsychosocial Welfare State?*, https://doi.org/10.1007/978-3-031-32793-3_5

come to include medicine and psychology in the discourse on poverty. The third part focuses on the German political discourse and on how political actors medicalize and psychologize this issue. The fourth section sheds light on the institutional setting of combatting poverty in Germany and investigates whether medical and psychological ideas were implemented during the early 2000s in the institutional reforms that led to the provision of minimum-income-replacement benefits.

5.1 Poverty Revisited: From Economic Measurements to the Concept of Multidimensionality

> 'Poverty' has joined that league of emotive words with slippery meanings—like 'freedom', 'liberty', 'justice', 'democracy' and 'dependency'; words which refer to powerful concepts, yet which are capable of being used or received in fundamentally different ways; words which convey diverse and complex associations, yet which can become so valorised or debased in ordinary discourse as to become meaningless or misleading. (Dean, 1992, p. 79)

The concept of poverty is difficult to define, and its meaning is highly context dependent. In the context of warzones and the poorest countries in the world, poverty is associated with fleeing from regions of crisis, with hunger, and with poor hygiene (United Nations, 2015). The lack of fulfillment of fundamental needs—such as access to clean drinking water and sufficient food—leads to the danger of malnutrition and death (United Nations, 2013). This *absolute poverty* ("having less than an objectively defined absolute minimum") is mainly found in the Global South. Poverty in the richer countries of the world, on the other hand, consists of *relative poverty*—that is, the inequal distribution of common goods ("having less than others")—or *subjective poverty* ("feeling you do not have enough to get along") (Förster, 1994). While extreme poverty means living on less than $1.25 a day and therefore also suffering from severe hunger, poverty in richer countries mostly involves having a specific income distribution of less than ca. 50%–60% of the median income (United Nations, 2013). This financial perspective on poverty is frequently used by a variety of indicators (e.g., the Gini-Coefficient, the Palma-Ratio, poverty rates before and after taxes and transfers, the poverty gap) (OECD, 2021a, b, c). Although even objective economic measures of the poverty line have always been subject to discussion, the core of this poverty line has always lain in material imbalance (Goedemé & Rottiers, 2011). Poverty indices are thus based on financial elements and only indirectly refer to social elements and/or to appropriate participation in society (Thomas Lampert, 2011).

However, the economic perspective on relative poverty has developed into one of many dimensions of poverty in recent decades. In addition to Armatya Sen's capability approach (Sen, 1999), other dimensions have been highlighted in the literature:

> Beginning with a focus on command over market-purchased goods (income), the definition of poverty has expanded to embrace other dimensions of living standards such as longevity, literacy, and healthiness. (Kanbur & Squire, 2001, p. 183)

While broadening the definition of poverty has not necessarily changed the target group that is considered to be poor (because many dimensions of poverty are closely correlated), it has broadened our understanding of poverty itself (Kanbur & Squire, 2001). Moreover, this shift to a multidimensional approach to poverty opens up new possibilities for interventions. The promotion of healthy living conditions and unrestricted access to health services represents one dimension of poverty that the OECD considers to be an important building block for breaking the cycle of poverty (OECD, 2003). These interdependences constitute major changes in our understanding of poverty because income and consumption measures provide information on who is poor and additionally on wider determinants of a person's well-being, including their economic and social participation.

International research has found poor health to be both an effect and a cause of various other dimensions of poverty, such as unemployment (Herber et al., 2019; Nichols et al., 2013; Vaalavuo, 2016; see also Chap. 4), employment income and wealth (Hajat et al., 2010), living conditions (Eikemo et al., 2016), migration (Gkiouleka & Huijts, 2020; Jayaweera & Quigley, 2010; Kirmayer et al., 2011; Missinne & Bracke, 2012), and education (van Zon et al., 2017). Similarly, for the case of Germany, illness and poor health have been shown to affect and be affected by various poverty dimensions (Kroll et al., 2016; T. Lampert & Kroll, 2006; Thomas Lampert & Ziese, 2005; Rathmann et al., 2018; Wittig et al., 2008). People in poverty experience a greater risk of a downward spiral that will eventually impair their mental health (Gallie et al., 2003): Indeed, unemployed people are at a higher risk of being poor and stigmatized and are therefore also at higher risk of being socially isolated. All of these factors decrease the chances that the unemployed will return to work and get out of poverty. Hence, health restrictions serve as an explanation as to *why* someone is suffering from poverty, but they are also an indication *that* someone is suffering from poverty. Focusing on the individual and their employability goes hand in hand with psychological concepts. Furthermore, the technologies of the self (Martin et al., 1988) include the responsibility that the individual has in creating resources that could lead to more stress and strain. In addition, psychological concepts appear to have generally become more important in society (Rose, 1998). In general, medicine—with its concepts of physical health—and psychology—with its concepts of mental health—are two major facets in the outlined shift of the concept of poverty away from an economic issue and toward a multidimensional issue. But how has this change in the *idea* of poverty come about? What *actors* have pushed and carried out this development? How is this new understanding translated in existing welfare state *institutions* that address poverty?

5.2 Scientific Actors in the Medicalization and Psychologization of Poverty

An important part of medicalization (and accordingly also of psychologization) is conceptual medicalization—that is, the use of medical concepts to understand certain problems. The process by which more and more elements of society are affected by medical knowledge is one key aspect of medicalization (Conrad, 1992). Various discourses have brought medical and psychological language into everyday life and into areas not commonly associated with medicine and have thus contributed to diffusing medical and psychological knowledge within society. Political, public, and scientific discourses shape the perception and interpretation of social phenomena (Bourdieu, 2015; Ferree et al., 2002; Keller, 2013; Ullrich, 2008; Peter Weingart et al., 2008). Whether these discourses are political (e.g., different parties express their values and attitudes on social issues), public (e.g., the media frames different perspectives), or scientific (e.g., new knowledge is generated and disseminated throughout society), they all contribute to the perception of a certain topic (Ferree et al., 2002). However, discourses do not develop on their own; rather, they are shaped by the actors who (are able to) participate in them. If particularly powerful actors propose a certain position, it is likely that this position will prevail on a broad scale (Ferree et al., 2002).

The scientific discourse and the scholars of various disciplines shape both how poverty is understood in the scientific community and how it can be taken up in political and public discourses. It is possible to measure which actors are important in the scientific discourse on poverty using two different methods—that is, we can measure the actors who publish extensively in a field and therefore gain attention on the one hand (quantity) or the actors who have a high reach via many citations and reads in the scientific community (quality) on the other hand. Hence, medicalization and psychologization in the scientific discourse take place if medical and psychological disciplines publish an increasing share of all scientific output on poverty and if the publications of medical and psychological disciplines are cited more frequently than are those of other disciplines.

The changing concept of poverty described in the previous section is evident in the scientific discourse, which has become more multidimensional over time through the growth of the disciplines of psychology and public health, in particular. A comprehensive scientific discourse analysis using research articles from the Social Science Citation Index (SSCI) from 1956 to 2019 that deal with issues of poverty in their title indicates that a shift is currently taking place. In the SSCI provided by the literature-citation database Web of Science (WoS), scientific disciplines are aggregated as research areas. In the last 30 years, "Public, Environmental & Occupational Health" and "Psychology" have replaced former top research areas to become the two fastest-growing areas in the SSCI in terms of research on poverty. The discourse in these areas is growing stronger than is the scientific poverty discourse in general. In the 1960s and 1970s, "Business & Economics" and "Government & Law" represented the majority of publications. Since the 1980s, however, "Public, Environmental & Occupational Health" and "Psychology" have grown substantially and have constituted the Top 2 research areas since the 1990s. These areas are growing at an above-average rate compared with the overall scientific poverty discourse such that today, one in three studies on poverty stems from one of these two disciplines (Krayter & Reibling,

2020). These findings indicate that the disciplines of public health[1] and psychology have increased their standing in the discourse. Although scholars from one discipline do not have a uniform perspective on one issue, their research is nevertheless shaped by the prevailing concepts and theories of their discipline. These findings mirror the transformation of the concept of poverty. This mere quantitative increase in the number of public health and psychology articles could be argued to be insufficient for substantiating the claim that the discourse on scientific poverty has been medicalized or psychologized. Indeed, researchers in health-related or psychological disciplines *may merely publish a lot but not be noticed in the overall scientific poverty discourse and may therefore also be less influential in public discourses.*

However, our data demonstrate that psychological and health-related research on poverty also matters in qualitative terms. We analyzed the amount of works cited in Web of Science from a health-related or psychological perspective, which yielded more information about whether research from this perspective matters in the overall discourse. We then examined the Top 50 cited research articles in each decade. Figure 5.1 reveals that in the 1960s, only about one-fifth of all citations in the Top 50 most-cited articles stemmed from health-related and psychological disciplines. On the other hand, in articles from the 2000s and 2010s, this figure increased to almost two-thirds, which demonstrates the ongoing and increasing impact of these disciplines. This finding reveals the importance of these research areas for further scientific research, which indicates that other researchers rely on findings from both a health-related and a psychological perspective.

Hence, health-related and psychological research on poverty gained significance in the scientific discourse between 1960 and 2019. Not only do these research areas publish more articles on poverty today compared with in earlier decades, which means that they shape the discourse in a quantitative manner, but they also shape the discourse by contributing the majority of the citations.

[1] In the present analysis, we only refer to the two individual WoS research areas of "Public, Environmental, & Occupational Health" and "Psychology." In upcoming analyses in this book, we expand our focus to include medical areas such as "General & Internal Medicine" and "Pediatrics." Our aggregation of the "health-related" perspective is therefore broader and includes strictly medical aspects and aspects of public health.

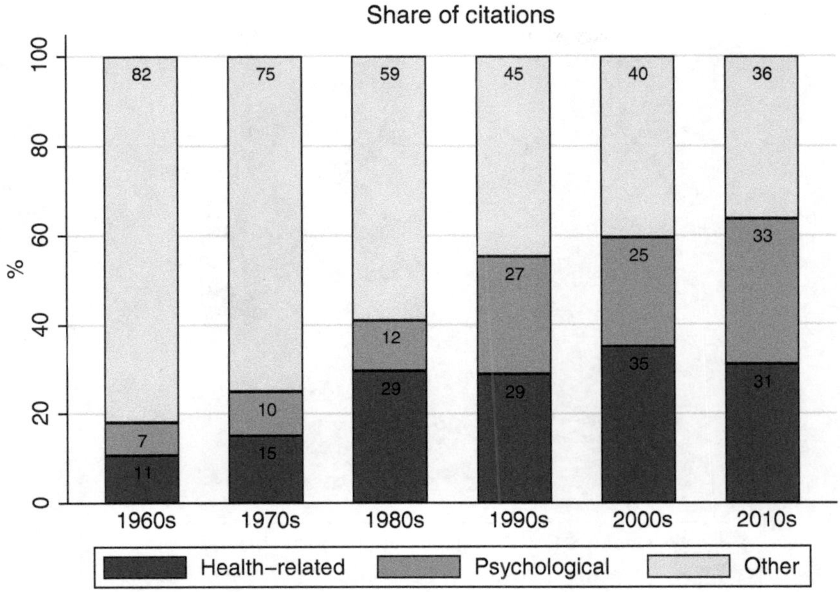

Fig. 5.1 Share of health-related and psychological research areas in the Top 50 most-cited articles on poverty

In delving deeper into the content of these Top 50 articles via a quantitative content analysis of the articles' abstracts, we uncovered interesting results. By creating the three distinctive categories of a *health & psychological dimension*, a *measuring poverty & economic dimension*, and a *social & political dimension*, we coded the abstracts of the Top 50 cited articles into these three categories by analyzing their focus and content.[2] About one-third of the abstracts discuss the *health and psychological* concepts of poverty, such as theories on the causal relationship between poverty and health, cognitive functioning, and brain development (e.g., children's developmental disabilities when exposed to poverty in their living environments, including poor parental health literacy). Seventeen percent of the abstracts discuss *measurements* of poverty, such as statistical methods

[2] Any given abstract can be assigned either to only one category if its focus is unambiguously related to only one field of research or to more than one category if its focus has a broader perspective and includes several areas.

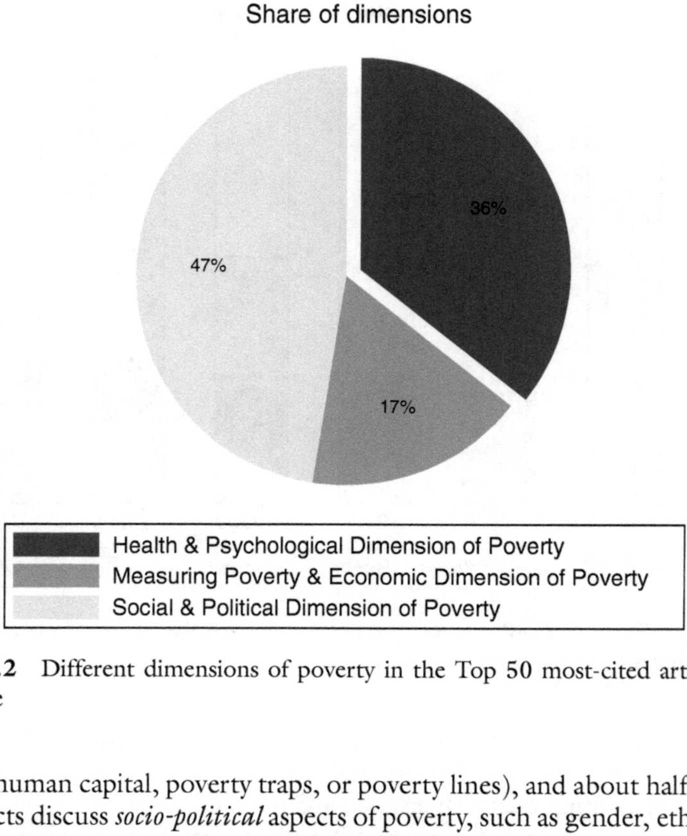

Fig. 5.2 Different dimensions of poverty in the Top 50 most-cited articles of all time

(e.g., human capital, poverty traps, or poverty lines), and about half of the abstracts discuss *socio-political* aspects of poverty, such as gender, ethnicity, geography, and education (see Fig. 5.2).[3]

In summary, these results establish a strong link between poverty and health and show that actors from health-related and psychological disciplines increasingly shape the scientific poverty discourse. In this way, ideas are created in which actors build up and expand their power of interpretation and might thus—in a further step—extend their influence to the political arena. These results are in line with findings on the medicalization and psychologization of poverty at the level of policies (Friedli, 2016; Mathieu, 1993; Schram, 2000; Wong, 2016). While medicalization and

[3] The high level of aggregation in the dimension of socio-political aspects was necessary to represent in a reasonable way the high number of subcategories that exist within the fields of sociology and political science.

psychologization could still be argued to be phenomena that unfold in the scientific arena, with health sciences and psychology being disciplines that stretch into the scientific poverty discourse, this argument would not necessarily mean that medicalization and psychologization are also found in arenas that are much more closely related to the poor—that is, in political arenas. The transfer of concepts from scientific debates to other arenas is complex and does not necessarily follow a certain pattern, meaning that only particular elements of the discourse will be transferred. However, science does have an impact in the political process (P. Weingart et al., 2009).

5.3 The Role of Political Actors in the Medicalization and Psychologization of Poverty

With the substantial increase of the use of the concepts of psychology and public health in the scientific discourse, it would be easy to wonder whether this increase has been echoed in the political discourse on poverty. Research ideas and results are often taken up by political actors, for example, by consulting scientific experts in political commissions (Falk et al., 2019). Hence, whether medicalization and psychologization processes have occurred not only in the scientific arena but also in the political arena is an open question. To answer this question, we analyzed the parliamentary debates on minimum-income-replacement benefits in Germany at two time points: after the introduction of a new minimum-benefit scheme via the Hartz reforms in 2002/2003 and after the changes made to this benefit scheme in 2016. At these time points, the German government implemented measures that were largely influenced by a neoliberal paradigm (2002/2003) on the one hand and by a social-investment paradigm (2016) on the other hand. These general ideas can be exemplified by two statements: Then-Chancellor Gerhard Schröder declared in 2001 that "people"—meaning the unemployed—had "no right to laziness" (Helm, 2001), whereas then-Minister of Labor Andrea Nahles argued in a press statement in 2016 that the unemployment agency should "actively support and accompany the unemployed" (Nahles, 2016).

We analyzed the two reforms using a quantitative content analysis that employed issue frames. Put simply, "framing is concerned with the presentation of issues" (Vreese, 2005, p. 53), and we investigated how important the issues or frames of medicine and psychology were in both reforms. Based on the different direction of the reforms and the different views on the unemployed—views that are guided by the neoliberal and the social-investment logic of the reforms—it was expected (1) that medical and psychological ideas *are* discussed by political parties because both paradigms can be connected to the spread of medicalization and psychologization and (2) that political parties employ medical and psychological ideas with a different intention. Our results reveal that the political parties do not medicalize or psychologize the issue of poverty, nor do they connect the implemented policies to medical or psychological categories. This non-medical and non-psychological framing was used both during the Hartz reforms and in the recent reforms. The issue framing in the Hartz reforms and in the reforms to the unemployment and poverty system in 2016[4] indicates that medical and psychological issues were nearly non-existent in the parliamentary debates on these reforms. Medical framing can be found in two paragraphs for the first time point and in four paragraphs for the second time point, amounting to 0.2% of all frames in 2002/2003 and 0.5% in 2016. Psychological framing was used more often than medical framing but still only accounted for a small proportion of issue framing. A total of 2.2% of all frames employed psychological terms and issues in 2002/2003, and this figure rose to 3.8% for the year 2016 (Fig. 5.3).

However, the use of psychological frames differs in qualitative terms between the two time points. In the Hartz reforms, psychological framing was targeted at large groups of "the people" or at "the unemployed and the economy." The psychological frames in 2016 mainly focused on the individual level. Key words that were used include "motivation," "self-confidence," and "stamina." This move from societal to individual psychology frames can be evaluated as a form of psychologization. However, in comparison with other issue frames, the extent of psychologization is still quite low.

> Additionally: Not only are the people against whom sanctions are imposed affected by these sanctions, but so too are many others because for them, there is a constant threat of having such a sanction arbitrarily imposed. This, of course, creates corresponding fears. (Deutscher Bundestag, 2016)

[4] The Hartz laws are called "laws on modern services in the labor market" (in short, "Hartz legislation," which was named after the head of the reform commission). They were passed in 2002 and 2003. The "law on strengthening further vocational training and the insurance coverage of unemployment insurance" (in short, AWStG) and "the ninth revision of Social Codebook II" were passed in 2016.

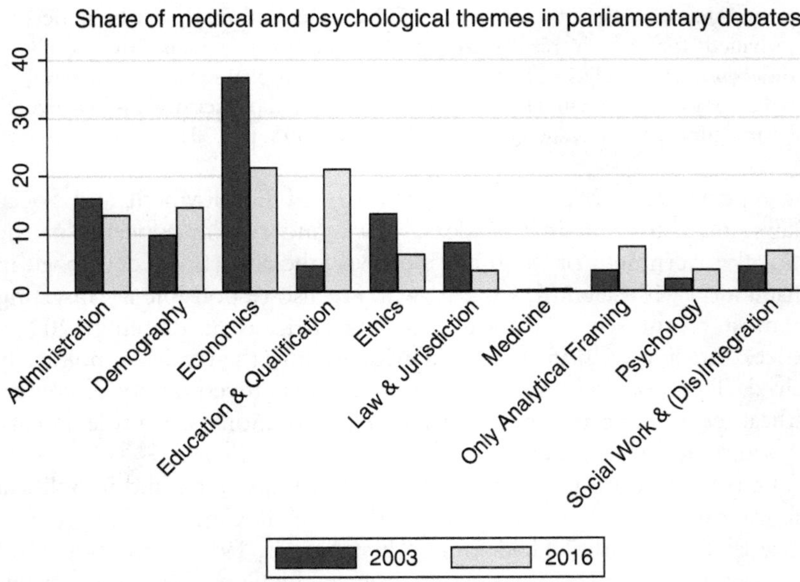

Fig. 5.3 Bar chart on the share of medical and psychological themes in parliamentary debates

While parliamentary debates on poverty-related policies are not framed using medical or psychological concepts and language, they do appear to matter in governmental reports on poverty. Since 2001, the Ministry for Employment and Social Affairs has published the Poverty and Wealth Reports (Armuts- und Reichtumsberichte) once per legislative period. The focus of these reports is on describing poverty (and wealth) trends and governmental actions that target poverty. We analyzed all five published reports from the years 2001, 2005, 2008, 2013, and 2017 and found that health was an important issue throughout the time period and that it had increased slightly in importance over time (Ariaans & Reibling, 2021). Health is mentioned in separate sections and in connection with other poverty-related items. As shown by the following quote, the fiscal risk of poverty is connected to social concepts of poverty and to various mental and physical health risks for children.

> The monetary poverty risk is only somewhat correlated with the limited chances for children to participate. Children and young people have particu-

> lar development deficits and social disadvantages and may even be underprovided for, which results in potential health problems. In socially disadvantaged families, children are often obese, display socially challenging behavior more frequently than in other families, and participate less in active leisure-time activities, such as sports. (BMAS, 2008, p. XXII)

The reports are published by the Ministry of Employment and Social Affairs and thus contain the ideas, views, and reform concepts of the national government of the time. However, the reports are developed in consultation with scientific experts, who are also responsible for inserting the most recent scientific ideas and data (Ariaans & Reibling, 2021). Hence, diffusing scientific ideas and evidence into the reports is politically desired. Thus, on the level of political-administrative-poverty discourse, medical terms, concepts, affiliations, and interventions play a role and are diffused by scientific experts.

The role of health in the public and political discourse and in political practice can also be exemplified via the annual German Congress of "Poverty and Health." Held for the first time in 1995 with about 200 participants and with a focus on three topics, the Congress now describes itself as the largest public health congress in Germany and includes about 2300 participants and 25 topics. The Congress brings together researchers, interest organizations, and policy-makers on the interrelations between poverty and health and contributes to disseminating scientific knowledge, evidence, and proposals throughout policy-making (Kongress Armut und Gesundheit, 2021).

While our empirical evidence only covers two reform packages for which we tested whether political actors have promoted medical and psychological frames, we can conclude that this has rarely been the case. Unlike in other countries, medical and psychological concepts in Germany are not important in high-level politics (Holmqvist, 2009; Mathieu, 1993). However, medical and psychological concepts have nevertheless gained in importance in poverty-related policy-making. Scientists are actively involved in disseminating medical and psychological frames through their involvement in key framing processes, which include writing and consulting on governmental reports and being involved in conferences, such as the "Poverty and Health" Congress, which bridges the gap between science and practice.

5.4 The Role of Institutions in Medicalizing and Psychologizing Poverty: Medical Status as a Determinant of the Eligibility for Benefits

The above-described findings establish that medical and psychological ideas are diffused into policies on poverty via scientific experts and interprofessional conferences. Hence, it is possible to wonder whether and how medical and psychological ideas have been intentionally or unintentionally integrated into and implemented in these institutions of the welfare state that target the poor. Germany is a highly developed and juridified welfare state in which the rights acquired by social-insurance contributions play an integral role. Institutions are often described as being coherent and stable entities and have—especially in the German context—been labeled as "frozen" (Esping-Andersen, 1996). However, neoliberal reforms—such as the Hartz reforms in the early 2000s and many small-scale social-investment reforms in the 2010s—have altered institutions of the German welfare state that deal with the issue of poverty. Thus, if we argue that the welfare state is transforming into a biopsychosocial welfare state, we should be able to find such a perspective in the institutions that constitute the German welfare state. However, institutions are not only the result of ideas and interests that actors have set in place; indeed, the institutions themselves create path dependencies. We therefore investigated the extent to which the institutional setup of the German welfare state has encouraged or hindered a medicalization or psychologization of social-policy programs that address poverty.

In general, the topic of poverty has gained political and societal importance in Germany due in large part to the increasing poverty rate. In Germany, poverty rates (defined as income that lies 50% under the median) since the 1990s both before and after taxes and transfers have increased (see Fig. 5.4). Since the 2000s, the poverty rate before taxes and transfers has been even higher than for the liberal welfare state of the United Kingdom. However, welfare state systems have reduced poverty in all countries by a large degree. All advanced welfare states now show lower poverty rates and economic inequality after taxes and social transfer. The social-democratic welfare state of Denmark shows the greatest reduction in poverty rates after taxes and transfers, and the liberal welfare state of the United Kingdom shows the lowest drop. In the conservative welfare regime of Germany, the level of poverty decreased by about 20 percentage points after taxes and transfers in 1990 and by about 22 percentage points in 2017. However, in 2017, the poverty rate after taxes and transfers was

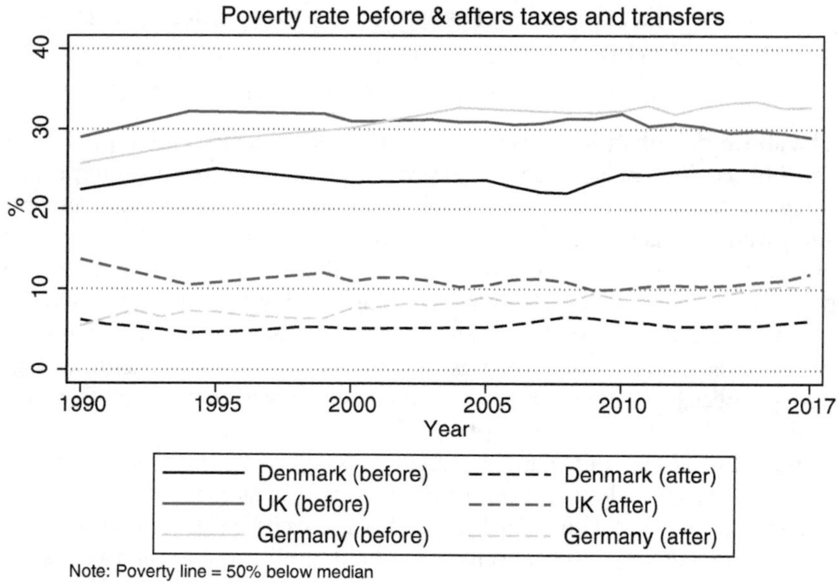

Fig. 5.4 Poverty rate before and after taxes and transfers

10.4%, whereas it was 5.5% in 1990. Hence, the German welfare state has become less effective at preventing poverty.

These increasing poverty rates have contributed to a developing public discourse on poverty in Germany—a discourse that was virtually non-existent until the early 1990s (Leisering, 1993). The term "poverty" has also come to be replaced by different concepts and terms, such as "unemployment" or "social assistance" (Leisering, 1993). This substitution of poverty by different concepts and its shift to other areas of discourse can be partly attributed to the design of the German welfare state, which is built around the principle of standard employment by a male breadwinner (Bender et al., 2007; Ferragina & Seeleib-Kaiser, 2014; Miller et al., 2021). In social-insurance contributions derived from labor market employment, basic social risks (illness, longevity, unemployment, disability) for employees and their spouses and children are covered. Hence, the risk of poverty is first tackled by these social-insurance systems. For those who are not employed, the history and future prospect of employment play an important role in determining how poverty is handled. Until 2005, the last safety net for the poor had two systems: The first system included people who had had a job in the past and who were able to search for a job. These people received unemployment assistance. This benefit followed after unemployment benefits had ceased, and the amount was based on prior wages. Although unemployment agencies administered this benefit, it was paid through general taxes (Berthold et al., 2000). The second system subsumed all other people who were not eligible for unemployment-assistance benefits but who fell below the poverty line. These people received social-assistance benefits. Benefits from social assistance were also tax-financed and were generally lower than unemployment-assistance benefits. Separating the poor into two systems—the unemployed poor on the one hand and the poor due to other reasons on the other hand—seemed reasonable in the 1950s and 1960s. However, beginning with the onset of—and increase in—mass unemployment in the 1980s, the boundaries between the two systems became blurred (Berthold et al., 2000). Criticism was directed at the dual structure of the system, at injustices between the people in both systems, and at the low incentives that both systems offered for gaining employment, which eventually led to the merger of the two systems (Knuth, 2006; Seeleib-Kaiser & Fleckenstein, 2007). The so-called Hartz reforms—which passed in 2002 and 2003 and have been in effect since 2005—merged both systems on the benefit level of social-assistance benefits. Furthermore, incentive structures for taking up employment and sanctions in the form of benefit cuts in case of non-compliance with general and individual obligations were tightened. In this new system, merely being poor (and having an employment history) does not qualify an individual for benefits. The new benchmark for receiving minimum-income benefits is determined by employability, which is defined as follows:

> Someone is considered able to work if they are not incapable of working at least three hours per day for the foreseeable future due to illness or disability under the usual conditions of the general labor market. (§8 (1), German Social Code (SGB) II)

Hence, employability is defined in negative terms as the absence of (severe) medical limitations. As a result, medical status instead of (prior) employment status—or the mere existence of material need—is now decisive for receiving minimum-income benefits.

Furthermore, the merger of unemployment assistance and social assistance means that poor people who are not able to work account for a significant portion of the eligible people in the system. However, the entire system was designed to promote and invest in employability and to sanction those who do not follow the conditions of the new unemployment system. People who are deemed healthy are assessed as being able to work. They must comply with all obligations and can be sanctioned in case of non-compliance. Obligations—which lead to sanctions if not met—include regular consultations with an unemployment agency and submitting a defined number of job applications each month. Exceptions to these obligations are only granted for caring duties or illness (see Chap. 4). Thus, illness is one of the few pathways out of actively seeking a job. People who are assessed as being physically or mentally ill do not need to follow most rules, and benefit cuts for them are practically impossible (§56 SGB II). Moreover, not only can illness mean that benefits are not allowed to be cut, but some illnesses can also lead to higher unemployment benefits (§21 Abs. 5 SGB II). For example, additional expenses for medically indicated nutritional needs are covered:

> In the case of beneficiaries with expensive nutrition requirements for medical reasons, an additional sum of a reasonable amount is to be granted. (§21 Abs. 5 SGB II (5))

5.5 Poverty: A Medicalized and Psychologized Issue in the Welfare State, But to What Extent?

In summary, this chapter focused on the question of whether poverty is becoming more frequently connected with medical and psychological ideas, actors, and institutions and also focused on developments to the German welfare state. Poverty—mostly in the sense of relative poverty—is a social problem that all developed welfare states face. How a welfare state conceptualizes and treats individuals with the lowest level of economic and social power might reveal a lot about its society and about the goals and ideas behind the state. Developments on the level of ideas, actors, and institutions might indicate how poverty is conceptualized and treated by the welfare state. Irrespective of whether medicalization and psychologization tendencies are intended or unintended processes, they might cause the social problem of poverty to become individualized. Medicalization and psychologization processes might also contribute to the further neglect of poverty as an issue, which has to be tackled mainly on the societal rather than on the individual level—especially in the German welfare state, where poverty has long been a neglected social-policy issue.

In general, the concept of poverty has changed in recent decades. Its definition has transformed from being mainly economic in nature to being a multidimensional concept. Both sociological and political dimensions on the one hand and health-related and psychological dimensions on the other hand have been added to the dominantly economic and financial understanding of poverty. However, medicine and psychology have not merely been added as dimensions to the concept of poverty; rather, they have risen to become the most significant areas in poverty research. The results in the political discourse are less clear cut. On the one hand, political parties rarely employ medical or psychological concepts in reforms of welfare state systems that target the poor. On the other hand, the Poverty and Wealth Reports that are published by the government have increasingly often adopted medicine and psychology as important topics. These topics are disseminated throughout the political discourse by scientific health experts, who have a consulting role in governmental reports and engage in promoting their ideas at conferences at which the scientific community and interest groups meet. Medicalization and psychologization are thus clearly not the top-down processes that the early scientific literature suggested (Ballard & Elston, 2005); rather, these processes take place at various levels. Accordingly, medicalization and psychologization are visible on the level of institutions that focus on the poor. Such institutions increasingly often incorporate medical and psychological ideas into their processes. German minimum-income-replacement schemes have been transformed and now focus less on prior employment status or need and more both on health status in determining obligations for receiving benefits and on the level of these benefits.

The receipt of minimum-income benefits is now based on the medically defined employability of the benefit claimant. However, minimum-income benefits are not only for the claimant; indeed, they are also for the claimant's children. In 2020, 33% of all households that received minimum-income benefits included underage children, and about half of these households had a single parent (Bundesagentur für Arbeit, 2020). Overall, in 2017, 20.4% of all minors were at risk of poverty and thus lived under conditions of less than 60% of the median income. This figure was about 5% higher than in the overall population (BMAS, 2021). Hence, children in—or at risk of—poverty are also an important target group for poverty interventions. As the citation in this chapter from the Poverty and Wealth Reports exemplifies, poverty-related problems and interventions increasingly often focus on health and psychology. In the following chapter, the way in which children and childhood are medicalized and psychologized is examined.

References

Ariaans, M., & Reibling, N. (2021). Die Rolle von Gesundheit und Krankheit im deutschen Armutsdiskurs: Eine Inhaltsanalyse der Armuts- und Reichtumsberichte. *Zeitschrift Für Sozialreform, 67*(2), 123–152. https://doi.org/10.1515/zsr-2021-0005

Ballard, K., & Elston, M. A. (2005). Medicalisation: A multi-dimensional concept. *Social Theory & Health, 3*(3), 228–241. https://doi.org/10.1057/palgrave.sth.8700053

Bender, C., Grassl, H., & Schaal, M. (2007). Der Schweizer Arbeitsmarkt: Sonderfall unter Modernisierungsdruck. In T. S. Eberle & K. Imhof (Eds.), *Sonderfall Schweiz* (pp. 172–187). Seismo Verlag.

Berthold, N., Thode, E., & von Berchem, S. (2000). Arbeitslosenhilfe und Sozialhilfe: zwei sind eine zuviel. *Wirtschaftsdienst, 80*(9), 576–584.

BMAS. (2008). *Lebenslagen in Deutschland: Der 3.* Armuts- und Reichtumsbericht der Bundesregierung.

BMAS. (2021). *Lebenslagen in Deutschland: Der 6.* Armuts- und Reichtumsbericht der Bundesregierung.

Bourdieu, P. (2015). *Die verborgenen Mechanismen der Macht: Schriften zu Politik & Kultur 1* (M. Steinrücke, Ed.). VSA.

Bundesagentur für Arbeit. (2020). K*inder in Bedarfsgemeinschaften – Deutschland,* West/Ost, Länder und Kreise (Monatszahlen): Dezember 2020. https://statistik.arbeitsagentur.de/SiteGlobals/Forms/Suche/Einzelheftsuche_Formular.html?nn=20656&topic_f=kinder.

Conrad, P. (1992). Medicalization and social control. *Annual Review of Sociology, 18*, 209–232.

Dean, H. (1992). Poverty discourse and the disempowerment of the poor. *Critical Social Policy, 12*(35), 79–88. https://doi.org/10.1177/026101839201203505

Deutscher Bundestag. (2016). *Stenografischer Bericht 165: Sitzung/ Plenarprotokoll 18/165.*

Eikemo, T. A., Bambra, C, Huijts, T., & Fitzgerald, R. (2016). The first Pan-European sociological health inequalities survey of the general population: The European social survey rotating module on the social determinants of health. *European Sociological Review*, 1–17. https://doi.org/10.1093/esr/jcw019.

Esping-Andersen, G. (Ed.). (1996). *Welfare states in transition: National adaptations in global economies.* SAGE. http://www.loc.gov/catdir/enhancements/fy0656/96068418-d.html

Falk, S., Glaab, M., Römmele, A., Schober, H., & Thunert, M. (Eds.). (2019). *Handbuch Politikberatung* (2., völlig neu bearbeitete Auflage). Springer VS. http://www.springer.com/https://doi.org/10.1007/978-3-658-03483-2.

Ferragina, E., & Seeleib-Kaiser, M. (2014). Determinants of a Silent ®evolution: Understanding the expansion of family policy in rich OECD countries. *Social Politics, 22*(1), 1–37. https://doi.org/10.1093/sp/jxu027

Ferree, M. M., Gamson, W. A., Gerhards, J., & Rucht, D. (2002). *Shaping abortion discourse: Democracy and the public sphere in Germany and the United States*. Cambridge University Press. Förster, M. (1994). Measurement of low incomes and poverty in a perspective of international comparisons. *OECD Labour Market and Social Policy Occasional Papers*. https://doi.org/10.1787/112854878327.

Friedli, L. (2016). Politics of tackling inequalitites. In K. E. Smith, S. Hill, & C. Bambra (Eds.), *Health inequalities: Critical perspectives*. Oxford University Press. https://doi.org/10.1136/bmj.f6750

Gallie, D., Paugam, S., & Jacobs, S. (2003). Unemployment, poverty and social isolation: Is there a vicious circle of social exclusion? *European Societies, 5*(1), 1–32. https://doi.org/10.1080/1461669032000057668

Gkiouleka, A., & Huijts, T. (2020). Intersectional migration-related health inequalities in Europe: Exploring the role of migrant generation, occupational status & gender. *Social Science & Medicine (1982), 267*, 113218. https://doi.org/10.1016/j.socscimed.2020.113218

Goedemé, T., & Rottiers, S. (2011). Poverty in the enlarged European Union. A discussion about definitions and reference groups. *Sociology Compass, 5*(1), 77–91. https://doi.org/10.1111/j.1751-9020.2010.00350.x

Hajat, A., Kaufman, J. S., Rose, K. M., Siddiqi, A., & Thomas, J. C. (2010). Long-term effects of wealth on mortality and self-rated health status. *American Journal of Epidemiology, 173*(2), 192–200. https://doi.org/10.1093/aje/kwq348

Helm, T. (2001). *Schröder threat to end dole for 'lazy'*. https://www.telegraph.co.uk/news/worldnews/europe/germany/1338111/Schroder-threat-to-end-dole-for-lazy.html.

Herber, G.-C., Ruijsbroek, A., Koopmanschap, M., Proper, K., van der Lucht, F., Boshuizen, H., Polder, J., & Uiters, E. (2019). Single transitions and persistence of unemployment are associated with poor health outcomes. *BMC Public Health, 19*(1), 740. https://doi.org/10.1186/s12889-019-7059-8

Holmqvist, M. (2009). Medicalization of unemployment: Individualizing social issues as personal problems in the Swedish welfare state. *Work, Employment and Society, 23*(3), 405–421. https://doi.org/10.1177/0950017009337063

Jayaweera, H., & Quigley, M. A. (2010). Health status, health behaviour and healthcare use among migrants in the UK: Evidence from mothers in the Millennium Cohort Study. *Social Science & Medicine (1982), 71*(5), 1002–1010. https://doi.org/10.1016/j.socscimed.2010.05.039

Kanbur, R., & Squire, L. (2001). The evolution of thinking about poverty: Exploring the interactions. In G. M. Meier & J. E. Stiglitz (Eds.), *Frontiers of development economics: The future in perspective* (pp. 183–226). World Bank; Oxford University Press.

Keller, R. (2013). Das Wissen der Wörter und Diskurse: Über Sprache und Wissen in der Wissenssoziologischen Diskursanalyse. In W. Viehöver, R. Keller, &

W. Schneider (Eds.), *Diskurs – Sprache – Wissen: Interdisziplinäre Beiträge zum Verhältnis von Sprache und Wissen in der Diskursforschung* (pp. 21–50). Springer VS.

Kirmayer, L. J., Narasiah, L., Munoz, M., Rashid, M., Ryder, A. G., Guzder, J., Hassan, G., Rousseau, C., & Pottie, K. (2011). Common mental health problems in immigrants and refugees: General approach in primary care. *CMAJ: Canadian Medical Association Journal = Journal De L'association Medicale Canadienne, 183*(12), E959–E967. https://doi.org/10.1503/cmaj.090292

Knuth, M. (2006). "Hartz IV" – die unbegriffene Reform. *Sozialer Fortschritt, 55*(7), 160–168.

Kongress Armut und Gesundheit. (2021). *Der Kongress Armut und Gesundheit begeht sein 25-jähriges Jubiläum*. https://www.armut-und-gesundheit.de/ueber-den-kongress/unser-25-jubilaeum.

Krayter, S., & Reibling, N. (2020). Medicalisation and psychologisation of poverty? An analysis of the scientific poverty discourse from 1956 to 2017. *Journal of Poverty and Social Justice, 28*(3), 361–381. https://doi.org/10.1332/175982720X15979441697421

Kroll, L. E., Müters, S., & Lampert, T. (2016). *Arbeitslosigkeit und ihre Auswirkungen auf die Gesundheit: Ein Überblick zum Forschungsstand und zu aktuellen Daten der Studien GEDA 2010 und GEDA 2012* [Unemployment and Health: An overview of current research results and data from the 2010 and 2012 German Health Update] (No. 2). https://doi.org/10.1007/s00103-015-2282-7.

Lampert, T. (2011). Armut und Gesundheit. In T. Schott & C. Hornberg (Eds.), *Gesundheit und Gesellschaft. Die Gesellschaft und ihre Gesundheit: 20 Jahre Public Health in Deutschland Bilanz und Ausblick einer Wissenschaft* (1st ed.). VS Verlag für Sozialwissenschaften.

Lampert, T., & Kroll, L. E. (2006). *Einkommensdifferenzen in der Gesundheit und Lebenserwartung – Quer- und Längsschnittbefunde des Sozio-oekonomischen Panels (SOEP)* [Income differences in health and life expectancy—cross-sectional and longitudinal findings of the German Socio-Economic Panel (GSOEP)] (No. 4). https://doi.org/10.1055/s-2006-926638.

Lampert, T., & Ziese, T. (2005). *Armut, soziale Ungleichheit und Gesundheit: Expertise des Robert Koch-Instituts zum 2. Armuts- und Reichtumsbericht der Bundesregierung*.

Leisering, L. (1993). *Zwischen Verdrängung und Dramatisierung: Zur Wissenssoziologie der Armut in der bundesrepublikanischen Gesellschaft* (Arbeitspapier No. 25). Bremen. Universität Bremen, SFB 186 Statuspassagen und Risikolagen im Lebensverlauf.

Martin, L. H., Gutman, H., & Hutton, P. H. (Eds.). (1988). *Technologies of the self: A seminar with Michel Foucault*. University of Massachusetts Press.

Mathieu, A. (1993). The medicalization of homelessness and the theater of repression. *Medical Anthropology Quarterly, 7*(2), 170–184.

Miller, B., Carter, J., MacRae, C., & Schulz, B. (2021). A comparative analysis of attitudes towards female and male breadwinners in Germany, Sweden and the United States. *Journal of Gender Studies, 30*(3), 358–370. https://doi.org/10.1080/09589236.2021.1872510

Missinne, S., & Bracke, P. (2012). Depressive symptoms among immigrants and ethnic minorities: A population based study in 23 European countries. *Social Psychiatry and Psychiatric Epidemiology, 47*(1), 97–109. https://doi.org/10.1007/s00127-010-0321-0

Nahles, A. (2016). *Stabiler Arbeitsmarkt auf sehr hohem Niveau: Pressekonferenz mit Bundesministerin Andrea Nahles am 30*. November 2016 in Berlin. https://www.bmas.de/SharedDocs/Videos/DE/Artikel/Arbeitsmarkt/arbeitsmarktzahlen-november-2016.html

Nichols, A., Mitchell, J., & Lindner, S. (2013). *Consequences of long-term unemployment*. The Urban Insitut.

OECD. (2003). *Poverty and health* (DAC guidelines and reference series). Paris, Geneva. DAC Network on Poverty Reduction.

OECD. (2021a). *Income inequality*. https://data.oecd.org/inequality/income-inequality.htm#indicator-chart

OECD. (2021b). *Poverty gap*. https://data.oecd.org/inequality/poverty-gap.htm#indicator-chart

OECD. (2021c). *Poverty rate*. https://data.oecd.org/inequality/poverty-rate.htm#indicator-chart

Rathmann, K., Lampert, T., Kuntz, B., Herke, M., & Loter, K. (2018). Die Bedeutung intergenerationaler Bildungsmobilität für die Gesundheit und die Lebenszufriedenheit von Schülerinnen und Schülern in Deutschland. *ZSE Zeitschrift Für Soziologie Der Erziehung Und Sozialisation, 38*(1), 80–99.

Rose, N. S. (1998). *Inventing our selves: Psychology, power and personhood* (1. paperback ed.). *Cambridge studies in the history of psychology*. Cambridge University Press.

Schram, S. F. (2000). In the clinic: The medicalization of welfare. *Social Text, 18*(1), 81–107.

Seeleib-Kaiser, M., & Fleckenstein, T. (2007). Discourse, learning and welfare state change: The case of German labour market reforms. *Social Policy & Administration, 41*(5), 427–448.

Sen, A. K. (1999). *Commodities and capabilities* (1st ed., 25th imp). *Oxford India paperbacks: Vol. 96*. Oxford University Press. https://doi.org/10.2307/2232999.

Ullrich, P. (2008). Diskursanalyse, Diskursforschung, Diskurstheorie. Ein- und Überblick. In U. Freikamp, M. Leanza, J. Mende, S. Müller, P. Ullrich, & H.-J. Voß (Eds.), *Texte/Rosa-Luxemburg-Stiftung: Vol. 42. Kritik mit Methode? Forschungsmethoden und Gesellschaftskritik* (pp. 19–32). Karl Dietz Verlag.

United Nations. (2013). *The OECD approach to measure and monitor income poverty across countries: Economic Commission for Europe*. Conference of European Statisticians.
United Nations. (2015). *The millennium development goals report 2015*. New York.
Vaalavuo, M. (2016). Deterioration in health: What is the role of unemployment and poverty? *Scandinavian Journal of Public Health, 44*, 347–353.
van Zon, S. K. R., Reijneveld, S. A., Mendes de Leon, C. F., & Bültmann, U. (2017). The impact of low education and poor health on unemployment varies by work life stage. *International Journal of Public Health, 62*(9), 997–1006. https://doi.org/10.1007/s00038-017-0972-7
Vreese, C. H. (2005). Identifying information and tenor in texts. *Information Design Journal, 13*(1), 51–62. https://doi.org/10.1075/idjdd.13.1.06vre
Weingart, P., Engels, A., & Pansegrau, P. (2008). *Von der Hypothese zur Katastrophe: Der Anthropogene Klimawandel im Diskurs zwischen Wissenschaft, Politik und Massenmedien* (2nd ed.). Barbara Budrich.
Weingart, P., Lentsch, J., Brown, M. B., Halffman, W., den Hoed, P., Keizer, A. G., Geffroy, L., Piriou, O., Zimmermann, B., & Joly, P. B. (Eds.). (2009). *Scientific advice to policy making: International comparison*. Verlag Barbara Budrich. https://books.google.de/books?id=1B9XtQtejlIC
Wittig, U., Lindert, J., Merbach, M., & Brähler, E. (2008). Mental health of patients from different cultures in Germany. *European Psychiatry, 23*(S1), 28–35. https://doi.org/10.1016/S0924-9338(08)70059-2
Wong, S. (2016). Geographies of medicalized welfare: Spatial analysis of supplemental security income in the U.S., 2000–2010. *Social Science & Medicine (1982), 160*, 9–19. https://doi.org/10.1016/j.socscimed.2016.05.018

CHAPTER 6

Childhood in Crisis: Are Medicine and Psychology Part of the Problem or Part of the Solution?

Nadine Reibling, Mareike Ariaans, and Lucas Hamel

6.1 Children and the Welfare State

Unlike poverty and unemployment, childhood is not a social problem; rather, it is simply a part of the human life course. However, upon closer inspection, childhood is rarely conceived as something that merely unfolds and it is instead approached as a problem that needs to be analyzed and managed. Rousseau's (1911 [1762]) *Émile, ou De l'éducation*, for instance, serves as a reminder that providing children with the right upbringing has occupied science and philosophy for decades. Over the course of the nineteenth and the beginning of twentieth centuries, medicine and psychology gained considerable authority over childhood, particularly—but not only—when it was considered problematic. Nolan (1998), for instance,

N. Reibling (✉)
Fulda University of Applied Sciences, Fulda, Germany
e-mail: nadine.reibling@pg.hs-fulda.de

M. Ariaans • L. Hamel
University of Siegen, Siegen, Germany

N. Reibling, M. Ariaans (eds.), *Toward a Biopsychosocial Welfare State?*, https://doi.org/10.1007/978-3-031-32793-3_6

exemplified how the legitimation of American public education moved from religious ideas and values to the psychological needs of children and their healthy development. Rafalovich (2001) traced the conceptual history of attention deficit hyperactivity disorder (ADHD) and demonstrated that medicine created various labels to categorize the disorder since at least 1877. In a more recent historical comparison, Clarke (2015) revealed that advice for mothers in Canada's most read woman's magazine was equally medicalized in the period from 1945 to 1956 as in the period from 1990 to 2010. These historical analyses indicate that the medicalization and psychologization of childhood are by no means new phenomena. Over the course of the twentieth century, medicine and psychology established themselves as two primary disciplines for dealing with childhood issues in contemporary societies. This characteristic was shown in an analysis of the scientific discourse on childhood problems in which medicine and psychology were found to have the greatest publication output in this area compared with all other disciplines covered in the Social Science Citation Index since the mid-twentieth century (Brase et al., 2022). However, if medicalization and psychologization have been historic phenomena *and* if both fields have such an established position today, why did we select childhood problems as a topic for this book?

One reason for our choice is that problems in childhood serve as a prime example for better understanding the link between medicalization, psychologization, and the welfare state. Children spend a large amount of their childhood in institutions that are funded and regulated by the welfare state. Public education is one of many ways in which the welfare state (e.g., family policy, children's and youth services, healthcare, minimum income for families) impacts children's lives in advanced, industrialized nations. Moreover, welfare states take a special interest in children whose lives are considered problematic. For these children, the welfare state usually offers additional programs, such as child protection services, assisted living, special education, and therapies. Thus, considering this collection of child-related programs and services, the welfare state has a strong influence on childhood and plays a key role in managing childhood problems.

Secondly, the role of children in the welfare state has changed dramatically over the last two decades. This change is strongly connected to the growing influence of the social investment paradigm. At the core of the paradigm is the idea of investing in human capital for future returns (i.e., in the form of productivity, social participation, and lower welfare expenditures), with investing in children "as an emblem of the future" (Adamson

& Brennan, 2014, p. 47) being seen as most profitable. For instance, Esping-Andersen (2002, 2005) prominently supports a "child-centred social investment strategy." This perspective has also been taken up by the European Commission, which issued a 2013 recommendation entitled "Investing in Children: breaking the cycle of disadvantage":

> (2) Children[1] are more at risk of poverty or social exclusion than the overall population in a large majority of EU countries; children growing up in poverty or social exclusion are less likely than their better-off peers to do well in school, enjoy good health and realise their full potential later in life; (3) Preventing the transmission of disadvantage across generations is a crucial investment in Europe's future, as well as a direct contribution to the Europe 2020 Strategy for smart, sustainable and inclusive growth, with long-term benefits for children, the economy and society as a whole. (European Commission, 2013)

This statement from the European Commission illustrates that children play an instrumental role in terms of how the social investment concept is used by the European Union to justify benefits and services that influence children's lives.

In the United States, economic Nobel laureate James J. Heckman is a prominent advocate for investing in early childhood. In his paper "Skill Formation and the Economics of Investing in Disadvantaged Children," which was published in Science in 2006, Heckman argues that "[m]any major economic and social problems can be traced to low levels of skill and ability in the population" (Heckman, 2006, p. 1901). He further suggests that these abilities are character skills, such as "motivation, perseverance, and tenacity" (Heckman, 2006, p. 1901), which disadvantaged children often lack because they are exposed to broken families and bad parenting. Heckman's work highlights the tendency of the social investment perspective to use psychological concepts such as motivation or resilience to tackle social problems. This psychologization of childhood problems is also visible in the expansion of parenting programs across advanced, industrialized countries (Betz et al., 2017).

In sum, children have become a central target of social investment initiatives (Esping-Andersen, 2005; European Commission, 2013; Kjørholt, 2013). Along with—and as a part of—educational reforms, fostering children's health and psychological competences has served as a cornerstone of these initiatives. Thus, we can identify a growing importance of medicine and psychology in the welfare state's monitoring of—and intervention in—children's lives (Ecclestone & Brunila, 2015). This monitoring includes the use of medical and psychological *ideas* to objectify childhood problems and to justify interventions (Gillies, 2005; Heckman & Kautz, 2013; Macvarish et al., 2015). Monitoring and intervening in children's lives can also mean managing childhood through medicalized and psychologized categories and interventions (*institutions*) (Odenbring et al., 2017; Ramey, 2020). Finally, this monitoring and intervening in children's lives can involve an increasing reliance on the expertise of medical doctors and psychologists (*actors*) (Liebsch, 2020).

In the present chapter, we investigate how the medicalization and psychologization of childhood have unfolded in Germany over the last two decades. In the following section, we provide an overarching perspective on how these processes have evolved based on existing literature and the analysis of policies and governmental reports. In the following part of the chapter, we present evidence from three studies that provide more information on how the processes of medicalization and psychologization work and how they compare and interact with other approaches of childhood and children's behavior (e.g., social or moral explanations). The first study illustrates how collective actors—specifically the German Professional Association of Pediatricians and the German Education Association—engage in or resist the medicalization or psychologization of problems in childhood. In the second study, we present the public's view on ADHD and the importance that the German public attaches to medical and psychological accounts of hyperactive behavior in children as compared with other explanations. Finally, we examine how learning difficulties are addressed in Germany and we provide examples of medicalization and psychologization in all three dimensions (i.e., ideas, institutions, actors). We end with an overarching conclusion from these three studies and provide some thoughts on how the COVID-19 pandemic might have impacted the medicalization and psychologization of childhood in Germany.

6.2 Medicalization and Psychologization of Childhood in Germany

Families have always been a focus of welfare statepolicies. However, since the end of the 1990s, children as an independent group have become increasingly important in the social policy discourse of the EU, in many international organizations, and in individual nations (Lister, 2006; Schiettecat et al., 2015), including Germany (Betz, 2016; Olk & Hübenthal, 2009). These discourses exhibit two main characteristics: (1) a new emphasis on the notion that child poverty is a central issue in advanced, industrialized countries (European Commission, 2013; Nygård & Krüger, 2012; Olk & Hübenthal, 2009) and (2) increasingly frequent references to the social investment model (Lister, 2006; Nygård & Krüger, 2012). Investing in children is considered instrumental for economic growth and for breaking the cycle of social disadvantage. For instance, in the draft of the so-called Good Daycare Law, the German government stated the following:

> For years, the OECD has pointed to the importance of early childhood education in cognitive and emotional development as well as in mitigating social inequality and promoting better overall student performance. [...] The Federal Ministry of Economics suggests that spending on early childhood education has high rates of return. For example, it has been shown that the real fiscal rate of return on quantity- and quality-enhancing spending in this area is roughly eight percent. [...] In the long term, the future employment opportunities of children improve, [...] and there are also further effects of investments in early childhood education, such as increased life satisfaction, reduced crime, and a greater willingness to engage in social activities. (Bundesregierung, 2018, pp. 11–12)

This quote demonstrates the high expectations set in policies which invest in children which should translate in improving society in various ways (economic growth, employment, life satisfaction, crime, civic engagement). While international organizations such as the OECD which is referenced in this legislation have promoted this view, social policy researchers have criticized these expectations as exaggerated (Cantillon & van Lancker, 2013).

In Germany, which has traditionally focused on a male-breadwinner model and familial childcare before the age of three, the social investment discourse has been accompanied by a fundamental change in policies.

Early childhood education and care (ECEC) has been substantially expanded ([Daycare expansion act] Tagesbetreuungsausbaugesetz, 2004), and in 2008, the government installed the social right of parents to receive childcare for children at the age of one ([Child promotion act] Kinderförderungsgesetz, 2008). Following the expansion of childcare, a debate and several initiatives for improving the quality of care were set in motion. Health promotion and child development were identified as key areas for the quality promotion initiatives in early childcare and education (Bundesregierung, 2022; [Daycare Quality and Participation Improvement Law] KiTa Qualitäts- und Teilhabeverbesserungsgesetz, 2018). In the accompanying discourse, quality childcare has been conceived as a strategy for combatting child poverty because it enables parents to be employed—which is considered the most effective way of overcoming material deprivation—and because childcare centers are supposed to provide stimulating environments that compensate for less stimulating environments in disadvantaged families (Lister, 2006; Olk & Hübenthal, 2009). In addition, parenting has become a focal point in discourses and policies. Parenting is considered the major factor that drives the successful development of children (Betz, 2016; Gillies, 2005), and a wide range of measures and initiatives have therefore been put in place to educate parents and improve their parenting skills (Betz, 2016).

While this new orientation toward children has been widely analyzed in the social policy literature (Cantillon & van Lancker, 2013; Lister, 2006; Schiettecat et al., 2015), little emphasis has been placed on the role of medicine and psychology in this development. The basis of the social investment paradigm is the human capital model, which is an economic theory. However, in the application of the social investment idea, medicine and psychology play an important role and provide individualistic perspectives that resonate well with the human capital model. Governmental reports and laws reveal how medical and psychological concepts and technologies are woven into these discourses and programs (Ariaans & Reibling, 2021; Wissenschaftlicher Beitrat für Familienfragen beim BMFSFJ, 2005). For instance, health and healthy development are central in this discourse and in policies that address the quality of childcare. Psychological concepts and evidence play a key role when it comes to justifying parenting programs that center around the psychological concept of parents' educational competence ("Erziehungskompetenz") (Wissenschaftlicher Beitrat für Familienfragen beim BMFSFJ, 2005). Similarly, psychological evidence is used to justify the necessity of services for improving the life of children who live in disadvantaged situations (Wissenschaftlicher Beitrat für Familienfragen beim BMFSFJ, 2005). Betz (2016) has also highlighted the fact that despite the investment perspective, there is a strong deficit orientation in childhood discourses, and epidemiological evidence is frequently used to justify the need for state monitoring and intervention. However, medicalization and psychologization have not only occurred on the level of ideas: Indeed, regular screening examinations with pediatricians have been offered since 1971. However, the range of—and tasks associated with—these screenings has been expanded to include screening for psychosocial preventive needs and child abuse. While these screenings are considered important for reasons of surveillance and monitoring children's development, they have created anxieties and led to a low tolerance for deviations from the norm (Liebsch, 2020). Pediatricians have become consultants and gatekeepers for educational decisions (e.g., regarding whether a child is ready for primary school) (Liebsch, 2020). Moreover, medical doctors and psychologists as well as other health professions have taken on a new role in child protection and have been approached as partners in several initiatives, such as early childhood intervention and prevention programs (e.g., Frühe Hilfen ("Early Childhood Intervention")—a national early parenting and intervention program). A specifically stated aim in such initiatives is to use the healthcare system as a door opener and gatekeeper for managing childhood (Deffte et al., 2018).

Finally, while the social investment paradigm casts a positive, future-oriented light on childhood, its narrative is accompanied by the analysis of problems in childhood and by the identification of children who are "at risk" (Betz, 2016). As a result, the new emphasis on children in the social policy discourse and the selected measures for intervention in children's lives may have contributed to a greater awareness of—as well as to the persistence of problems in—childhood. First, the focus in policymaking has been intentionally placed on emphasizing education and services as well as on activating parents to work rather than on redistributing resources (Olk & Hübenthal, 2009). Despite the stated hopes of these policies, structural inequalities and child poverty have hardly been affected: Indeed, child poverty has remained mostly stable over the last 15 years, with around one in five children at risk of poverty (Schmitz-Kießler, 2022), and the poverty risk of single parents—and particularly of families with three and more children—has even increased in recent years (Schmitz-Kießler, 2022). Moreover, there is no indication that the expansion of early childhood education has reduced the influence of social origin on educational success (Hußmann et al., 2017).

Second, the increased surveillance of childhood—combined with the high expectations associated with investing in children has led to an increased attention toward childhood problems. This heightened problem awareness exists because children who are not happy, healthy, and successful constitute a threat to social investment logic (Lister, 2006). If such childhood problems arise, medicine and psychology are professions that are regularly approached to deal with these problems (by parents, teachers, and policymakers). The right of these professions to provide diagnoses is essential, as these diagnoses constitute official explanations for childhood problems. Moreover, medical doctors and psychologists serve as gatekeepers to treatment and access to specialized services that are provided by the German welfare system, such as logopedic, physical therapy, and educational training for children with learning difficulties. In a focus group in our research project conducted with professionals who work with children in Germany, one pediatrician stated:

> From the perspective of pediatricians, our work has changed a lot in the last few decades. We deal much less with acute illness and infectious diseases than we used to, and we are consulted by parents regarding educational problems, behavioral problems, learning problems, and [...] and social and psychological problems. And [...] we are paid by health insurances, [so] we of course can only take action if a diagnosis is made [...]. [W]e always have to have a justification for creating costs. (Pediatrician, focus group, 25 June 2021)

In line with this assessment, diagnoses of mental illnesses in children and adolescents rose in Germany between 2005 and 2015, with more than one in four children having received a diagnosis within the previous year (Grobe, 2017; Steffen et al., 2018). Moreover, there was also a steep upward trend in the consumption of methylphenidate (i.e., the most common medication for treating ADHD) between 1993 and 2012 (Bundesinstitut für Arzneimittel und Medizinprodukte, 2015). However, this development was perceived critically and led to a debate on overmedicating children in Germany (Karsch, 2018). In reaction, the prescription guideline for stimulants for children became more restrictive in 2010, which led to the stabilization and partial reduction of prescriptions for stimulants that had commonly been prescribed for ADHD (Grimmsmann

& Himmel, 2021). However, in 2017, a new treatment guideline was issued that referenced existing UK recommendations provided by National Institute for Health and Care Excellence (NICE). The new guideline lowered the clinical criteria for prescribing stimulants and suggested using these stimulants for moderate-intensity ADHD based on evidence on the relative effectiveness of pharmacotherapy and psychotherapy. The implications of these changes cannot yet be identified with available data (Grimmsmann & Himmel, 2021).

This debate on the diagnosis and treatment of childhood mental illness conditions reveals the dynamics in the role of medicine and psychology in the field of childhood problems. While the medicalization and psychologization of childhood in Germany can be detected in current discourses and policies, there is no indication that childhood is exclusively or primarily viewed from a medical or psychological perspective. Instead, medical and psychological ideas, categories, and actors are integrated with economic, social, and educational elements (NZFH Beirat, 2016). Moreover, over-medicalizing childhood (albeit not over-psychologizing childhood) has also met with critique and resistance. In the following section, we examine the role of two professional organizations in the discourse on childhood problems and discuss how medicalization—and the resistance to medicalization—can be identified in their public communication.

6.3 Childhood Discourses: How Pediatricians and Educators Construct Problems in Childhood

In our theoretical framework, we outlined three dimensions of medicalization and psychologization. In this section, we examine the dimension of *ideas* and specifically address whether and how medical and psychological ideas are used to describe and explain problems in childhood. In order to do this, we systematically analyzed the ideas that two specific actors—namely the German Professional Association of Pediatricians (Berufsverband der Kinder- und Jugendärzte—BVKJ) and the German Education Association (Verband Bildung und Erziehung—VBE)—have used in their public communication on childhood problems. We investigate these two associations because the existing literature has shown that pediatricians and educators are important agents in medicalizing childhood behavior (Brault et al., 2022; Klasen, 2000; Malacrida, 2004; Rafalovich, 2005a). However, the role of these groups has thus far been analyzed on the micro-level. For instance, studies have examined how teachers and pediatricians influence families in seeking a diagnosis for problematic childhood behavior (Brault et al., 2022; Klasen, 2000; Lavin, 2016; Malacrida, 2004; Rafalovich, 2005b). From these studies, we know that the influence of both groups can vary. In some cases and contexts, pediatricians and educators encourage the medicalization and/or treatment of children's behavior, while in other cases, these pediatricians and educators actively resist this process and try to de-medicalize children's behavior, for instance, by trying to convince parents with other explanations for the behavior, by refusing to make a diagnosis or referral, or by refusing to prescribe medication. However, what has been largely unexplored is the influence that pediatricians and educators have as collective actors on ideas about childhood problems through their professional associations. These professional associations are important since they are the mouthpiece of the profession. Through their public communication and lobbying work, the professions have the potential to influence public discourses and policy decisions.

Therefore, we investigate how these associations construct childhood behavior. Specifically, we examine when and how these associations medicalize/psychologize or de-medicalize/de-psychologize childhood. To shed light on this issue, we conducted a qualitative content analysis of 48 press releases made by the German Professional Association of Pediatricians and of 104 press releases made by the German Education Association that these organizations had published between 2009 and 2019. We would have liked to additionally examine the ideas put forth by one of the psychological associations in the field, but sufficient data were not available to conduct a comparable analysis.

6.3.1 German Professional Association of Pediatricians, 2009–2019

The German Professional Association of Pediatricians issues press releases on a wide variety of issues, including social problems such as poverty, child protection, early education, problematic childhood behavior, and learning difficulties. In part of the press releases, the association unequivocally advocates for a medicalized perspective of childhood problems, for example, in its position on ADHD:

> ADHD is a predominantly biological and genetic disorder that is modified by environmental and social factors. [...] Pharmaceutical treatment for ADHD has been established for over 60 years and has been scientifically validated by countless studies. The therapy is highly effective, with serious, undesirable side effects being rare [as well as] reversible and tolerable with careful monitoring. (Berufsverband der Kinder- und Jugendärzte, 2012c)

Moreover, the association is committed to prevention and health promotion in childhood, for instance, by calling for more health professionals in schools (Berufsverband der Kinder- und Jugendärzte, 2017a, b) and by more extensively including health topics in school curricula (Berufsverband der Kinder- und Jugendärzte, 2017b, 2018).

In contrast, in other press releases, the association has argued that social problems such as poverty are the cause of many problems that are encountered in their clinical practice. For instance, the association claims that poverty leads to health issues such as respiratory infections (Berufsverband der Kinder- und Jugendärzte, 2016). Moreover, in several press releases, the association has highlighted how children in poor or socially disadvantaged families more frequently have developmental disorders due to their low-stimulus environment (Berufsverband der Kinder- und Jugendärzte, 2009b, 2011c, 2012a, b, 2013a, 2014, 2015b). The association thus demands more, earlier, and better early childhood education in order to help these children (Berufsverband der Kinder- und Jugendärzte, 2009a, 2010a, b, 2011a, 2013b, 2015b, 2019).

In several press releases, The German Professional Association of Pediatricians has constructed the medicalization of children as a result of the failing educational system. For instance, the association has found inadequate educational structures and teachers to be responsible for sending these children to the medical system. Pediatricians claim that teachers are quick to refer children to medical help (Berufsverband der Kinder- und Jugendärzte, 2014, 2015d) and that children are increasingly often "pathologized" in the facilities of the educational system. For example, children with behavioral problems are not treated with educational methods and are instead advised by teachers to go to the medical doctor (Berufsverband der Kinder- und Jugendärzte, 2011a). Due to insufficient social and pedagogical measures and interventions, physicians respond with the tools of their own system—namely diagnosis and therapy—(Berufsverband der Kinder- und Jugendärzte, 2011a) even though these immanent tools have not been evaluated to be effective in most cases

(Berufsverband der Kinder- und Jugendärzte, 2010c, 2011a, 2015b, c). Thus, physicians argue that they have no other option than to medicalize children:

> If we had a quantitatively and qualitatively adequate pedagogical system of socially compensatory early childhood support, such children would certainly be better off there than in the medical system. Those who denounce the increase in spending on prescription drugs for treating children must ask themselves why society does not provide sufficient early intervention facilities and does not equip childcare facilities in such a way that they can fulfil their educational mandate. (Berufsverband der Kinder- und Jugendärzte, 2011a)

Overall, the German Professional Association of Pediatricians views problems in childhood as both medical and social problems. To some extent, the association resists medicalizing childhood by explicitly discussing the phenomenon of medicalization and criticizing the educational system's quick tendency to look for help from the medical system. However, the association has also argued that pediatricians have no other choice than to diagnose and treat children due to the lack of alternative strategies—thus legitimizing medicalization of childhood problems.

Moreover, our analysis of the association's press releases additionally indicates an implicit form of medicalization that derives from two mechanisms: (a) *Boundary expansion*: The German Professional Association of Pediatricians comments on many topics that lie far outside its professional boundaries (e.g., the quality of the educational system), which can be interpreted as an extension of the boundaries of the association's jurisdiction. This development has also been described in the United States, where scholars have shown how pediatricians extended the scope of their practice in the second half of the twentieth century to also include childhood behavior and the psychosocial needs of children, which today constitute major components of their work (Halpern, 1990; Pawluch, 1983). In comparison, educators have addressed the healthcare system far less frequently, which reveals how medical expertise can often be leveraged to comment as experts on many topics while medicine can mostly be critiqued within its own professional circle. (b) *Medical framing*: The language used in the press releases is interspersed with medical terms. Thus, even if the association calls for social measures, the framing of an issue is often medical due to the references to medical diagnoses and treatments.

6.3.2 German Education Association, 2009–2019

The German Education Association encompasses a wide range of professions and institutions, including educators in early childhood centers and kindergartens as well as schoolteachers in various tracks. The existing medicalization literature has highlighted the importance of educators and schools in the initiation and implementation of medicalizing childhood behavior (Brault et al., 2022; Malacrida, 2004; Rafalovich, 2005b). One of the reasons for the prominent role of these of educators is that they interact with the same group of children on a daily basis *and* have "the opportunity to constantly compare a student's behaviors to those of other students" (Brault et al., 2022, 3). However, cross-national comparisons of the role of teachers in labeling ADHD have indicated that in North America (USA, Canada), teachers' tendency to medicalize children's behavior is much more pronounced than in Europe (UK, Belgium), where teachers are often critical of medicalizing children's behavior (Brault et al., 2022; Malacrida, 2004).

Our analyses of press releases made by the German Education Association indicate that the association's conceptualization of children's problems is similar to what can be found in teachers' practices in other European nations. If the association writes about problems in childhood, these problems are most often attributed to the socio-economic context of the children's family, such as poverty or migration background. The solutions that the association advocates predominantly focus on the educational system and include *structural measures*, such as (financial) investment in pre-school education, more hours of education in schools, and smaller class sizes (Verband Bildung und Erziehung, 2016a, b, d). More often, however, *individual measures* are proposed as solutions, such as special classes and educational counseling for children with problematic behavior or support for difficult circumstances (Verband Bildung und Erziehung, 2009a, 2010, 2015, 2016a).

Although social and educational reasoning and measures for problematic childhood behavior are promoted, some press releases relate to medical and psychological descriptions and measures. Similar to pediatricians, educators advocate for more health competencies and prevention (e.g., measures against obesity) in schools as well as for individual care and assistance of chronically ill children, which should be done by healthcare workers who are employed at schools (Verband Bildung und Erziehung, 2017a, 2018a, b). Furthermore, low social and emotional development in children should be given greater importance and should be supported by additional special-needs education (Verband Bildung und Erziehung, 2017b).

> The state must therefore also ensure [that] basic medical care [is provided] by school health professionals in all schools. [...] School health professionals should make preventive offers and thus contribute to a healthier lifestyle for [their] students. (Verband Bildung und Erziehung, 2018b)

However, educators are also concerned about the medicalization and pharmaceuticalization of childhood problems, as demonstrated by the following quote from 2012, which was the peak year in the strong upward trend of methylphenidate consumption in Germany:

> Children should be allowed to remain children; they should be allowed to romp around and be loud without it being immediately interpreted as an illness. Only in severe cases and in the event of behavioral problems should medication be reached for. Before that, Beckmann [Chairman of the VBE] demands, children with behavioral problems should be treated with smaller classes and better support. (Verband Bildung und Erziehung, 2012a)

Nevertheless, the association additionally uses psychological categories—such as "burnout" and "stress"—to draw attention to increased performance pressure in schools (Verband Bildung und Erziehung, 2009b, 2010, 2016c). According to the German Education Association, "The pressure on the children must not be allowed to get out of hand. Students who are burned out are no longer a rarity" (2016c). This statement indicates that while educators in Germany seem to be mostly opposed to the medicalization of childhood behavior, they nevertheless engage with psychological explanations. This finding is in line with the existing literature, which has highlighted how the educational system has embraced psychological concepts and technologies (Alexander, 2018; Ecclestone & Brunila, 2015).

Table 6.1 summarizes the main results of the analyses of the press releases by the German Education Association and the German Professional Association of Pediatricians. The table displays the diverging general approaches of both organizations and presents a concept of problematic childhood behavior from the perspective of educators that stresses social and educational causes while pediatricians focus on medical causes.

Table 6.1 Medicalization and resistance to medicalization by the German Education Association and the German Professional Association of Pediatricians

	German Education Association	*German Professional Association of Pediatricians*
Problem explanations and suggested solutions	Social causes of problems and individual, educational solutions	Individual and social causes of problems and medicalization of solutions
Concept of problematic childhood behavior	*Medicalization*: psychological stress and burnout due to high pressure in schools *Resistance*: hyperactive and inattentive children are seldom due to a medical condition; children should be allowed to run free	*Medicalization*: ADHD as a disease/disorder with medical diagnosis and treatment
Advocated measures and actions regarding childhood problems	*Medicalization*: call for more healthcare workers in schools *Resistance*: individual educational support and smaller class sizes; pharmaceuticals as a last resort	*Medicalization*: call for more healthcare workers in schools and implementation of health education in curricula; pediatricians as contact people for social problems; treatment of ADHD with pharmaceuticals *Resistance*: learning disorders can and should be dealt with via early education and in schools

Educators mainly demand more social and educational measures and investment in children and view medical, psychological, and pharmaceutical treatment as a means of last resort. In contrast, pediatricians portray pharmaceutical treatment for ADHD as a common, non-dangerous solution. These medical actions for deviant childhood behavior prevail in the German Professional Association of Pediatricians but also highlight the fact that more social and educational investment in children is needed. Nevertheless, as long as this greater investment remains lacking, children are diagnosed and treated within the healthcare system.

6.4 Medicine and Psychology in the Public's View of Children with Problems

The welfare state is more than merely a conglomeration of policies, programs, and institutions: Indeed, its influence is also exerted through ideas and narratives from welfare discourses. These ideas are shaped by many different actors, including professional associations, such as the ones analyzed in the previous section, as well as by policymakers, journalists, scientists, social movements. However, ideas not only circulate among these elite discourses, but also form part of the understanding and beliefs of individual citizens. The public's attitudes are critical for the public legitimacy of the welfare state and also shape the experiences of welfare recipients, who encounter these ideas in social interactions (van Oorschot et al., 2017). Therefore, welfare state research has been increasingly interested in examining the public opinion of welfare policies and the target groups of such policies (van Oorschot et al., 2017). There are many ways in which we can investigate the ideas of the welfare state and its recipients. One prominent way has been through the study of public opinions of welfare policies and target groups. However, despite the growing influence of children as a target group of the welfare state, the social legitimacy literature has not yet examined the public's views on children and their problems as a way of understanding ideas about childhood and the welfare state.

Therefore, in this section, we investigate the public's views on children with problems. To do so, we developed several vignettes of children with problematic behavior. These vignettes were launched as a self-designed factorial survey that was fielded in an online access panel from YouGov Germany in September 2019. The sample was quota-based and represented the German adult population in terms of sex, age, education, and region. We presented respondents with hypothetical case descriptions of children. Here, we compare the descriptions of a child with normal (albeit not perfect) behavior and a child who represents a characteristic case of behavior that would indicate a diagnosis of ADHD. The case descriptions were developed and pre-tested with three trained psychologists. In the descriptions, both children were eight years old and attended a public elementary school. The description of the children, however, varied with respect to gender and ethnicity as well as in terms of the characteristics of their families (i.e., educational status, one-parent/two-parent family, sexual orientation of parents). The varying vignettes were assigned to respondents via randomization. One vignette of the child with hyperactive behavior appeared as follows:

> Ben is 8 years old, attends 2nd grade in elementary school, and lives with his mother, Sandra, who did not graduate school. Ben is a bright and intelligent boy. Nevertheless, he has been having more and more problems in school, especially because he finds it difficult to concentrate on individual tasks, which he often does not complete. On Parents Day, Ben's class teacher reported that Ben is easily distracted and needs to be reminded frequently to focus on his task. He often gets up from his seat without being asked, walks around the classroom, or suddenly starts talking loudly to classmates. Ben has a couple of friends in the neighborhood with whom he meets regularly to pursue common hobbies, but he finds it difficult to make new friends. Sandra has also noticed that Ben increasingly often forgets his homework and loses his toys. He also has frequent problems with getting up in the morning and going to sleep on time in the evening.

After presenting the vignette, we first asked respondents what they thought were the likely causes of the described child's behavior. Figure 6.1 displays

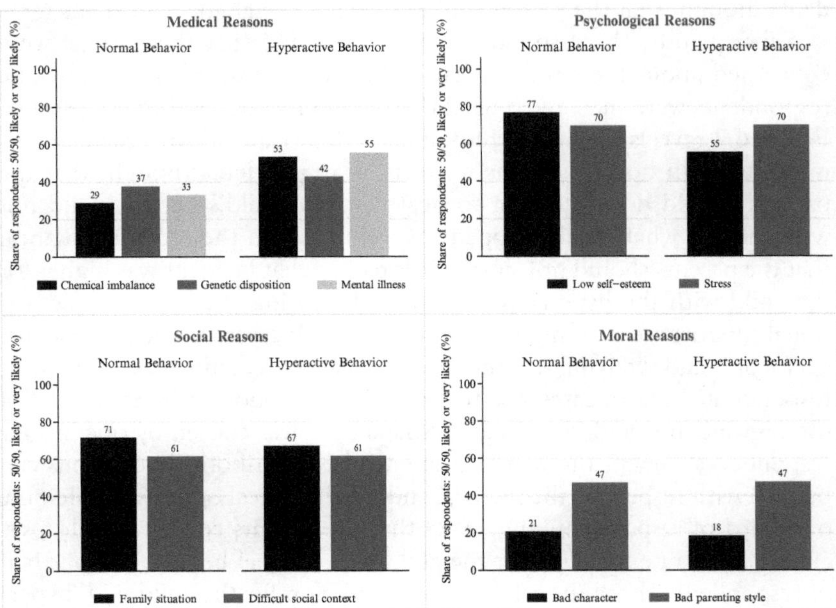

Fig. 6.1 Weighted share of respondents who assessed the various reasons provided as 50/50, likely, or very likely causes of the described child's behavior. Categorization into medical, psychological, social, and moral reasons based on theoretical reasoning. Source: vignette study, Wave 1 (in 2019) ($N = 2093$), own calculations

the percentage of respondents who indicated that the given reason was very likely, likely, or at least had a 50-50 chance of being a cause of the behavior. Overall, we can see that psychological and social reasons were more frequently selected than medical and moral reasons as causes of the child's behavior. Thus, the behavior of both children was attributed by most respondents to psychological reasons, such as "low self-esteem" or "stress," and social reasons, such as the "family situation" or "a difficult social context." Except for "low self-esteem," these causes were considered equally or similarly likely for both children. In contrast, medical reasons—such as a "chemical imbalance in the brain," a "genetic predisposition," or a "mental illness"—were perceived as likely by more respondents for the child who was described as showing hyperactive behavior than for the child with normal behavior. Thus, about half of the respondents considered biomedical reasons to be a potential cause for the child's behavior. Additionally, about half of the respondents thought that the behavior might be the result of a bad parenting style, while only one in five respondents thought that the reason could be due to the child's bad character.

Subsequently, the respondents were informed that the parents were concerned about the child's behavior but were unsure what to do. The respondents were then asked what they would recommend to the parents. Figure 6.2 reveals how many respondents (fully) agreed with each recommendation. In both cases, the majority of respondents thought that the parents should do something to deal with the child's behavior and not wait and see what would happen. Agreement with the recommendation that the parents should not simply wait to see what happens was higher for the child with the hyperactive behavior. Parenting strategies and educational support received high agreement for both cases. "Love and encouragement" and "talking to the teacher" were recommended by most respondents in both cases, "setting rules" was supported by about half of the respondents, and "warning to 'shape up'" was chosen by one in four respondents. Again, the major difference between both descriptions can be seen with respect to the medical and psychological options. While only one-third of respondents suggested that the parents consult a child psychologist or a pediatrician for the child with normal behavior, about half of respondents chose the same recommendation for the child with hyperactive behavior. Interestingly, support for consulting a child psychologist was even higher than for consulting a pediatrician.

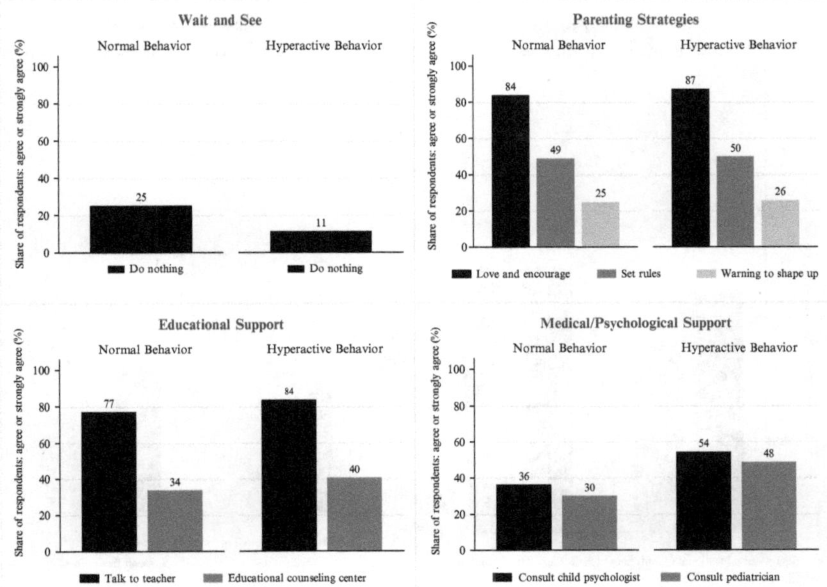

Fig. 6.2 Weighted share of respondents who agreed or strongly agreed with different parental recommendations. Source: vignette study, Wave 1 (in 2019) (N = 2307), own calculations

Finally, we aimed to obtain a better impression as to how much respondents would support potential welfare entitlements and obligations for the described children and their families (see Fig. 6.3). Support for entitlements—namely an "entitlement to free educational counseling (8 sessions)" and an "entitlement to free family therapy (1 year or longer)"—were supported by a greater share of respondents than were obligations. Support was higher for the child who was characterized by hyperactive behavior, with 58% of respondents supporting "short educational counseling" for this child compared with 53% for the normal child description, and 54% of respondents supporting "long family therapy" for the child with hyperactive behavior compared with 42% for the normal child description. Requirements such as "being obligated to attend family counseling," "being obligated to consult a pediatrician," and "being obligated to take medication" were supported by between one-fourth and one-third of respondents, with support for all options being somewhat higher for the

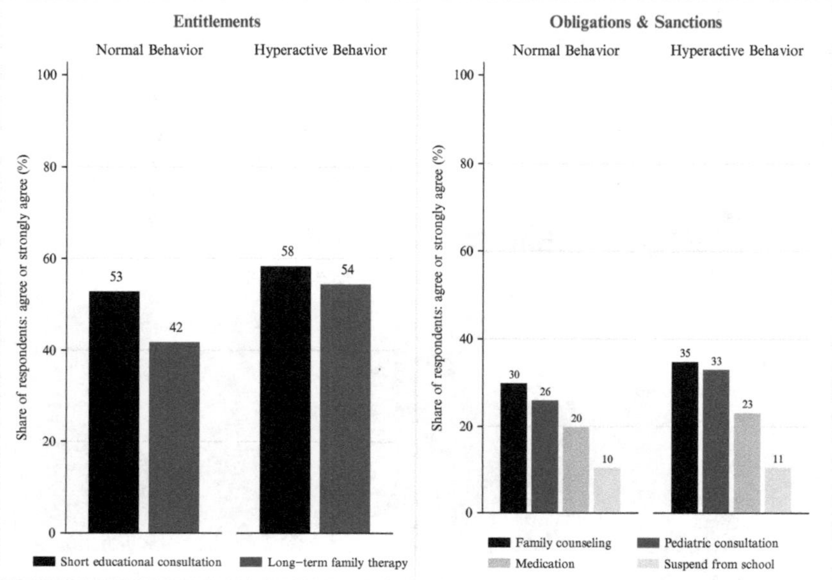

Fig. 6.3 Weighted share of respondents who agreed or strongly agreed with entitlements, obligations, and sanctions. Source: vignette study, Wave 1 (in 2019) ($N = 2289$), own calculations

child with hyperactive behavior. Support for sanctions in the form of removing the child from school until a medical examination has been performed was low, with only one in ten respondents agreeing with this option. Support for sanctions did not differ between the two descriptions.

Our analyses indicate that psychological explanations—such as stress and low self-esteem—are popular and are among the most frequently selected options for explaining childhood behavior. On the other hand, medical explanations are much less popular but are seen as being much more relevant in the case of hyperactive behavior. Medical doctors and psychologists are clearly considered important professions in dealing with childhood problems. However, parenting and educational measures receive even greater support. About half of the respondents support providing parents who are concerned about their child's behavior with access to (even potentially costly) therapeutic options, while only a minority of the respondents support medical or psychological obligations or removing children from school. In sum, medicine and psychology are clearly part of the societal repertoire for dealing with childhood problems. Nevertheless, they are neither the only nor the collectively shared answer to childhood problems. However, the greater support for medical and psychological explanations and interventions in the case of hyperactive behavior indicates that this childhood diagnosis has become part of the public discourse.

6.5 Learning Difficulties and the Medicalization and Psychologization of the German Educational System

Behavioral problems among children—and specifically ADHD—have long been a central topic when it comes to understanding medicalization and psychologization in childhood (Conrad & Schneider, 1992; Malacrida, 2004). Learning difficulties are another interesting issue with a specific link to the educational system (Holmqvist, 2020; Katchergin, 2012). Medical diagnostic categories in the ICD-10 (F81.0, F81.1, and F81.2) and the DSM-5 (Kaufmann & Aster, 2020) as well as clinical practice guidelines have been developed for dyslexia and dyscalculia in many countries, including Germany. Unlike for ADHD, however, no medical or psychological treatments exist for dyslexia and dyscalculia; instead, treatment consists of special educational measures and programs that are designed to foster competencies in writing, reading, and mathematics (Kaufmann & Aster, 2020; Schulte-Körne, 2010). Assessing a student as not having generally low intelligence is important for diagnosing these learning disorders. Therefore, previous studies have investigated learning disorders as examples of "positive stigmas" (Katchergin, 2012) or even as "consecrating medicalization" (Holmqvist, 2020). This labeling means that the diagnosis of a learning disorder often allows children from privileged families to maintain their status despite their low educational performance in specific areas and even gives them appreciation by others that they can succeed despite this impairment (Holmqvist, 2020). Hence, the diagnosis of learning disorders can contribute to the reproduction of social stratification. In a recent study from the US, for instance, Suhr and Johnson (2022) reported that not only has test-seeking for learning disorders increased, but the results of these tests have also led to inequalities:

> There are disparities in who receives accommodations. For children, receipt of diagnosis and high stakes test accommodations has increased more, and is overall much higher, among students attending high performing districts in communities with high socioeconomic status relative to middle class or lower-income school districts. (Suhr & Johnson, 2022, p. 1)

In the following section, we reveal how learning difficulties have resulted in medicalization and psychologization in different dimensions (i.e., actors, institutions, and ideas) in Germany. Moreover, we discuss how the institutional setup in Germany shapes whether, when, and where learning difficulties are medicalized/psychologized. In so doing, we highlight (a) how learning disorders are socially constructed and (b) how diagnostic categories become linked to social rights in the educational system.

In Germany, about 5% of school-aged children are diagnosed with dyslexia (Schulte-Körne, 2017), while the more recently acknowledged dyscalculia is only diagnosed in 1–2% of children (Wyschkon et al., 2009). Learning disorders are accepted diagnoses in the ICD-10 and the DSM-5, and children receive the diagnosis from psychiatrists and psychologists (medicalization/psychologization in the dimension of *actors*). Nevertheless, these diagnostic categories are not acknowledged by the German public healthcare system as a disease (Gemeinsamer Bundesausschuss, 2020; Schulte-Körne, 2010). This regulation means that all forms of therapies for learning disorders are explicitly not covered by health insurance (Gemeinsamer Bundesausschuss, 2020). Only if learning disorders are accompanied by other diagnoses such as depressive symptoms or ADHD can psychological and/or medical treatment be accessed (Schulte-Körne, 2010). This institutionalization of learning disorders reflects the core controversy surrounding this issue in which certain actors argue for medicalizing/psychologizing learning disorders while others resist this process.

In Germany, for instance, the Federal Association of Dyslexia and Dyscalculia (Bundesverband Legasthenie und Dyskalkulie)—an advocacy organization for people with learning disabilities—adopts a biomedical framing. By referring to the ICD-10 and the DSM-5, genetic and neurological predispositions are viewed as the primary causes of dyslexia and dyscalculia (Bundesverband Legasthenie und Dyskalkulie e. V., 2018a, b). In contrast, the German Education Association (VBE) and the German Professional Association of Pediatricians (BVKJ) both argue that social background is mostly a factor for children who have difficulties in reading

(Berufsverband der Kinder- und Jugendärzte, 2010d; Verband Bildung und Erziehung, 2012b). While the German Professional Association of Pediatricians acknowledges possible neurological causes of dyslexia (Berufsverband der Kinder- und Jugendärzte, 2015a) and uses the medical term *learning disorders* (Berufsverband der Kinder- und Jugendärzte, 2011b), the German Education Association exclusively employs exclusively the term *learning weakness*, which does not implicate a biomedical framing (Verband Bildung und Erziehung, 2016a). The biomedical and non-medical framing of learning difficulties in the discourse reflects the general scientific debate on learning difficulties, which has not yet reached a firm consensus as to the origins of these difficulties and has highlighted diagnostic problems (Elliott & Gibbs, 2008; Elliott & Grigorenko, 2014; Suhr & Johnson, 2022).

As mentioned earlier, from a welfare state perspective, it is interesting that a diagnosed learning disorder does not entitle the diagnosed individual to a benefit in the German healthcare system. However, a diagnosis can imply entitlements in the educational system (i.e., medicalization/psychologization in the dimension of *institutions*). In Germany, the entitlements granted for learning disabilities in the educational system vary across the 16 federal states because educational regulations are state-specific. Thus, in essence, 16 different rules and regulations on how to deal with learning disorders exist. In other words, federalism shapes how learning difficulties are acknowledged and dealt with and thereby creates variation in the degree of medicalization and psychologization of learning difficulties within Germany. This variation notwithstanding, there are two main options for schools to respond to students with learning difficulties: compensating for disadvantages ("Nachteilsausgleich") and safeguarding grades ("Notenschutz") (Schulte-Körne, 2017). Compensating for disadvantages is based on the principle of equal treatment. Thus, the compensation aims to establish equal conditions for all students during the test. For example, a student may receive compensation (e.g., more time, access to a dictionary) for a test, but the test would then be graded the same as all other tests. In contrast, safeguarding grades means that the parts of a student's performance that can be affected by a learning disorder are not taken into account in the grading scheme. For example, a student might take the same test as everyone else, but the grading would be adjusted (e.g., orthography may not be graded). Compensating for disadvantages is not allowed to be mentioned in school reports, whereas safeguarding grades usually must be mentioned in reports and school graduation certificates.

However, it is not only the federal states and the educational policies on the state level that shape how learning difficulties are dealt with: Indeed, court decisions also play a role. Court decisions shape how compensation for disadvantages is handled and also play a critical role in safeguarding grades for the federal state of Bavaria, the second-most populous state in Germany. Court decisions have been reached on cases concerning safeguarding grades for students with dyslexia by the Munich Administrative Court, the Bavarian Administrative Court, and the National Administrative Court, the latter of which made changes to the Bavarian Law on Education and Schooling (BayEUG). Based on all of these courts' rulings, the Bavarian state amended its federal education and schooling law by including a new section (Art. 52 Abs. 5 BayEUG) that proclaims that safeguarding grades is permissible under certain circumstances (e.g., approved disorder, request by parents) and that it must be noted in all reports and diplomas. In general, schools decide whether and how compensating for disadvantages and safeguarding grades for a child are carried out (§ 35 Abs.1 BayScho). In order to prove dyslexia, children are required to submit a school psychological statement (§ 35 Abs.2 BayScho). An assessment by a school psychologist is now required when families wish to receive an acknowledgment of their child's dyslexia by the school. In essence, the court ruling stimulated the psychologization of reading and spelling difficulties by tying educational benefits to a psychological expert opinion. However, although court decisions led to this psychologization, this development cannot be evaluated as an intentional process by the involved courts. The courts' decisions only call for clarifying the existing law for safeguarding grades, but exactly how this clarification is done and whether it involves a psychological assessment are decisions that were made by the Bavarian government. Therefore, this example reveals that legal institutions shape medicalization and psychologization processes, though this effect was not intended by the courts. Nevertheless, the Bavarian government probably would also not have changed the existing law and included psychological assessments for cases of dyslexia, but it did so because it had been required to create an explicit law.

Upon investigating other states, we see that regulations for learning difficulties—and thus also the rights of individual students—can differ. In North Rhine-Westphalia (the state with the highest resident population in Germany), for instance, the diagnosis of dyslexia does not have to be proven by a psychological assessment, and an evaluation by a teacher is usually sufficient (Ministerium für Schule und Bildung des Landes Nordrhein-Westfalen, 1991). Nevertheless, compensating for disadvantages and safeguarding grades are both possible (Ministerium für Schule und Bildung des Landes Nordrhein-Westfalen, 1991). However, safeguarding grades is generally not possible for students after grade 10, i.e. for those aspiring to the highest schooling degree (Ministerium für Schule und Bildung des Landes Nordrhein-Westfalen, 1991).

Our analyses of state guidelines and laws also found medicalization and psychologization in the dimension of *ideas*: The guideline from the schooling ministry of North Rhine-Westphalia, for instance, uses the term "particular difficulties in learning to read and write" throughout its text and avoids the terms "disorder" and "weakness," both of which are used in the Bavarian laws. A comprehensive word search of all federal schooling legislations found that many federal states have not yet integrated learning difficulties into their schooling legislations. However, the states might have done so in other directives and regulations. Of the federal states that have adopted passages on learning difficulties in their schooling laws, the adopted terms range from conveying no medicalization to conveying a high degree of medicalization. Some federal states have adopted the phrase "difficulties in reading, writing, and calculating" (Berlin, Brandenburg), whereas others use the term "weakness" (Bavaria, Saxony, Lower Saxony), and still others employ the medical term "disorder" (Bavaria, Hesse, Mecklenburg-Vorpommern).

Overall, the handling of learning difficulties in Germany indicates that political and legal institutions and policy legacies shape the extent to which—and the dimension in which—medicalization and psychologization unfold. The two cases of Bavaria and North Rhine-Westphalia indicate that rules and procedures for handling learning difficulties within Germany can vary substantially. However, for both states, national diagnostic guidelines apply, and their federal institutions provide for different pathways. In North Rhine-Westphalia, institutions support a resistance to medicalizing and psychologizing learning difficulties because these difficulties are mainly assessed by teachers rather than by medical doctors or psychologists. Furthermore, safeguarding grades is usually not employed after grade ten and is thus not performed for children aspiring to the highest schooling degree. On the contrary, Bavarian institutions have psychologized learning disorders by requiring both a psychological assessment and parental requests in order to safeguard grades. These rules might have repercussions on the individual level and might also lead to inequalities in access to safeguarding grades. As parents need to be highly involved in the process of having their children's learning disorders (officially) acknowledged in Bavaria, parents with a higher social status might go through this process with their child more often than parents with a lower social status.

6.6 Conclusion

Medicine and psychology play a prominent role in how advanced, industrialized countries such as Germany address children. This role is visible in the current social investment discourse, which highlights health, character skills, and competences as forms of investment in the future of children and entire societies. These concepts have various disciplinary sources and can be interpreted from a biopsychosocial perspective that reveals how medicine and psychology are part of an interdisciplinary form of investing in children. In addition to this future-oriented and investment-focused adoption of medical and psychological perspectives and the integration of the two professions, medicalization and psychologization are also visible when children have, or, are perceived to have problems. While the discourse acknowledges the socio-economic origin (e.g., child poverty) of many of these problems, thereby showing a clear link to the two social problems discussed in the previous chapters, medical and psychological concepts are used to characterize and diagnose various childhood problems. Moreover, medical and psychological diagnoses and treatment are often the way that these problems are addressed in practice in the absence of alternative solutions, such as redistribution, social security, and adequate resources in the educational system.

The tendency to medicalize and psychologize childhood problems has been resisted by professional organizations and to some extent also by public opinion. However, high and rising rates of diagnosing mental illnesses in childhood suggest that in practice, there is still a tendency to medicalize and psychologize these problems. For instance, an analysis of the most comprehensive data sources that relied on ambulatory physician billing claims found that the proportion of children and adolescents with a diagnosed mental disorder within the preceding year had increased from 23% in 2009 to 28% in 2017 (Steffen et al., 2018). Nevertheless, there is a lack of comparable longitudinal data that would be necessary to investigate trends over a longer time period (i.e., over several decades).

In the second year of the COVID-19 pandemic, the implications of the situation for children became quite an important issue in the German discourse. While this discourse has been interdisciplinary, the recurring reference to epidemiological studies that "provide evidence" of the problematic situation that children face is one indication as to how medical and psychological accounts have been influential in this debate. Thus, childhood problems in the discourse have been quite often understood through the lens of medical and psychological concepts and interventions:

> Two-thirds of the children and adolescents reported being highly burdened by the COVID-19 pandemic. They experienced significantly lower HRQoL (40.2% vs. 15.3%), more mental health problems (17.8% vs. 9.9%) and higher anxiety levels (24.1% vs. 14.9%) than before the pandemic. Children with low socioeconomic status, migration background and limited living space were affected significantly more. Health promotion and prevention strategies need to be implemented to maintain children's and adolescents' mental health, improve their HRQoL, and mitigate the burden caused by COVID-19, particularly for children who are most at risk. (Ravens-Sieberer et al., 2021, p. 879)

The long-term impact of the pandemic on discourses and policies on childhood remains to be empirically determined, but there are good reasons to believe that medicalization and psychologization have and will represent an important strategy in terms of how societies discuss and manage the long-term effects of the pandemic on children.

References

Adamson, E., & Brennan, D. (2014). Social Investment or private profit? Diverging notions of 'investment' in early childhood education and care. *International Journal of Early Childhood, 46*(1), 47–61. https://doi.org/10.1007/s13158-013-0098-x

Alexander, P. A. (2018). Past as prologue: Educational psychology's legacy and progeny. *Journal of Educational Psychology, 110*(2), 147–162. https://doi.org/10.1037/edu0000200

Ariaans, M., & Reibling, N. (2021). Die Rolle von Gesundheit und Krankheit im deutschen Armutsdiskurs. *Zeitschrift Für Sozialreform, 67*(2), 123–152. https://doi.org/10.1515/zsr-2021-0005

Berufsverband der Kinder- und Jugendärzte. (2009a, February 2). *Kinder leben in sozialer Armut in Deutschland: "Wir brauchen neue Konzepte früher Hilfen"* [Press release]. Köln.

Berufsverband der Kinder- und Jugendärzte. (2009b, February 25). *Kinder leben in sozialer Armut in Deutschland: "Wir brauchen neue Konzepte früher Hilfen"* [Press release]. Köln.

Berufsverband der Kinder- und Jugendärzte. (2010a, February 8). *Kinder- und Jugendärzte begrüßen Hartz-IV-Revision: Weg frei für sinnvolle Reformen zu Gunsten sozial benachteiligter Kinder – Bildungschancen wichtiger als alles Materielle - Sachleistungen sinnvoller als Geldleistungen* [Press release]. Köln.

Berufsverband der Kinder- und Jugendärzte. (2010b, June 13). *Kinder – und Jugendärzte fordern: "Arme Kinder dürfen nicht weiter benachteiligt werden"* [Press release]. Köln.

Berufsverband der Kinder- und Jugendärzte. (2010c, August 5). *Kinder- und Jugendärzte: "Bildungsgutscheine für Kinder sind eine sinnvolle Maßnahme und ein richtiges Signal – für alle Kinder! Kinder- und Jugendärzte sind bereit, sich an Bildungsprojekten für Kinder zu beteiligen."* [Press release]. Köln.

Berufsverband der Kinder- und Jugendärzte. (2010d, December 6). *Kinder- und Jugendärzte zur PISA-Studie: "Endlich ernst machen mit Aktion Lesestart!"* [Press release]. Köln.

Berufsverband der Kinder- und Jugendärzte. (2011a, August 24). *"Kein Kind vergessen"* [Press release]. Köln.

Berufsverband der Kinder- und Jugendärzte. (2011b, November 8). *Kein Platz für Kinder – Familienpolitik verfehlt ihr Ziel* [Press release]. Berlin.

Berufsverband der Kinder- und Jugendärzte. (2011c, December 22). *Sprechen lernen nur möglich mit emotionaler Bindung! Wie Eltern die Sprachentwicklung ihrer Kinder fördern und überflüssige Therapien vermeiden können* [Press release]. Düsseldorf.

Berufsverband der Kinder- und Jugendärzte. (2012a, January 3). *Wenn Arbeitslosigkeit und sozialer Status der Eltern das Wachstum von Kindern hemmen, müssen wir mit unseren Präventionsanstrengungen noch früher beginnen…* [Press release]. Köln.

Berufsverband der Kinder- und Jugendärzte. (2012b, January 31). *BVKJ: Sprachentwicklungsstörungen sind nicht nur ein Problem der Krankenkassen* [Press release]. Köln.

Berufsverband der Kinder- und Jugendärzte. (2012c, March 11). *Pressemitteilung BVKJ, AG ADHS AG NP: ADHS ist keine Modeerscheinung, keine Fiktion, sondern ein medizinisch definiertes Störungsbild* [Press release]. Köln.

Berufsverband der Kinder- und Jugendärzte. (2013a, May 14). *Vom Verstehen zum Verständnis – Kinder und Jugendliche mit Migrationshintergrund können sich gut auf unterschiedlichen Kulturhintergründen bewegen. Aber Sprachverstehen ist Voraussetzung: Pressemeldung des Berufsverbandes der Kinder- und*

Jugendärzte (BVKJ): Vom Verstehen zum Verständnis – Kinder und Jugendliche mit Migrationshintergrund können sich gut auf unterschiedlichen Kulturhintergründen bewegen. Aber Spracheverstehen ist Voraussetzung [Press release]. Berlin.

Berufsverband der Kinder- und Jugendärzte. (2013b, July 30). *Pressemeldung des Berufsverbandes der Kinder- und Jugendärzte (BVKJ e. V.)* [Press release]. Köln.

Berufsverband der Kinder- und Jugendärzte. (2014, September 23). *Kinder- und Jugendärzte: Bundesregierung vernachlässigt Kindeswohl* [Press release]. Köln.

Berufsverband der Kinder- und Jugendärzte. (2015a, March 10). *Lese-Rechtschreibstörungen im Kindes- und Jugendalter* [Press release]. Köln.

Berufsverband der Kinder- und Jugendärzte. (2015b, April 30). *"Kinderbetreuungseinrichtungen kommt eine ähnliche Bedeutung bei der Bildung zu wie den Schulen!": Berufsverband der Kinder- und Jugendärzte fordert den Ausbau und die Qualifizierung von Kinderbetreuungseinrichtungen* [Press release]. Köln.

Berufsverband der Kinder- und Jugendärzte. (2015c, May 7). *Kinder- und Jugendärzte sprechen sich für einheitliche strukturierte Förderangebote für Kinder aus schwierigen Lebensverhältnissen aus* [Press release]. Berlin.

Berufsverband der Kinder- und Jugendärzte. (2015d, August 11). *Kinder- und Jugendärzte geben Tipps für guten Schulstart* [Press release]. Köln.

Berufsverband der Kinder- und Jugendärzte. (2016, February 25). *Kinder- und Jugendärzte fordern: Kinderarmut in NRW energischer bekämpfen!* [Press release]. Köln.

Berufsverband der Kinder- und Jugendärzte. (2017a, March 20). *VBE und BVKJ: Medikamentenabgabe ist keine Aufgabe von Lehrkräften Rechtssicherheit herstellen – Schulgesundheitsfachkräfte einstellen!* [Press release].

Berufsverband der Kinder- und Jugendärzte. (2017b, September 14). *Weltkindertag am 20. September: Gesundheit beginnt mit der Politik - Impfschutz, Früherkennung und Schutz vor Gewalt und Missbrauch in Deutschland nicht ausreichend* [Press release]. Köln.

Berufsverband der Kinder- und Jugendärzte. (2018, July 20). *Kinder- und Jugendärzte zur Diskussion um Notaufnahmen: "Viele Fälle gehören nicht in die Notaufnahmen. Wir brauchen endlich umfassende Gesundheitsbildung ab der Kita."* [Press release].

Berufsverband der Kinder- und Jugendärzte. (2019, July 11). *Kinder- und Jugendärzte: Neues NRW-Kita-Gesetz reicht nicht aus, um Chancengleichheit zu garantieren* [Press release]. Köln.

Betz, T. (2016). Frühe Kindheit im Risikodiskurs: Charakteristika, Problemstellungen und Funktionen. In R. Anhorn & M. Balzereit (Eds.), *Perspektiven kritischer Sozialer Arbeit: Band 23. Handbuch Therapeutisierung und Soziale Arbeit* (pp. 429–450). Springer VS.

Betz, T., Honig, M.-S., & Ostner, I. (Eds.). (2017). *Parents in the spotlight: Parenting practices and support from a comparative perspective*. Barbara Budrich Publishers: Sonderheft der Zeitschrift für Familienforschung 11(2016). https://ebookcentral.proquest.com/lib/kxp/detail.action?docID=4916649

Brase, J., Krayter, S., & Reibling, N. (2022). Scientific discourses on three social problems: what is the role of medicine and psychology? *Working Paper*.

Brault, M.-C., Degroote, E., & van Houtte, M. (2022). Disparities in the prevalence of ADHD diagnoses, suspicion, and medication use between Flanders and Québec from the lens of the medicalization process. *Health (London, England: 1997)*, 136345932210934. https://doi.org/10.1177/13634593221093492

Bundesinstitut für Arzneimittel und Medizinprodukte. (2015). *Infografik: Erwerb von Methylphenidat durch Apotheken in Form von Fertigarzneimitteln 1993–2014*. Bonn. https://www.bfarm.de/SharedDocs/Pressemitteilungen/DE/2015/pm7-2015.html

Bundesregierung. (2018). *Entwurf eines Gesetzes zur Weiterentwicklung der Qualität und zur Teilhabe in der Kindertagesbetreuung* (Drucksache 469/18). https://www.bundesrat.de/SharedDocs/drucksachen/2018/0401-0500/469-18.pdf?__blob=publicationFile&v=1

Bundesregierung. (2022). *Entwurf eines Zweiten Gesetzes zur Weiterentwicklung der Qualität und zur Teilhabe in der Kindertagesbetreuung: KiTa Qualitätsgesetz* (Drucksache 408/22). https://dserver.bundestag.de/brd/2022/0408-22.pdf

Bundesverband Legasthenie und Dyskalkulie e. V. (2018a). *Dyskalkulie: Ratgeber zum Thema Dyskalkulie – Erkennen und Verstehen*.

Bundesverband Legasthenie und Dyskalkulie e. V. (2018b). *Legasthenie: Ratgeber zum Thema Legasthenie – Erkennen und Verstehen*.

Cantillon, B., & van Lancker, W. (2013). Three shortcomings of the social investment perspective. *Social Policy and Society, 12*(4), 553–564. https://doi.org/10.1017/S1474746413000080

Clarke, J. N. (2015). Advice to mothers about managing children's behaviours in Canada's premier woman's magazine: A comparison of 1945–1956 with 1990–2010. *Child & Family Social Work, 20*(3), 310–321. https://doi.org/10.1111/cfs.12079

Conrad, P., & Schneider, J. W. (1992). *Deviance and medicalization: From badness to sickness*. Temple University Press.

Deffte, V., Kohlscheen, J., Köhler, S., & Hartlieb, J. (2018). *Entwicklungsgruppe Einbindung des Gesundheitswesens in die kommunalen Präventionsketten*. https://www.kinderstark.nrw/fileadmin/user_upload/Fachmagazin/Gesundheitswesen_WEB.pdf

Ecclestone, K., & Brunila, K. (2015). Governing emotionally vulnerable subjects and 'therapisation' of social justice. *Pedagogy, Culture & Society, 23*(4), 485–506. https://doi.org/10.1080/14681366.2015.1015152

Elliott, J. G., & Gibbs, S. (2008). Does dyslexia exist? *Journal of Philosophy of Education, 42*(3–4), 475–491.

Elliott, J. G., & Grigorenko, E. L. (2014). *The dyslexia debate*. Cambridge University Press.

Esping-Andersen, G. (2002). A child centred social investment strategy. In G. Esping-Andersen, D. Gallie, A. Hemerijck, & J. Myles (Eds.), *Why we need a new welfare state* (pp. 26–67). Oxford University Press.

Esping-Andersen, G. (2005). Children in the welfare state: A social investment approach. *Universitat Pompeu Fabra DemoSoc Working Paper*. https://repositori.upf.edu/bitstream/handle/10230/275/Esping-Andersen_Children.pdf?sequence=3

European Commission. (2013). Investing in children: Breaking the cycle of disadvantage: (2013/112/EU) (No. 5). *Official Journal of the European Union, 59*.

Gemeinsamer Bundesausschuss. (2020). *Richtlinie des Gemeinsamen Bundesausschusses: Richtlinien über die Verordnung von Heilmitteln in der vetragsärztlichen Versorgung (Heilmittel-Richtlinie/HeilM-RL)*.

Gesetz zum qualitätsorientierten und bedarfsgerechten Ausbau der Tagesbetreuung für Kinder, 76 Bundesgesetzblatt 3852 (2004). https://www.bgbl.de/xaver/bgbl/start.xav?startbk=Bundesanzeiger_BGBl&bk=Bundesanzeiger_BGBl&start=//*[@attr_id=%27bgbl104s3852.pdf%27]#__bgbl__%2F%2F*%5B%40attr_id%3D%27bgbl104s3852.pdf%27%5D__1665106778529

Gesetz zur Förderung von Kindern unter drei Jahren in Tageseinrichtungen und in Kindertagespflege, 57 Bundesgesetzblatt 2403–209 (2008). https://www.bgbl.de/xaver/bgbl/start.xav?startbk=Bundesanzeiger_BGBl#__bgbl__%2F%2F*%5B%40attr_id%3D%27bgbl108s2403.pdf%27%5D__1665107157625

Gesetz zur Weiterentwicklung der Qualität und zur Teilhabe in der Kindertagesbetreuung, 49 Bundesgesetzblatt 2696 (2018). https://www.bgbl.de/xaver/bgbl/start.xav?startbk=Bundesanzeiger_BGBl&start=//*[@attr_id=%27bgbl117s1228.pdf%27]#__bgbl__%2F%2F*%5B%40attr_id%3D%27bgbl118s2696.pdf%27%5D__1665107035388

Gillies, V. (2005). Raising the 'meritocracy'. *Sociology, 39*(5), 835–853. https://doi.org/10.1177/0038038505058368

Grimmsmann, T., & Himmel, W. (2021). The 10-year trend in drug prescriptions for attention-deficit/hyperactivity disorder (ADHD) in Germany. *European Journal of Clinical Pharmacology, 77*(1), 107–115. https://doi.org/10.1007/s00228-020-02948-3

Grobe, T. G. (2017). Regionale Unterschiede von ADHS-Diagnoseraten in Krankenkassendaten 2005 bis 2015: Methodische Überlegungen und Ergebnisse [Regional differences of ADHD diagnosis rates in health insurance data from 2005 to 2015: Methodological considerations and results].

Bundesgesundheitsblatt, Gesundheitsforschung, Gesundheitsschutz, 60(12), 1336–1345. https://doi.org/10.1007/s00103-017-2640-8

Halpern, S. A. (1990). Medicalization as professional process: Postwar trends in pediatrics. *Journal of Health and Social Behavior, 31*(1), 28–42.

Heckman, J. J. (2006). Skill formation and the economics of investing in disadvantaged children. *Science*, 312(5782), 1900–1902. https://doi.org/10.1126/science.1128898

Heckman, J. J., & Kautz, T. (2013). *Fostering and measuring skills: Interventions that improve character and cognition*. National Bureau of Economic Research.

Holmqvist, M. (2020). Medical diagnosis of dyslexia in a Swedish elite school: A case of "consecrating medicalization". *The British Journal of Sociology, 71*(2), 366–381.

Hußmann, A., Stubbe, T. C., & Kasper, D. (2017). Soziale Herkunft und Lesekompetenzen von Schülerinnen und Schülern. In A. Hussmann, H. Wendt, W. Bos, A. Bremerich-Vos, D. Kasper, E.-M. Lankes, N. McElvany, T. C. Stubbe, & R. Valtin (Eds.), *Waxmann-E-Books Empirische Erziehungswissenschaft. IGLU 2016: Lesekompetenzen von Grundschulkindern in Deutschland im internationalen Vergleich* (pp. 195–218). Waxmann Verlag.

Karsch, F. (2018). The medicalization of Fidgety Philip: Adhd in Germany. In M. R. Bergey, A. M. Filipe, P. Conrad, & I. Singh (Eds.), *Global perspectives on ADHD: Social dimensions of diagnosis and treatment in 16 countries* (pp. 97–117). Johns Hopkins University Press.

Katchergin, O. (2012). Between negative stigma (cultural deprivation) and positive stigma (learning disability): The historical development of two special education tracks. *Culture, Medicine and Psychiatry, 36*(4), 679–711. https://doi.org/10.1007/s11013-012-9281-z

Kaufmann, L., & von Aster, M. (2020). Umschreibende Entwicklungsstörungen schulischer Fertigkeiten. In M. Kölch, M. Rassenhofer, & J. M. Fegert (Eds.), *Klinikmanual Kinder- und Jugendpsychiatrie und -psychotherapie* (3rd ed., pp. 435–454). Springer.

Kjørholt, A. T. (2013). Childhood as social investment, rights and the valuing of education. *Children & Society, 27*(4), 245–257. https://doi.org/10.1111/chso.12037

Klasen, H. (2000). A name, what's in a name? The medicalization of hyperactivity, revisited. *Harvard Review of Psychiatry, 7*(6), 334–344. https://doi.org/10.1093/hrp/7.6.334

Lavin, M. F. (2016). They call us problem child: Delinquency, medicalization, and social class in primary education. *Deviant Behavior, 37*(11), 1276–1287. https://doi.org/10.1080/01639625.2016.1174517

Liebsch, K. (2020). Medikalisierung als Spannungsfeld von sozialer Kontrolle und Problembearbeitung: das Beispiel 'Medikalisierung des Kindesalters'. In A. Riedel & S. Lehmeyer (Eds.), *Springer Nature Living Reference Medicine.*

Ethik im Gesundheitswesen (pp. 1–17). Springer. https://doi.org/10.1007/978-3-662-58685-3_81-1

Lister, R. (2006). Children (but not women) first: New Labour, child welfare and gender. *Critical Social Policy, 26*(2), 315–335. https://doi.org/10.1177/0261018306062588

Macvarish, J., Lee, E., & Lowe, P. (2015). Neuroscience and family policy: What becomes of the parent? *Critical Social Policy, 35*(2), 248–269. https://doi.org/10.1177/0261018315574019

Malacrida, C. (2004). Medicalization, ambivalence and social control: Mothers' descriptions of educators and ADD/ADHD. *Health (London, England: 1997), 8*(1), 61–80. https://doi.org/10.1177/1363459304038795

Ministerium für Schule und Bildung des Landes Nordrhein-Westfalen. (1991). *14–01 Nr. 1 Förderung von Schülerinnen und Schülern bei besonderen Schwierigkeiten im Erlernen des Lesens und Rechtschreibens (LRS)*. https://bass.schul-welt.de/280.htm#pgfId-1802839

Nolan, J. L. (1998). *The therapeutic state: Justifying government at century's end.* New York University Press.

Nygård, M., & Krüger, N. (2012). Poverty, families and the investment state. *European Societies, 14*(5), 755–777. https://doi.org/10.1080/14616696.2012.726368

NZFH Beirat. (2016). *Leitbild Frühe Hilfen.* Köln. https://www.fruehehilfen.de/fileadmin/user_upload/fruehehilfen.de/pdf/Publikation_NZFH_Kompakt_Beirat_Leitbild_fuer_Fruehe_Hilfen.pdf

Odenbring, Y., Johansson, T., & Hunehäll Berndtsson, K. (2017). The many faces of attention deficit hyperactivity disorder: Unruly behaviour in secondary school and diagnostic solutions. *Power and Education, 9*(1), 51–64. https://doi.org/10.1177/1757743817693026

Olk, T., & Hübenthal, M. (2009). Child poverty in the German social investment state. *Zeitschrift Für Familienforschung, 21*(2), 150–167. https://www.ssoar.info/ssoar/bitstream/document/33526/1/ssoar-zff-2009-2-olk_et_al-Child_poverty_in_the_German.pdf

Pawluch, D. (1983). Transitions in pediatrics: A segmental analysis. *Social Problems, 30*(4), 449–465.

Rafalovich, A. (2001). The conceptual history of attention deficit hyperactivity disorder: Idiocy, imbecility, encephalitis and the child deviant, 1877–1929. *Deviant Behavior, 22*(2), 93–115. https://doi.org/10.1080/016396201750065009

Rafalovich, A. (2005a). Exploring clinician uncertainty in the diagnosis and treatment of attention deficit hyperactivity disorder. *Sociology of Health & Illness, 27*(3), 305–323. https://doi.org/10.1111/j.1467-9566.2005.00444.x

Rafalovich, A. (2005b). Relational troubles and semiofficial suspicion: Educators and the medicalization of "unruly" children. *Symbolic Interaction, 28*(1), 25–46. https://doi.org/10.1525/si.2005.28.1.25

Ramey, D. M. (2020). Punitive versus medicalized responses to childhood behavior problems and high school graduation. *Sociological Perspectives, 63*(2), 201–227. https://doi.org/10.1177/0731121419849094

Ravens-Sieberer, U., Kaman, A., Erhart, M., Devine, J., Schlack, R., & Otto, C. (2021). Impact of the COVID-19 pandemic on quality of life and mental health in children and adolescents in Germany. *European Child & Adolescent Psychiatry*.

Rousseau, J.-J. (1911). *Émile, Or Education*. J.M Dent & Sons (Original work published in 1762).

Schiettecat, T., Roets, G., & Vandenbroeck, M. (2015). Do families in poverty need child and family social work? *European Journal of Social Work, 18*(5), 647–660. https://doi.org/10.1080/13691457.2014.953916

Schmitz-Kießler, J. (2022). *Mehr Ausgaben, weniger Einnahmen: Armut von Kindern, Alleinerziehenden und kinderreichen Familien steigt weiter.* Institut Arbeit und Qualifikation der Universität Duisburg-Essen. https://www.sozialpolitik-aktuell.de/files/sozialpolitik-aktuell/_Politikfelder/Einkommen-Armut/Datensammlung/PDF-Dateien/abbVII106_Thema_Monat_07_2022.pdf

Schulte-Körne, G. (2010). Diagnostik und Therapie der Lese-Rechtschreib-Störung. *Deutsches Ärzteblatt International, 107*(41), 718–727.

Schulte-Körne, G. (2017). Lese- und/oder Rechtschreibstörung: Symptomatik, Diagnostik und Behandlung. *Monatsschrift Kinderheilkunde, 165*, 476–481.

Steffen, A., Manas K. Akmatov, Holstiege, J., & Bätzing, J. (2018). *Diagnoseprävalenz psychischer Störungen bei Kindern und Jugendlichen in Deutschland: eine Analyse bundesweiter vertragsärztlicher Abrechnungsdaten der Jahre 2009 bis 2017.* https://doi.org/10.20364/VA-18.07

Suhr, J. A., & Johnson, E. E. H. (2022). First do no harm: Ethical issues in pathologizing normal variations in behavior and functioning. *Psychological Injury and Law.* Advance online publication. https://doi.org/10.1007/s12207-022-09455-z

van Oorschot, W., Roosma, F., Meuleman, B., & Reeskens, T. (2017). *The social legitimacy of targeted welfare: Attitudes to welfare deservingness. Globalization and welfare series.* Edward Elgar Publishing. https://doi.org/10.4337/9781785367212

Verband Bildung und Erziehung. (2009a, April 16). *Frühkindliche Bildung aufwerten: VBE: Voraussetzungen schaffen, um für die Jüngsten die Besten zu gewinnen* [Press release].

Verband Bildung und Erziehung. (2009b, August 27). *VBE für längeres gemeinsames Lernen* [Press release].

Verband Bildung und Erziehung. (2010, June 16). *Unsinnig unterm Deckmantel des Förderns: VBE zum Sonderprogramm für Hauptschüler* [Press release].

Verband Bildung und Erziehung. (2012a, February 24). *Nicht zu früh zu Ritalin greifen: Doping in der Schule* [Press release].
Verband Bildung und Erziehung. (2012b, September 7). *Lesekompetenz so früh wie möglich fördern* [Press release].
Verband Bildung und Erziehung. (2015, March 27). *VBE: Nur vermessen macht Schule nicht besser: 5. Internationaler Kongress zum Lehrerberuf (ISTP) in Banff* [Press release].
Verband Bildung und Erziehung. (2016a, February 10). *Bildungsgerechtigkeit bedeutet individuelle Förderung sichern: PISA-Studie 2015* [Press release].
Verband Bildung und Erziehung. (2016b, April 5). *"Gewalt darf keine Schule machen"* [Press release].
Verband Bildung und Erziehung. (2016c, September 20). *Kindeswohl ist nicht vermessbar! Weltkindertag von UNICEF und Deutschem Kinderhilfswerk* [Press release].
Verband Bildung und Erziehung. (2016d, November 25). *Individuelle Förderung sichert den Bildungserfolg aller Kinder* [Press release].
Verband Bildung und Erziehung. (2017a, March 20). *VBE und BVKJ: Medikamentenabgabe ist keine Aufgabe von Lehrkräften: Rechtssicherheit herstellen - Schulgesundheitsfachkräfte einstellen!* [Press release].
Verband Bildung und Erziehung. (2017b, April 24). *Jeder zweite ESE-Schüler benötigt intensivpädagogische Förderung: Expertise: "Welchen Förderbedarf haben Kinder mit emotional-sozialen Entwicklungsstörungen?"* [Press release].
Verband Bildung und Erziehung. (2018a, February 15). *Bessere Bildungschancen durch bessere Gesundheitsversorgung* [Press release].
Verband Bildung und Erziehung. (2018b, March 15). *Wer Prävention will, muss Schulgesundheitsfachkräfte einstellen!* [Press release].
Wissenschaftlicher Beitrat für Familienfragen beim BMFSFJ. (2005). *Stärkung familialer Beziehungs- und Erziehungskompetenzen*. Berlin. https://www.bmfsfj.de/resource/blob/95354/076596362455af26733a2bedf0a32d6e/staerkung-familialer-beziehungs-und-erziehungskompetenzen-data.pdf
Wyschkon, A., Kohn, J., Ballaschk, K., & Esser, G. (2009). Sind Rechenstörungen genau so häufig wie Lese-Rechtschreibstörungen? *Zeitschrift für Kinder- und Jugendpsychiatrie und Psychotherapie, 37*(6), 499–512.

CHAPTER 7

Neoliberalism and Social Investment: Paving the Way for Medicalization and Psychologization

Mareike Ariaans and Nadine Reibling

In the three previous chapters, we illustrated examples of medicalization and psychologization in the context of unemployment, poverty, and childhood (problems). While each social problem has its unique characteristics that shape the specific form and consequences of medicalization and psychologization dynamics, these changes nevertheless need to be evaluated in the light of a common political and societal context. Over the last three decades, neoliberalism and social investment thinking have shaped public discourses and guided the substantial restructuring of the German welfare state (Olk, 2007; Sowa & Zapfel, 2015). Although neoliberalism and social investment are not commonly associated with medicine and psychology in the welfare state literature, both medicalization and

M. Ariaans (✉)
University of Siegen, Siegen, Germany
e-mail: ariaans@soziologie.uni-siegen.de

N. Reibling
Fulda University of Applied Sciences, Fulda, Germany
e-mail: nadine.reibling@gw.hs-fulda.de

N. Reibling, M. Ariaans (eds.), *Toward a Biopsychosocial Welfare State?*, https://doi.org/10.1007/978-3-031-32793-3_7

psychologization have been part of this contemporary welfare state transformation.

Neoliberalism and social investment are the two policy paradigms that have shaped the reform agendas of many European welfare states over the past three decades (Hemerijck, 2018). Generally, the neoliberal agenda preceded the implementation of social investment policies; however, the scope and timeline of both policy paradigms differ from country to country (Hemerijck, 2018) Although the welfare state literature has analyzed the two paradigms, their implementation and consequences in various countries (Abrahamson, 2010; Morel et al., 2012b), the link to medicalization and psychologization processes has received little attention in this work. Instead, the medicalization and psychologization literature has considered the role of neoliberalism quite extensively (Adams et al., 2019; Barbee et al., 2018; Esposito & Perez, 2014; Foster, 2016; LaMarre et al., 2019; Madsen, 2018; Sugarman, 2015), but rarely with a focus on social policies or on the welfare state (Hansen et al., 2014; for exceptions see: Holmqvist et al., 2013; Mills, 2015; Peeters, 2019; Wong, 2016). In the present chapter, we follow the assumption that neoliberalism and social investment constitute the discursive context in which actors have operated and in which institutional changes within the welfare state have been designed and legitimized. We reveal that due to the resonance of both paradigms with the medical and psychological construction of social problems, the co-evolution of medicalization and psychologization in welfare states during the rise of these paradigms has been overlooked.

The present chapter first describes how neoliberalism can be defined and how the neoliberal agenda entered welfare state policies in many European welfare states. Adopting a focus on Germany, we discuss neoliberal welfare state reforms and the manner in which they have contributed to medicalization and psychologization processes. In so doing, we focus primarily on examples from the previous chapters and interpret them in the light of the neoliberal agenda. Second, we describe the process of implementing social investment policies and explain this process's similarities to and differences with the neoliberal paradigm. Focusing on Germany, we then exemplify how the social investment paradigm has contributed in different ways to the rising importance of medicine and psychology in social policy. In the third and final section, we discuss the role of the political context for medicalization and psychologization processes during the past 30 years. We conclude that both paradigms set the stage for medicalization and psychologization processes both as promising solutions intentionally selected by certain actors to achieve political goals and as unintended effects of policy reforms, changing discourses and institutions.

7.1 Neoliberalism and the Individual Responsibility for Health

Neoliberalism can be described as a policy paradigm that relies on the market to organize and structure virtually all aspects of society. In a stricter definition, "neoliberalism signifies an ensemble of ideological and institutional forces whose primary purpose is to create a social reality where all facets of human life are reduced to economic concerns" (Esposito & Perez, 2014, p. 432). Consequently, the influence of neoliberalism has gone beyond the economy and the welfare state and now stretches to issues such as marriage (Marzullo, 2011), imprisonment (Wacquant, 2010), and sleep (Barbee et al., 2018). Generally, the Reagan and Thatcher administrations of the 1980s are considered as the starting point of neoliberal transformations of the welfare state. Neoliberal ideas have been implemented in policy agendas with the aim of limiting state intervention in the economy and in the life of individuals. Neoliberal reforms include policy measures such as cutting taxes, reducing government spending (particularly for benefits and social services), and deregulating political institutions (Harvey, 2010).

In the field of social policy, neoliberalism entails three components: the individualization of risks, the privatization of social services, and the decentralization of regulation (McGregor, 2001). Furthermore, social policy measures—such as limiting and targeting passive social benefits, deregulating social welfare markets by incentivizing the privatization of social services, and limiting the power of trade unions—have transformed many welfare states over the last three decades (Putzel, 2020). These policy measures were designed with the individual as the main target of intervention in mind and with the aim of shifting the responsibility for life course risks from society to the individual (Peeters, 2019). In particular, the market integration—and thus, also the employment and employability—of each individual marks the central policy aim of neoliberal welfare state policy (Morel et al., 2012a):

> I think we have gone through a period when too many children and people have given to understand 'I have a problem, it is the Government's job to cope with it!' or 'I have a problem, I will go and get a grant to cope with it!'

> [or] 'I am homeless, the Government must house me!' and so they are casting their problems on society, and who is society? There is no such thing! There are individual men and women, and there are families, and no government can do anything except through people, and people look to themselves first. (Thatcher, 1987)

The neoliberal agenda has been pushed and supported by international institutions and organizations such as the OECD, the Word Bank, and the EU (Fougère et al., 2017; Hermann, 2007). In fact, the EU has been an influential actor in spreading the neoliberal agenda on an ideational level but has also actively pursued the paradigm through its fiscal and monetary policies (Hermann, 2007). For example, the Maastricht Treaty and the strict budgetary requirements that were included within it were designed to keep EU member states' welfare state spending under control (Hemerijck, 2018). Furthermore, in 1993, the EU launched a white paper entitled "Growth, Competitiveness and Employment," which included many neoliberal policy ideas on employment, such as promoting the flexibility of workers by reducing social benefits in case of unemployment, reducing employment protection rights, and investing more in active—and less in passive—labor market benefits (European Commission, 1993).

Another welfare state area in which neoliberal ideas have been disseminated by international organizations is education policy. In this area, employability has also been the main target of policy-making. One major actor in pushing neoliberal ideas into education policy has been the OECD. Via the Programme for International Student Assessment (PISA), which provides an international assessment of education systems, 15-year-old school children in a growing number of countries have been tested on their reading, mathematics, and scientific literacy since 2000. Both the fact that children's competencies are tested and the selection of tested skills have been evaluated as a form of dissemination of neoliberal educational ideas (Bouhali, 2015; Martens, 2007). International educational testing leads to the dissemination of a specific educational agenda of skills that are most important in the (global) labor market, thereby leaving little room for national or local characteristics (Bouhali, 2015; Rutkowski, 2007). These scientific evaluations can also be found in the reasoning of the OECD for its first PISA study, which states that "[t]he assessments [are] designed to contribute to an understanding of the extent to which education systems [...] are preparing their students to become lifelong learners and to play constructive roles as citizens in society" (OECD, 1999, p. 8).

Furthermore, the OECD clarifies that the emphasis on the competencies that PISA tests lies in the "mastery of broad concepts, [which] is particularly significant considering the concern among nations to develop human capital," which the OECD defines as "[t]he knowledge, skills, competencies and other attributes embodied in individuals that are relevant to personal, social and economic well-being" (OECD, 1999, p. 11).

7.1.1 *The Role of Health and Psychology in the Neoliberal Agenda*

Individual responsibility, market integration, and employability are thus key aspects of neoliberal social policy. The question now involves how health and psychology come into this picture and which role they play. In general, being and remaining in good health is a precondition for being able to find employment, remaining employed, and increasing the time spent in employment. Nevertheless, references to healthcare, rehabilitation, or prevention are rarely found in the overall neoliberal agenda. For example, the EU white paper "Growth, Competitiveness and Employment" (European Commission, 1993) uses the term "health care" only five times. Thus, at first glance, medicine and psychology do not appear to be a central part of the neoliberal agenda as viewed from the social policy perspective. However, the fact that neoliberalism and its three central dimensions—namely individualization, privatization, and decentralization—have reorganized our understanding of health and illness is obvious when we examine policy documents from international organizations that focus specifically on healthcare, rehabilitation, and prevention. These documents take up neoliberal ideas, for instance, by demonstrating how healthcare contributes to growth, productivity, and employment. For example, the World Health Organization (WHO) has experienced decreasing significance and a worsening reputation since the 1980s, when the World Bank began to promote the view that health and healthcare should contribute to economic growth (Chorev, 2013). Hence, the WHO has been forced to react to the World Bank's view—which called into question whether health is an aim in itself—by adopting neoliberal policy frames and connecting to these communication frames:

> an effective way to earn the support of finance ministers was not to talk about health, but to talk about finance. Hence, the WHO abandoned its long-held position that health was an aspect of social development that

> should be pursued independently of economic concerns and, accepting the neoliberal reduction of social development to economic development, adopted instead the premise that health was good for economic growth. (Chorev, 2013, p. 643)

One of the key ideas and consequences of neoliberalism is that the individual is responsible for their own life course and the risks associated with their own life course decisions. Thus, if life course risks hit and interventions are necessary, then these interventions are more commonly focused on the individual. This idea resonates with medicine and psychology, which as disciplines (with the exception of specific subfields) take the individual (organism) as their focal point: "biomedicine and neoliberalism have made natural bedfellows, sharing as they do an emphasis on individuals as being autonomous and rational consumers ultimately responsible for their own risk behaviours and their own wellbeing" (Rushton & Williams, 2012, p. 154).

Instead of being targeted at the societal level, both health and the responsibility for being healthy have been transferred to the individual (Esposito & Perez, 2014). As Barbee et al. (2018, 5) put it, "[I]n a neoliberal society where people are expected to maximize and protect their own welfare [...], 'good' health is also an individual, moral project [...] designed to maximize workplace productivity." On the institutional level, this development has been underlined, for example, by state policies that foster individual prevention measures that focus predominantly on the behavior of individuals instead of on the social context (Michailakis & Schirmer, 2010), Furthermore, individual responsibility has also been strengthened through the reconfiguration of the patient as a consumer on the healthcare market. In this vein, choice and health literacy have become central concepts, with patients now being "put in the driver's seat" of their own healthcare journeys: "The shift from patient to medical consumer puts the responsibility for medical decisions and their outcomes on those seeking help, guidance, and care from the medical system" (Sulik & Eich-Krohm, 2008, p. 8).

These developments of medicalization and psychologization through individualization are further underlined by another dimension of neoliberalism: the privatization of welfare services. Privatization developments have unfolded differently in different OECD countries. In some countries, privatization can be seen via an increase in the number of private health insurers and providers, which leaves the individual with more choices to insure against individual health risks. Germany has borne witness to strong privatization in the hospital sector, with the share of privately owned hospitals having increased from 15.5% in 1992 to 38.5% in 2020 (Institut für Arbeit und Qualifikation, 2022). For example, both per capita expenditure for voluntary healthcare schemes and out-of-pocket expenditure have increased in almost all OECD countries since the 1980s. In Germany, expenditure rose from about $200 in 1980 to $420 in 1990 and $630 in 2000 (current prices, current PPPs) (OECD, 2023). In other countries, privatization has also increased the need for individuals to be insured individually against all necessary health risks and to choose a provider. For example, in the Netherlands, the large healthcare reform in 2006 has left individuals with a choice regarding the extent to which they want to be insured against risks that do not fall within the basic benefit package (Kroneman et al., 2016).

7.1.2 The Case of Germany: Neoliberal Policies and (Un)intended Medicalization and Psychologization

This turn to being responsible for one's own health during neoliberal reforms can also be seen in the era of neoliberal policy implementation in Germany. Neoliberal policies were gradually implemented during the early 1990s under the Christian Democrats and the Liberal Party (Hinrichs, 2021). However, these reforms can be labeled small-scale first- or second-order policy changes and have therefore rarely been discussed in the public discourse as a neoliberal turn. The neoliberal turn in German welfare state policy is mainly associated with the Social Democratic—Green government, which took office in 1998 under Chancellor Gerhard Schröder (Hinrichs, 2021). This coalition government implemented third-order changes in pension and unemployment systems, which increased individual responsibility and decreased publicly ensured benefit levels (Eichhorst et al., 2010; Hinrichs, 2021). These reforms were based on two expert commissions, one of which—the Rürup Commission—developed policy proposals on social security, whereas the other of which—the Hartz Commission—developed policy proposals on (un)employment. The final reports of both commissions promoted a neoliberal welfare agenda. The Rürup Commission's report focused on reforming social security systems in the light of "growth and employment" (Rürup-Kommission, 2003, p. 1) and stressed the future economic impact of the proposed reforms while largely neglecting the societal and individual consequences of the reforms (Rürup-Kommission, 2003, pp. 20–22). One proposal made in the Rürup Commission's report was to increase the pension age. The report explicitly stressed that there should be no exceptions regarding having a higher pension age for the long-term insured or for those who are insured in a physically demanding job (Rürup-Kommission, 2003, p. 8). As this recommendation would have led to high pressure on incapacity pensions, the commission advised keeping incapacity benefits at a low level and further decreasing the incentives for applying for incapacity pensions (Rürup-Kommission, 2003, p. 9). The Hartz Commission displayed a tight connection between both welfare and (un)employment policies on the one hand and both economic and fiscal policies on the other hand. Furthermore, unemployed individuals were given a central role in overcoming the situation of being unemployed (Hartz-Kommission, 2002). The Hartz Commission's report emphasized the notion that unemployed individuals must search for employment and that if they are deemed to have not sufficiently engaged in the job search process, sanctions are to be applied (Hartz-Kommission, 2002, pp. 24–25). Thus, both documents stressed individual responsibility for market integration and therefore also for health, which was required to be maintained individually.

The Hartz Commission laid the groundwork for the reforms of the unemployment system in the early 2000s, which mainly implemented neoliberal ideas (Marx & Schumacher, 2013). The implemented policies and institutions were designed to increase individual responsibility for (un)employment. Although the political intention was not to strengthen the role of medicine or psychology in unemployment policy (see the analysis of parliamentary debates in Chap. 5), the reform constructed ill health as the only specified path out of the logic of active job search, Thus, the medicalization and psychologization of unemployment became the path-dependent result of these decisions, as can be seen in the increasing importance of sick leave for the unemployed in Germany following these reforms (see Chap. 4). Our analyses of public opinion data have additionally revealed that the quid-pro-quo idea of activation is also seen as being adequate for health problems, with a large portion of the population supporting mandatory rehabilitation measures for physically and mentally ill unemployed individuals (see Chap. 4). Moreover, activation and the notion of increasing employability rely in many ways on psychological concepts and technologies. For instance, profiling motivation and personality characteristics has become important within activation regimes across countries (International Labour Organization/European Commission,

2017). This is also true for Germany, where the testing and development of competence profiles have been essential in creating measures for unemployed people and where psychologists may act as coaches in activation training programs (Ott, 2016).

Similar to unemployment, educational policy in Germany was also transformed in the early 2000s with the aim of redirecting curricula more toward skills that are considered necessary on the (international) labor market (Tillmann et al., 2008). The results of the international education system evaluation (PISA) conducted by the OECD spurred a vast discussion about the quality of the German education system and the competitiveness of the future generation of workers in the knowledge society (Seitz, 2003). Hence, German school systems and curricula have been transformed to cater to the neoliberal principle of future employability. This transformation has included focusing curricula on reading, mathematics, and natural science competencies as well as on (creative) problem-solving and much less in social or cultural competencies. Furthermore, these competencies are now regularly assessed via standardized tests (Seitz, 2003). These assessments set standards that children are expected to achieve. If children fail to achieve a given standard, this is considered a problem that stems from the individual level and triggers the search for individual explanations and solutions. As we outlined in Chap. 6, medicine and psychology are two primary disciplines that are called upon by the education system, for example, when conducting an assessment for a learning disorder which is a common explanation when students fail to achieve standards in mathematics or reading.

7.1.3 Medicalization as an Unintended Effect of Neoliberal (Employment) Policy

Political decision-makers in most European countries—including Germany—have implemented neoliberal policies with the aim of increasing the efficiency and decreasing the costs of the welfare state system. Instead, the aim of medicalizing and psychologizing welfare was hardly part of the discourse and the specific political goals during this period (see also the policy analysis in the Chap. 5). However, neoliberal reforms have in fact included or resulted in these processes. For example, Holmqvist (2010) revealed that the activation turn in unemployment policy has led to more processes in which unemployed individuals are constructed as "disabled" in order to deal with problems of activation and employability in Sweden. Similarly, Wong (2016) demonstrated that welfare retrenchment in the United States has increased access to medicalized welfare benefits, especially in areas with high poverty rates and low educational attainment. In our analyses, we found the category of sick leave for the unemployed to play a significant role as an institutional mechanism for dealing with long-term unemployed people who have difficulties accessing the restrictive German incapacity pensions (see Chap. 4).

Internationally, a theoretical debate on the medicalization and psychologization of poverty has been ongoing (Hyman, 2018). In our research, we could show empirically that medicine, psychology, and public health have played an increasingly larger role in the international poverty discourse over time. This research literature has established a strong connection between poverty and ill health, which is also well acknowledged in governmental reports and public discourses in Germany. The policy consequences are often seen in health promotion and prevention, where several new programs have been developed over the last decades, such as the German Collaborative Network for Equity in Health[1] (founded in 2003) or the Federal Foundation for Early Childhood Interventions[2] (founded in 2012). Thus, the political reaction to the well-established link between poverty and ill health has generally focused on illness, while it is well-known that ill health does not only cause poverty, but poverty primarily causes ill health. However, at the same time as the German government has launched these new programs toward reducing health inequalities and supporting the health of individuals and specifically children in socially disadvantaged situations, other policies such as the reform of unemployment and minimum income schemes—have resulted in rising poverty rates and a reduced effectiveness of the welfare state at preventing poverty (see Chap. 5).

Children are among the group most affected by poverty in Germany, and poor socio-economic conditions are considered major contributing factors to ill health as well as to various childhood problems. Nevertheless, both the increasing number of diagnoses and our analyses of professional discourses suggest that medicalization and psychologization is often the strategy with which these problems are addressed rather than improving the socio-economic situation of children (see Chap. 6).

[1] https://www.gesundheitliche-chancengleichheit.de/
[2] https://www.fruehehilfen.de/

7.2 Social Investment and the Turn to Health and Personality as Assets

By the end of the 1990s, a new social policy paradigm had entered the stage: the social investment approach (Jenson, 2010). This paradigm—which was centrally developed by Giddens (2013) and Esping-Andersen (2002)—argues that the welfare state has to reorient itself toward investing in human capital that enables individuals to participate in the labor market and to be productive. The social investment approach could be viewed as an alternative to, an advancement of, or a complement to neoliberalism. In the social policy discourse, in particular, the social investment paradigm has gradually replaced the neoliberal paradigm, whose limitations have been increasingly often documented (Jenson, 2010). The strong focus on the individual and on the goal of labor market participation mark the continuity from neoliberalism to social investment (Deeming & Smyth, 2015; Jenson, 2010, 2017). Therefore, social investment has not abolished neoliberal thinking; rather, social investment can be viewed a derivative of neoliberalism (Jenson, 2010):

> governments adjusted their social policies to incorporate the social investment perspective. In doing so they did not try to return to the Keynesian past; they did not reject all of the social thinking of neoliberalism. They did, however, begin to retreat from classical neoliberalism's emphasis on markets and communities as the main pillars of wellbeing and started to identify ways to better address the new social risks of contemporary economic and social relations. In doing so, they were redesigning social citizenship and relations between the state and citizens more broadly. (Jenson, 2014, p. 61)

While the focus on the individual—particularly the emphasis on participating in the labor market—remains in the social investment perspective, all responsibility is not left to individual citizens. Instead, the social investment perspective stresses the notion that the state has—and should assume—responsibility for its (most vulnerable) citizens and that state activities are often a prerequisite for individuals' ability to participate in social life. Prominently, Esping-Andersen (2002) argued that the state should invest more in children, education, and family policy due to the positive effects that such investments have on other welfare state areas, such as employment:

> Active training and mobility policies can only be effective if they complement a strategy of prevention and this means, once again, the need for major social investments in childhood and youth. Or, to put it differently, our employment policies need to join hands with our family policies. (Esping-Andersen, 2002, p. 24)

Following these ideas, social investment policies no longer hold the view that the main role of the welfare state is to decommodify and financially protect individuals from social risks (e.g., old-age, illness, unemployment, poverty). Instead, the welfare state should provide benefits, which should first prevent people from getting into situations in which they need societal help and second enable people to find (individual) solutions for getting out of situations such as unemployment, poverty, or illness (Hemerijck, 2017; Midgley, 1999). These two main aims are often supported by the provision of social services, but targeted benefits can also be implemented to achieve these goals (Busemeyer et al., 2018; Choi et al., 2020). In principle, a large variety of measures are possible because the meaning and particular aims of social investment can vary to a large degree (Jenson, 2010).

Investing before social problems arise—in order to prevent them—is a key notion behind social investment policies. Therefore, measures concerning the acquisition of skills as early in life as possible represent the heart of social investment policies (Hemerijck, 2018). Social investment policies hence stretch across the entire life course and even target children through childcare services and public health interventions. This investment in children reflects the intention to foster their future employability (Lister, 2003). In unemployment policies, social investment focuses on training and re-training unemployed individuals in order to enable them to find and remain in employment and to transition from job to job rather than from work to unemployment (Choi et al., 2020; van Berkel & van der Aa, 2015).

The social investment paradigm has been promoted by international organizations such as the OECD, the World Bank, the EU, and the WHO (Chorev, 2013; Jenson, 2017; Mahon, 2019). As early as in the mid-1990s, the World Bank's policy documents initiated a paradigm shift from a neoliberal perspective to a social investment perspective by stressing the importance of education and human capital development and by beginning to invest in education and skills in early childhood (Jenson, 2017). In 1998, the World Bank published a paper entitled *Beyond the Washington Consensus: Institutions Matter* (Burki & Perry, 1998), in which it stated that the expected decline in poverty due to neoliberal policies had not taken place and that instead, social inequality had increased (Abrahamson, 2010). Hence, the World Bank called for a new series of institutional reforms, which have been labeled "after-neoliberalism"—or social investment—reforms (Jenson, 2010). Not only has this shift taken place in the global South (i.e., the World Bank's main focus), but it has also gained ground in the OECD and thus in the global North for similar reasons (i.e., concerns about social cohesion and increasing social inequalities) (Jenson, 2017). The OECD's shift to social investment began with two conferences in the mid-1990s that focused on social cohesion, but policy recommendations only began to evolve during the early and mid-2000s. For example, the OECD series *Babies and Bosses* focused predominantly on labor inflow by promoting childcare and parental leave programs designed to keep workers in the labor force, though less focus was placed on early childhood education (Jenson, 2017).

7.2.1 Health in the Social Investment Paradigm

We next turn to the role that medicine and psychology play in social investment policy and investigate how this role differs compared with in neoliberal policies. Goijaerts et al. (2022) have theoretically discussed how health is—and should be—considered part of social investment policies. Focusing on the different functions of social investment policies (e.g., stock, flow, buffer, institutional complementarity) (Hemerijck, 2017), the authors explained how health prevention programs, investments in health (both before and after sickness, and particularly for groups that are inactive in the labor market), expenditures on "old" social risks in the light of lifelong health promotion, and the triangulation of these measures foster the activation, lifelong learning, and productivity rationality of the social investment paradigm.

Both the fact that health and psychology play a role in social investment concepts and the way in which the role of health and psychology changes over time are exemplified by EU policy documents and the policy-making of the WHO. Indeed, the WHO is an example of how an international organization adopts social investment measures as a reaction to the international neoliberal policy agenda. With the spread of neoliberal thinking on the international level, the WHO had to present new argumentation as to why health is an important issue. It was thus no longer enough to state that both individual and public health are an aim in their own right;

instead, the WHO needed to stress the role of health in economic growth in order to legitimize its own function as an organization (Chorev, 2013). In line with neoliberal thinking, the WHO adopted policies that took up economic growth as the guideline for health policy interventions. However,

> the WHO's programs and policies also significantly altered the neoliberal logic. The WHO staff used the concern with economic growth to justify greater financial investment in health and relied on cost-effective logic to call for a 'new universalism'—the delivery of high-quality essential care to all—while maintaining a focus on infectious diseases affecting the poor. (Chorev, 2013, p. 654)

EU policy documents reveal the role that the issue of health plays within the social investment concept. Although the European Commission states that "health is a value in itself" (European Commission, 2013a, p. 1), it also stresses that health expenditures are "growth-friendly" and promote a "job-rich recovery" and that "[p]eople's health influences economic outcomes in terms of productivity, labour supply, human capital and public spending" (European Commission, 2013a, p. 1). Furthermore, the European Commission has stated that investments in health—particularly in preventative measures—are particularly important for children from weak economic backgrounds and for people living in poverty because these investments are cost-effective and thus result in lower costs in other welfare state systems (European Commission, 2013b):

> Children who grow up in poverty often stay in poverty for their entire lives. For example, significant disadvantages faced in childhood in education and health are often compounded over life. Addressing health determinants throughout people's lives is therefore important. (European Commission, 2013b, p. 6).

Thus, investing in health from an early age is expected to (1) allow people to remain active and in better health for a longer period of time, (2) increase the productivity of the workforce, and (3) lower the financial pressures on health systems. Health promotion and preventative healthcare are considered particularly important including investing in health and safety at work (European Commission, 2013b). Hence, both health and investments in health from an early age constitute a central element of the assumptions behind social investment and are actively pursued in welfare state policies.

The social investment logic has also been defined through psychological concepts and relies on psychological technologies and actors. While some conceptions of social investment policies have a narrow understanding of skills, many other conceptions specifically highlight psychological concepts such as optimism, self-efficacy, self-regulation, motivation, or resilience (Friedli, 2015). Services that aim to improve these personal competencies and that more generally seek to improve social and labor market participation through individual coping mechanisms have been part of labor market measures, parental training programs, and services for children and adolescents (Friedli, 2015; Gillies, 2005; Ott, 2016). Parenting programs are an important example. Daly (2017), for instance, outlined how psychological theories such as parenting styles (Baumrind, 1967) and attachment theory (Bowlby, 1958) have been central to the evolution and popularity of parenting as a concept and evolved to a field of government intervention. Moreover, the comparatively higher use of mental healthcare services by children and adults with a lower socio-economic status means that the mental healthcare sector plays a central role in dealing with socio-economic problems (Buffel et al., 2015; Lampert et al., 2018; Reiß et al., 2021). This includes in Germany services offered by psychologists such as psychological psychotherapy. In sum, the long-acknowledged role of psychology in the governmentality of individuals in liberal democracies has been stimulated by the social investment discourse. Psychological concepts are discursively used to re-interpret and individualize marginalization and deprivation:

> Theories of 'individualization' and 'risk' have shifted attention away from the material and structural roots of inequality and sanctioned a psychologized view of class distinctions in terms of personal qualities. (Gillies, 2005, p. 835)

7.2.2 Health and Psychology in the German Turn to Social Investment

In Germany, the stepwise shift from neoliberal to social investment policies was triggered by the public and political criticism following the Hartz reforms and the implemented neoliberal agenda (Brettschneider, 2008).

Although social investment approaches had begun to be discussed internationally in the mid-1990s and in Germany in the early 2000s, these approaches have only been *thoroughly* discussed and implemented in Germany since the mid-2010s (Brussig, 2019). Concerning childcare, social investment strategies have gradually been implemented since the mid-2000s in the form of strengthening and expanding the rights of parents to access leave policies and public childcare (West et al., 2020). In other areas, such as poverty and elderly care, social investment policies have also been implemented since the early 2010s (Brettschneider & Klammer, 2020). For example, the Federal Participation Act (Bundesteilhabegesetz)—which began to be gradually implemented in 2016—has strengthened the rights of disabled people as well as of people in rehabilitation and focuses on (re-)integrating these people into both society and the labor market. Concerning unemployment, social investment was part of the Hartz reforms, but this component was underdeveloped and instead activation and sanctioning was the focus of the initial reforms (Dingeldey, 2020). Hence, the turn to social investment in unemployment policy has gradually increased since the early 2010s via various small-scale reforms that have focused on young unemployed people and on further qualifications for all age groups (Ariaans & Reibling, 2022; Dingeldey, 2020).

However, this focus on investment in qualification and skills has failed to "activate" its most important target group: the long-term unemployed (Brussig, 2019). For Germany, the share of long-term unemployed has not decreased significantly since 2011 (Brussig, 2019). Furthermore, before the turn to social investment, unemployed people who were (evaluated as being) not able to (re-)enter the labor market had shifted to early or incapacity pensions (Giddens, 1998). However, transitions to these programs have been blocked for many individuals in many welfare states during the past century (Ebbinghaus, 2006; Hinrichs, 2021) due to the aim of investing in the employability of these people. Thus, despite social investments in skills and qualifications, the large group of long-term unemployed people who cannot be reached with these types of social investment policies remains unaddressed. And how does the welfare state deal with these unemployed people? Instead of social investments in skills and qualifications, policies have turned to investments in health. As shown in the previous section, health in the form of prevention and rehabilitation has also been introduced in various forms into welfare state policies in Germany in order to promote healthy aging and to increase individual and societal productivity (Gerlinger, 2018). For example, the Federal Participation Act (Bundesteilhabegesetz) initiated a program (rehapro) that focuses on the medical and occupational rehabilitation of (often long-term) unemployed individuals. This program furthermore establishes a cooperation between various health and welfare state actors, such as employment agencies, health insurers, rehabilitative centers, and employers (rehapro, 2022). Thus, investment in health has become more important on the German policy agenda in recent years. Although this increased focus on health has been a clear political goal, "'Health' alone is still not a particularly strong motive of health policy, but [it] comes into play primarily when it promises to contribute to the achievement of other—primarily economic—goals" (own translation, Gerlinger, 2018, p. 200).

7.3 Conclusion

The present chapter revealed that the neoliberal paradigm and the turn to the social investment paradigm have both created a societal and political climate in which medicalization and psychologization processes have unfolded. The two paradigms have been actively promoted by international political institutions and organizations and have been implemented as guiding principles in welfare state policy in advanced welfare states since the 1980s. Table 7.1 compares the two paradigms: Neoliberalism and social investment both focus on the individual and on the individual's personal responsibility for their own unique life course risks. Nevertheless, neoliberalism and social investment diverge in terms of how they view self-responsibility and the role of the individual within the market. In a strict sense, the neoliberal paradigm promotes the notion that individuals are solely responsible for themselves when it comes to falling into and getting out of existential life course risks, whereas the social investment paradigm highlights the function of the welfare state to enable individuals from an early stage onward to take responsibility for not entering existential life crisis events and to give these individuals the necessary skills and prerequisites to exit such situations.

Medicalization and psychologization are not found prominently in contemporary discussions of neoliberalism and social investment debates. However, we have shown in this chapter how medicine and psychology have played a part in these discourses and reforms. Medical doctors and psychologists are not at the forefront of social policy debates, but they are included on the micro- and meso-level because they use their specific

Table 7.1 Key characteristics of neoliberalism and social investment

	Neoliberal paradigm	*Social investment paradigm*
Role of the welfare state	The state provides the minimum requirements for societal and economic participation.	Provides services/benefits in order to enable social and economic participation. Prevents individuals from falling into existential life course risks.
Dominant view of the individual	The individual is viewed as the subject in the market.	The individual is viewed as the subject in the market.
Individual responsibility	The individuals are responsible for themselves.	The state supports individuals to be responsible for themselves.
Impact on medicalization/ psychologization	Illness is the only way out of the activation logic. Illness is a hindrance to market integration.	Services/benefits are provided for health promotion, rehabilitation and the development of psychological competences deemed important for a successful life/ labor market participation. Illness should be prevented/ health should be promoted.

professional expertise and abilities to deal with the externalities of neoliberal reforms or to support investment programs through individualized services.

The neoliberal agenda contributes to medicalization and psychologization via individual enhancement and the notion of illness as a state that individuals have to overcome as soon as possible. However, both of these processes appear to also come into play as unintentional side-effects of neoliberal reforms. They take the role of escape routes that buffer neoliberal policies and the consequences of these policies. Health and psychological competencies play an even stronger role in the social investment paradigm as forms of capital that the state invests in. However, the welfare state invests in the health of the population before people become unemployed and additionally helps people to become healthy and consequently to increase their chances of finding a job. Thus, medicalization and psychologization might be more intentional policy processes during the current phase of social investment than they were during the neoliberal policy era.

Medicalization and psychologization from the perspective of both neoliberal and social investment thinking have a highly instrumental nature. The concepts of recovery, labor market participation, and growing up successfully create strong expectations and can lead to the neglect and stigmatization of groups for which these goals are not attainable. Moreover, the new focus on health and psychological competences entails the risk to de-emphasize structural aspects of social problems, e.g., social inequalities (Lister, 2003) or the structure of labor markets (Lindsay & Houston, 2011).

With respect to Germany, medicalization and psychologization have been part of neoliberal and social investment reforms, as we demonstrated and documented in our empirical analyses in the Chaps. 4–6. However, in the social investment period (thus in the more recent years), we can also find discourses and reforms that focus on structural explanations, new redistributive and social security policies, or investments in social infrastructures (e.g., schools). While these changes may have been smaller-scaled and were (not yet) able to affect (child) poverty, long-term unemployment, and social inequality, this socio-economic perspective has not been crowded out by medicalization and psychologization. Instead, social policies that have addressed unemployment, poverty, and childhood problems have moved toward an integrative biopsychosocial approach.

References

Abrahamson, P. (2010). European welfare states beyond neoliberalism: Toward the social investment state. *Development and Society, 39*(1), 61–95. https://doi.org/10.21588/dns.2010.39.1.003

Adams, G., Estrada-Villalta, S., Sullivan, D., & Markus, H. R. (2019). The psychology of neoliberalism and the neoliberalism of psychology. *Journal of Social Issues, 75*(1), 189–216. https://doi.org/10.1111/josi.12305

Ariaans, M., & Reibling, N. (2022). Constructions of unemployed individuals in German parliamentary debates on active labour market policy reforms: A comparative analysis of 2003 and 2016. *Social Policy and Society*, 1–18. https://doi.org/10.1017/S1474746421000890

Barbee, H., Moloney, M. E., & Konrad, T. R. (2018). Selling slumber: American neoliberalism and the medicalization of sleeplessness. *Sociology Compass, 12*(10), e12622. https://doi.org/10.1111/soc4.12622

Baumrind, D. (1967). Child care practices anteceding three patterns of preschool behavior. *Genetic Psychology Monographs, 75*(1), 43–88. https://psycnet.apa.org/record/1967-05780-001

Bouhali, C. E. (2015). The OECD neoliberal governance. In A. A. Abdi, L. Shultz, & T. Pillay (Eds.), *Decolonizing global citizenship education* (pp. 119–129). Sense Publishers. https://doi.org/10.1007/978-94-6300-277-6_10

Bowlby, J. (1958). The nature of the child's tie to his mother. *International Journal of Psychoanalysis, 39*(5), 350–373.

Brettschneider, A. (2008). On the way to social investment? The normative recalibration of the German Welfare State. *German Policy Studies, 4*(2), 19–66.

Brettschneider, A., & Klammer, U. (2020). *Vorbeugende Sozialpolitik: Grundlinien eines sozialpolitischen Forschungsprogramms*. Forschungsinstitut für gesellschaftliche Weiterentwicklung e.V. (FGW).

Brussig, M. (2019). Was kommt nach der Aktivierung? Neue Leitbilder der Arbeitsmarktpolitik. *Arbeit, 28*(2), 101–123. https://doi.org/10.1515/arbeit-2019-0008

Buffel, V., Dereuddre, R., & Bracke, P. (2015). Medicalization of the uncertainty? An empirical study of the relationships between unemployment or job insecurity, professional care seeking, and the consumption of antidepressants. *European Sociological Review, 31*(4), 446–459. https://doi.org/10.1093/esr/jcv004

Burki, S. J., & Perry, G. E. (1998). *Beyond the Washington consensus: Institutions matter*. The World Bank.

Busemeyer, M. R., de La Porte, C., Garritzmann, J. L., & Pavolini, E. (2018). The future of the social investment state: Politics, policies, and outcomes. *Journal of European Public Policy, 25*(6), 801–809. https://doi.org/10.1080/13501763.2017.1402944

Choi, Y. J., Huber, E., Kim, W. S., Kwon, H. Y., & Shi, S.-J. (2020). Social investment in the knowledge-based economy: New politics and policies. *Policy and Society, 39*(2), 147–170. https://doi.org/10.1080/14494035.2020.1782577

Chorev, N. (2013). Restructuring neoliberalism at the World Health Organization. *Review of International Political Economy, 20*(4), 627–666. https://doi.org/10.1080/09692290.2012.690774

Daly, M. (2017). Parenting: Critical insights from a sociological perspective. In T. Betz, M.-S. Honig, & I. Ostner (Eds.), *Sonderheft der Zeitschrift Für Familienforschung: Parents in the spotlight: Parenting practices and support from a comparative perspective* (pp. 41–56). Barbara Budrich Publishers.

Deeming, C., & Smyth, P. (2015). Social investment after neoliberalism: Policy paradigms and political platforms. *Journal of Social Policy, 44*(2), 297–318. https://doi.org/10.1017/S0047279414000828

Dingeldey, I. (2020). Mehr als 50 Jahre Arbeitsförderungsgesetz: Die Entwicklung der deutschen Arbeitsmarktpolitik als Fortschritt oder Rückschritt? *Momentum Quaterly. Zeitschrift Für Sozialen Fortschritt, 9*(1), 35–49. https://doi.org/10.15203/momentumquarterly.vol9.no1.p35-49

Ebbinghaus, B. (2006). *Reforming early retirement in Europe, Japan and the USA*. Oxford University Press.

Eichhorst, W., Grienberger-Zingerle, M., & Konle-Seidl, R. (2010). Activating labor market and social policies in Germany: From status protection to basic income support. *German Policy Studies, 6*(1), 65–106.

Esping-Andersen, G. (2002). *Why we need a new welfare state.* Oxford University Press.

Esposito, L., & Perez, F. M. (2014). Neoliberalism and the commodification of mental health. *Humanity and Society, 38*(4), 414–442. https://doi.org/10.1177/0160597614544958

European Commission. (1993). *Growth, competitiveness, employment: The challenges and ways forward into the 21st century.* Luxembourg.

European Commission. (2013a). *Investing in Health.* SWD (2013) 43 final. Brussels.

European Commission. (2013b). *Towards social investment for growth and cohesion – including implementing the European Social Fund 2014–2020.* COM (2013): 83 final. Brussels.

Foster, R. (2016). Therapeutic culture, authenticity and neo-liberalism. *History of the Human Sciences, 29*(1), 99–116. https://doi.org/10.1177/0952695115617384

Fougère, M., Segercrantz, B., & Seeck, H. (2017). A critical reading of the European Union's social innovation policy discourse: (Re)legitimizing neoliberalism. *Organization, 24*(6), 819–843. https://doi.org/10.1177/1350508416685171

Friedli, L. (2015). The politics of tackling inequalities: The rise of psychological fundamentalism in public health and welfare reform. In K. E. Smith, C. Bambra, & S. E. Hill (Eds.), *Health inequalities: Critical perspectives* (pp. 206–221). Oxford University Press.

Gerlinger, T. (2018). Der Public Health-Gedanke in der Gesundheitspolitik. *Public Health Forum, 26*(3), 198–200. https://doi.org/10.1515/pubhef-2018-0066

Giddens, A. (1998). The social investment state. In A. Giddens (Ed.), *The third way: Renewal of social democracy* (pp. 99–128). Polity Press.

Giddens, A. (2013). *The third way: The renewal of social democracy.* Wiley.

Gillies, V. (2005). Raising the 'meritocracy'. *Sociology, 39*(5), 835–853. https://doi.org/10.1177/0038038505058368

Goijaerts, J., van der Zwan, N., & Bussemaker, J. (2022). Health and the social investment state. *Journal of European Public Policy*, 1–21. https://doi.org/10.1080/13501763.2022.2038239

Hansen, H., Bourgois, P., & Drucker, E. (2014). Pathologizing poverty: New forms of diagnosis, disability, and structural stigma under welfare reform. *Social Science & Medicine, 1982*(103), 76–83. https://doi.org/10.1016/j.socscimed.2013.06.033

Hartz-Kommission. (2002). *Moderne Dienstleistungen am Arbeitsmarkt: Kurzfassung*. Hartz-Kommission.

Harvey, D. (2010). *A brief history of neoliberalism*. Oxford University Press.

Hemerijck, A. (2017). The social investment and its critics. In A. Hemerijck (Ed.), *The uses of social investment* (pp. 3–42). Oxford University Press.

Hemerijck, A. (2018). Social investment as a policy paradigm. *Journal of European Public Policy, 25*(6), 810–827. https://doi.org/10.1080/13501763.2017.1401111

Hermann, C. (2007). Neoliberalism in the European Union. *Studies in Political Economy, 79*(1), 61–90. https://doi.org/10.1080/19187033.2007.11675092

Hinrichs, K. (2021). A social insurance state withers away. Welfare state reforms in Germany – or: Attempts to turn around in a Cul-de-Sac. In B. Palier (Ed.), *A long goodbye to bismarck?* (pp. 45–72). Amsterdam University Press. https://doi.org/10.1017/9789048512454.003

Holmqvist, M. (2010). The 'active welfare state' and its consequences. *European Societies, 12*(2), 209–230. https://doi.org/10.1080/14616690903388960

Holmqvist, M., Maravelias, C., & Skålén, P. (2013). Identity regulation in neoliberal societies: Constructing the 'occupationally disabled' individual. *Organization, 20*(2), 193–211. https://doi.org/10.1177/1350508412438704

Hyman, D. A. (2018). The medicalization of poverty: A dose of theory. *The Journal of Law, Medicine & Ethics: A Journal of the American Society of Law, Medicine & Ethics, 46*(3), 582–587. https://doi.org/10.1177/1073110518804200

Institut für Arbeit und Qualifikation. (2022). *Krankenhäuser und Betten nach Trägerschaft*. Universität Duisburg-Essen. https://www.sozialpolitik-aktuell.de/files/sozialpolitik-aktuell/_Politikfelder/Gesundheitswesen/Datensammlung/PDF-Dateien/abbVI32b.pdf

International Labour Organization/European Commission. (2017). *Profiling youth labour market disadvantage: A review of approaches in Europe*. International Labour Organization.

Jenson, J. (2010). Diffusing ideas for after neoliberalism. *Global Social Policy, 10*(1), 59–84. https://doi.org/10.1177/1468018109354813

Jenson, J. (2014). Redesigning citizenship regimes after neoliberalism: Moving towards social investment. In N. Morel, B. Palier, & J. Palme (Eds.), *Towards a social investment welfare state? Ideas, policies and challenges* (pp. 61–88). Policy. https://doi.org/10.1332/policypress/9781847429247.003.0003

Jenson, J. (2017). Developing and spreading a social investment perspective: The World Bank and OECD compared. In A. Hemerijck (Ed.), *The uses of social investment*. Oxford University Press.

Kroneman, M., Boerma W., van den Berg M., Groenewegen P., de Jong J., & van Ginneken E. (2016). *The Netherlands: health system review* (Health Systems in Transition 18(2)).

LaMarre, A., Smoliak, O., Cool, C., Kinavey, H., & Hardt, L. (2019). The normal, improving, and productive self: Unpacking neoliberal governmentality in therapeutic interactions. *Journal of Constructivist Psychology, 32*(3), 236–253. https://doi.org/10.1080/10720537.2018.1477080

Lampert, T., Prütz, F., Rommel, A., & Kuntz, B. (2018). Soziale Unterschiede in der Inanspruchnahme medizinischer Leistungen von Kindern und Jugendlichen in Deutschland – Querschnittergebnisse aus KiGGS Welle 2. *Journal of Health Monitoring, 3*(4), 38–56. https://doi.org/10.17886/RKI-GBE-2018-091

Lindsay, C., & Houston, D. (2011). Fit for purpose? Welfare reform and challenges for health and labour market policy in the UK. *Environment and Planning a: Economy and Space, 43*(3), 703–721. https://doi.org/10.1068/a43442

Lister, R. (2003). Investing in the Citizen-workers of the future: Transformations in citizenship and the state under new labour. *Social Policy & Administration, 37*(5), 427–443. https://doi.org/10.1111/1467-9515.00350

Madsen, O. J. (2018). *The psychologization of society: On the unfolding of the therapeutic in Norway*. Routledge. https://doi.org/10.4324/9781351118347

Mahon, R. (2019). Broadening the social investment agenda: The OECD, the World Bank and inclusive growth. *Global Social Policy, 19*(1–2), 121–138. https://doi.org/10.1177/1468018119826404

Martens, K. (2007). How to become an influential actor – The 'comparative turn' in OECD educational policy. In K. Martens, A. Rusconi, & K. Leuze (Eds.), *Transformations of the state series. New arenas of education governance: The impact of international organizations and markets on educational policy making* (pp. 40–56). Palgrave Macmillan.

Marx, P., & Schumacher, G. (2013). Will to power? Intra-party conflict in social democratic parties and the choice for neoliberal policies in Germany, the Netherlands and Spain (1980–2010). *European Political Science Review, 5*(1), 151–173. https://doi.org/10.1017/S1755773912000070

Marzullo, M. (2011). Through a glass, darkly: U.S. Marriage discourse and neoliberalism. *Journal of Homosexuality, 58*(6-7), 758–774. https://doi.org/10.1080/00918369.2011.581919

McGregor, S. (2001). Neoliberalism and health care. *International Journal of Consumer Studies, 25*(2), 82–89. https://doi.org/10.1111/j.1470-6431.2001.00183.x

Michailakis, D., & Schirmer, W. (2010). Agents of their health? How the Swedish welfare state introduces expectations of individual responsibility. *Sociology of Health & Illness, 32*(6), 930–947. https://doi.org/10.1111/j.1467-9566.2010.01262.x

Midgley, J. (1999). Growth, redistribution, and welfare: Toward social investment. *Social Service Review, 73*(1), 3–21. https://doi.org/10.1086/515795

Mills, C. (2015). The psychiatrization of poverty: Rethinking the mental health-poverty nexus. *Social and Personality Psychology Compass, 9*(5), 213–222. https://doi.org/10.1111/spc3.12168

Morel, N., Palier, B., & Palme, J. (2012a). Social investment: A paradigm in search of a new economic model and political mobilisation. In N. Morel, B. Palier, & J. Palme (Eds.), *Towards a social investment welfare state? Ideas, policies and challenges* (pp. 353–376). Policy Press.

Morel, N., Palier, B., & Palme, J. (Eds.). (2012b). *Towards a social investment welfare state? Ideas, policies and challenges*. Policy Press.

OECD. (1999). *Measuring student knowledge and skills: A new framework for assessment*. Franz. Ausg. U.D.T.: Mesurer les connaissances et compétences des élèves. *OECD Programme for International Student Assessment (PISA)*. OECD.

OECD. (2023). *OECD.stats*. https://stats.oecd.org/

Olk, T. (2007). Children in the 'social investment state'. *Zeitschrift für Soziologie der Erziehung und Sozialisation, 27*(1), 43–57.

Ott, M. (2016). (In-)Kompetenzen aktivieren in Praktiken des Testens – wie Erwerbslosigkeit praktisch personalisiert wird. In R. Anhorn (Ed.), Perspektiven Kritischer Sozialer Arbeit. Handbuch Therapeutisierung und Soziale Arbeit (pp. 709–724). Springer Fachmedien Wiesbaden GmbH. https://doi.org/10.1007/978-3-658-10870-0_25

Peeters, R. (2019). Manufacturing responsibility: The governmentality of behavioural power in social policies. *Social Policy and Society, 18*(1), 51–65. https://doi.org/10.1017/s147474641700046x

Putzel, J. (2020). The 'populist' right challenge to neoliberalism: Social policy between a rock and a hard place. *Development and Change, 51*(2), 418–441. https://doi.org/10.1111/dech.12578

Rehapro. (2022). *Innovative Wege zur Teilhabe am Arbeitsleben – rehapro*. https://www.modellvorhaben-rehapro.de/DE/Home/home_node.html

Reiß, F., Schlack, R., Otto, C., Meyrose, A.-K., & Ravens-Sieberer, U. (2021). Zur Rolle des sozioökonomischen Status bei der Inanspruchnahme fachspezifischer Versorgung von psychisch auffälligen Kindern und Jugendlichen in Deutschland: Ergebnisse der BELLA-Studie [The Role of the Socioeconomic Status in Mental Health Care Utilization by Children and Adolescents in Germany: Results of the BELLA Study]. *Gesundheitswesen, 83*(11), 919–927. https://doi.org/10.1055/a-1335-4212

Rürup-Kommission. (2003). *Bericht der Kommission Nachhaltigkeit in der Finanzierung der Sozialen Sicherungssysteme: Kurzfassung*. Rürup-Kommission.

Rushton, S., & Williams, O. D. (2012). Frames, paradigms and power: Global health policy-making under neoliberalism. *Global Society, 26*(2), 147–167. https://doi.org/10.1080/13600826.2012.656266

Rutkowski, D. J. (2007). Converging us softly: How intergovernmental organizations promote neoliberal educational policy. *Critical Studies in Education, 48*(2), 229–247. https://doi.org/10.1080/17508480701494259

Seitz, K. (2003). Der schiefe Turm von PISA – nur die Spitze eines Eisbergs? Der PISA-Schock und der weltweite Umbau der Bildungssysteme. *ZEP: Zeitschrift für internationale Bildungsforschung und Entwicklungspädagogik, 26*(1), 2–8. https://doi.org/10.25656/01:6154

Sowa, F., & Zapfel, S. (2015). Aktivierung als globales Modell der Weltpolitik? Konzeptionelle Überlegungen zum Wandel der Arbeitsmarktpolitik in europäischen Wohlfahrtsstaaten. *Sozialer Fortschritt, 64*(3), 47–54. https://doi.org/10.3790/sfo.64.3.47

Sugarman, J. (2015). Neoliberalism and psychological ethics. *Journal of Theoretical and Philosophical Psychology, 35*(2), 103–116. https://doi.org/10.1037/a0038960

Sulik, G. A., & Eich-Krohm, A. (2008). No longer a patient: The social construction of the medical consumer. In *Advances in medical sociology. Patients, consumers and civil society* (Vol. 10, pp. 3–28). Emerald (MCB UP). https://doi.org/10.1016/S1057-6290(08)10002-X

Thatcher, M. (1987, September 23). *Interview by D. Keay [Thatcher Archive (THCR 5/2/262): COI transcript]*. No. 10 Downing Street.

Tillmann, K.-J., Dedering, K., Kneuper, D., Kuhlmann, C., & Nessel, I. (2008). *PISA als bildungspolitisches Ereignis: Fallstudien in vier Bundesländern. Schule und Gesellschaft: Vol. 43*. VS Verl. für Sozialwiss.

van Berkel, R., & van der Aa, P. (2015). New welfare, new policies: Towards preventive worker-directed active labour-market policies. *Journal of Social Policy, 44*(3), 425–442. https://doi.org/10.1017/S0047279415000082

Wacquant, L. (2010). Crafting the neoliberal state: Workfare, prisonfare, and social insecurity. *Sociological Forum, 25*(2), 197–220. https://doi.org/10.1111/j.1573-7861.2010.01173.x

West, A., Blome, A., & Lewis, J. (2020). What characteristics of funding, provision and regulation are associated with effective social investment in ECEC in England, France and Germany? *Journal of Social Policy, 49*(4), 681–704.

Wong, S. (2016). Geographies of medicalized welfare: Spatial analysis of supplemental security income in the U.S., 2000–2010. *Social Science & Medicine (1982), 160*, 9–19. https://doi.org/10.1016/j.socscimed.2016.05.018

CHAPTER 8

The Biopsychosocial Welfare State: A New Perspective on Social Policy

Nadine Reibling

Throughout this book, we sought to understand (1) *the roles that medicine and psychology play in the welfare state.* Our guiding hypothesis was that both disciplines play an important role in a wide range of issues that are addressed by the welfare state in fields other than healthcare. We investigated this issue specifically for three social problems that are key to the welfare state's fields of action: unemployment, poverty, and problems in childhood. In order to grasp the role of medicine and psychology in the welfare state, we proposed a theoretical model that conceptualizes medicalization and psychologization along three levels (i.e., micro, meso, macro) and three dimensions (i.e., ideas, actors, institutions) (see Chap. 3). We employed this framework in the analyses of our three social problems, which we described throughout Chaps. 4–7. For instance, on the micro-level, medicalization and psychologization were visible in the dimension of *ideas* in terms of how individuals use information on physical and psychological health in their assessment of unemployed people (e.g., whether

N. Reibling (✉)
Fulda University of Applied Sciences, Fulda, Germany
e-mail: nadine.reibling@gw.hs-fulda.de

N. Reibling, M. Ariaans (eds.), *Toward a Biopsychosocial Welfare State?*, https://doi.org/10.1007/978-3-031-32793-3_8

these unemployed people are blamed for becoming or remaining unemployed; see Chap. 4). On the meso-level, we discussed how social security branches use medical categories in their organizational procedures—such as "sick leave" (*institutions*)—and have their own medical service agencies (*actors*) for managing long-term unemployment (see Chap. 4). On the macro-level, which we studied most extensively, we illustrated how *ideas* from medicine and psychology shape scientific discourses and the definition of poverty in policy reports and public debates (see Chap. 5). Moreover, we showed how medical and psychological categories have become integrated into social law and thus influence access to benefits and services on the dimension of *institutions* (see the institutional analyses of medicalized benefit receipt in Chap. 4 and the analyses of learning difficulties in Chap. 6). Finally, we illustrated how medical profession associations engage as *actors* in public discourses and therein simultaneously medicalize and de-medicalize childhood (see Chap. 6). Thus, the results we found throughout Chaps. 4–7 revealed that the role of both medicine and psychology in the three problem areas is in fact quite extensive.

Nevertheless, our systematic empirical analyses also uncovered little evidence that medicine, psychology or "a therapeutic culture" have become the dominant form of legitimization or governmentality in the welfare state. For instance, some of our analyses revealed no medicalization or psychologization at all (e.g., our analysis of plenary debates on unemployment in Germany in Chap. 5), and empirical examples of de-medicalization and de-psychologization were even found, such as with the restriction of access to incapacity benefits (see Chap. 4), with policies that limit the pharmaceuticalization of ADHD, and with the resistance of German states to a medicalized/psychologized practice of dealing with learning difficulties (see Chap. 6). Moreover, medical and psychological regulation are often integrated with each other as well as with social elements (e.g., education, social work, income benefits). Thus, the notion of the "layering of institutional control and [the] increasing multi-institutional management of social problems" suggested by Medina and McCraine (2011) more adequately describes the empirical patterns of medicalization and psychologization that we found in the German welfare state. We argued that this idea can be taken a step further by viewing the medicalization and psychologization of social problems and social policies as a move toward a biopsychosocial welfare state—that is, as a move toward a welfare state that integrates biomedical, psychological, and social ideas, technologies, and actors in addressing social problems.

Finally, we set out to explicitly compare medicalization and psychologization across social problems. While this endeavor was certainly limited by the need to use problem-specific data sources and methodological approaches, we can tentatively conclude that the influence of medicine and psychology differs across social problems. Psychology seemed to be least relevant in Germany for unemployment and most significant in the case of childhood problems, whereas medicine proved relevant to all three social problems. Despite the rapidly increasing growth and relevance of psychology, medicine has remained the more powerful profession. This finding is particularly true in the case of Germany, where the medical profession has a powerful position in the self-regulatory bodies of the healthcare system and where medical doctors represent the majority of healthcare professionals who are employed or contracted by the various branches of social security. Nevertheless, Rose's (1996) thesis—that is, that the influence of psychology unfolds not by monopolizing, but rather, by sharing its ideas and methods—was also found in our data analyses, in which, for example, psychological concepts such as self-efficacy and parenting style were important without necessarily being associated with the discipline of psychology.

A second question that we posed in this book involved (2) *how medicalization and psychologization in the welfare state have developed over time*. For all social problems, we could find historical examples of how medicine and (sometimes) psychology were relevant as early as at the end of the nineteenth century, such as in the discourses on unemployment and incapacity and in the regulation of problematic childhood behavior. This research area would certainly greatly benefit from a systematic quantitative longitudinal analysis that explicitly tests the importance of medicine and psychology in the welfare stare over time. However, in practice, such an overarching analysis is precluded by the lack of available data as well as by methodological challenges. Nevertheless, the existing literature (e.g., Furedi, 2008; Olafsdottir, 2007; Pulkingham & Fuller, 2012; Wong, 2016)—as well as our own analyses—have assessed medicalization and psychologization trends for specific issues and/or over more limited periods of time. For instance, we conducted bibliographical analyses of the share of disciplines among all three social problems (this book includes analyses for poverty; see also Brase et al., 2022; Krayter & Reibling, 2020), which revealed that poverty had become more medicalization and psychologized between 1960 and 2019. These results and further data—such as the rising number of medical doctors and psychologists (see Chap. 1)—provide evidence of the increasingly important role that medicine and psychology play in the welfare state. However, when we take other results from our studies into account, we agree with Halfmann's (2012) observation that a more detailed analysis often reveals both medicalization and de-medicalization, which sometimes even occur simultaneously. Thus, for certain periods, we found an increasingly strong role of medicine and psychology in terms of how modern welfare states intervene in specific social problems. Moreover, medicine and psychology can certainly be seen to have become more powerful if we simply consider the increasing size of both professions (see Chap. 1). However, in addition to considering the absolute magnitude and pervasiveness of medicalization and psychologization, it is important to think about *how* and *why* medicine and psychology work within the welfare state. We suggested that the medicalization and psychologization dynamics of recent decades need to be viewed in the context of neoliberal and social investment discourses and reforms, which have influenced medicalization and psychologization processes in Western welfare states. One example is how the importance of sick leave among the unemployed changed in the context of the increased conditionality of unemployment and minimum income benefits (see Chap. 4).

Finally, we also investigated (3) *the effects of the processes of medicalization and psychologization—that is, the implications of a move toward a bio-psychosocial welfare state.* These implications are both manifold and mixed (i.e., they are both positive and negative). These mixed consequences of medicalization and psychologization can be understood through Foucault's (1979) notion of power as a positive, productive phenomenon on the one hand and a negative, oppressive phenomenon on the other hand. To begin, the growing role of medicine and psychology in the welfare state has many positive, productive, and liberating implications. For instance, a medical and psychological perspective gives more attention to the perspective of individuals within the welfare state—that is, regarding how individuals experience social problems and the welfare state's involvement in these individuals' lives (e.g., Jo, 2013; Linden et al., 2018; Stenner & Taylor, 2008). Another major liberating aspect of the role of medicine is that individuals' problems and experiences are legitimized through medical and psychological diagnoses, which explains why individuals actively pursue these diagnoses (e.g., Hansen et al., 2014; Klasen, 2000). In addition, from a practical perspective, a medical (and sometimes psychological) diagnosis is a necessary precondition for receiving certain benefits and services from the welfare state, such as incapacity benefits, sick leave benefits, or services/changed rules for learning disabilities. Moreover, medical and psychological ideas have broadened the concept of social investment by including individuals' health and psychological characteristics in the discussion (rather than only including these individuals' labor market qualifications) (Goijaerts et al., 2022). Thus, our results indicate that medicalization and psychologization can also be interpreted as a learning process that has revealed that unemployment, poverty, and childhood are complex, multifaceted phenomena that require multiple and intersectoral forms of action from the welfare state (e.g., Ariaans & Reibling, 2021; European Network of Public Employment Services, 2020). Such interventions (e.g., early childhood intervention (i.e., "Frühe Hilfen") in Germany) rely on health professionals—due to the required trust and the low-access threshold—to act as a door-opener for further welfare state interventions. Finally, as medical doctors and psychologists are regularly confronted with patients who have problems that originate from their social and economic situations rather than from their bodies, psyches, or behavior (Wilfer et al., 2018), these professionals can act as advocates for their clients. We demonstrated this finding, for instance, in our analyses of the public communication of the German Professional Association of Pediatricians (see Chap. 6).

In contrast, medicalization and psychologization in the welfare state can be oppressive and constraining. Medicine and psychology not only legitimize access to benefits/services and refrain from labor market participation, but they also legitimize the intervention of welfare organizations in people's lives. The major point of criticism of this element of social control served as the source of inspiration for the development of medicalization theory in the 1960s. Over time, as Nye (2003, p. 127) pointed it out, this critique has moved somewhat out of focus: "Scholars [who] investigat[e] [...] long-term development and present [the] effects of medicalization remain warily suspicious of [the] close alliance of medical power and the state, but regularly find, in the modern welfare state at least, less cause for concern." While our results do not stand in opposition to Nye's assessment, it is important to underline the idea that the implications for the social control and surveillance of medicalization and psychologization are central when we study these processes in the context of the welfare state. Moreover, the recent restructuring of the welfare state toward more conditionality (under neoliberalism) and the resurgence of paternalistic interventions (based on social investment thinking) reveal how significant this implication of medicalization and psychologization currently is.

Moreover, as Lupton (1997, p. 156) noted, the repressive effects of discourses (in her case, public health discourses) are not equal for all individuals but "do frequently serve to perpetuate relations of social inequality, [which are] often organized around the drawing of distinctions between gender, categories of sexual preference, ethnicity and social class." This point is also particularly relevant to our social policy perspective, and existing research has pointed out how medical and psychological ideas and technologies have been used in "the politics of tackling inequalities" (Friedli, 2015, p. 206). We also found support for this observation in our vignette study, in which citizens widely supported obligatory medical/psychological interventions for recipients of minimum income benefits with a medical or psychological diagnosis (see Chap. 4). Finally, in their current practices, medicalization and psychologization usually imply that social problems such as unemployment, poverty, or problems in childhood are individualized. This means that these problems are interpreted as problems of individual health, personal resources, actions, and so on and are therefore subject to individual, therapeutic interventions (Conrad, 2007; Madsen, 2014). In its ideal typical version, medicalization individualizes problems by pathologizing them, thereby relieving individuals of responsibility for their own state, whereas psychology holds individuals responsible for finding the solution to their problems, which is understood to lie in these individuals' thoughts, emotions, and actions (Brickman et al., 1982). In practice, both medicine and psychology contain ideas and practices that involve pathologizing and responsiblizing individuals. However, in either case, the structural, socio-economic causes of these problems—which would require macro-level political action—receive little attention in medicine or psychology (important exceptions such as social medicine and critical psychology notwithstanding). While this individualization of social problems is one of the most pertinent downsides of medicalization and psychologization discussed in the literature (e.g., Adams et al., 2019; Friedli, 2015), it is important to point out that in our analyses of the German cases (and specifically of parliamentary debates, governmental reports, and public attitudes), we found that medical and psychological measures in Germany are often discussed together with social or economic interventions or are considered secondary. However, despite the awareness of the need for economic measures, the reforms over the last two decades have not increased social security enough to lead to reduced poverty and child-poverty rates (see Chaps. 5–6).

8.1 Medicalization, Psychologization, and Welfare State Research

The aim of this book was to trigger a fruitful academic dialogue between two research areas—namely, ***medicalization and psychologization research*** on the one hand and ***welfare state research*** on the other hand. Both earlier (e.g., Conrad, 1980; Nolan, 1998; Stone, 1984; de Swaan, 1988) and more contemporary (e.g., Buffel et al., 2017; Ecclestone & Brunila, 2015; Holmqvist, 2008; Olafsdottir, 2007) research have examined the intersection of the two fields in terms of specific social problems. In this book, however, we built on existing work and extended it through our own analyses and research in order to move toward a synthesis of how medicalization and psychologization matter to the welfare state more generally. To that end, we brought these two research areas into dialogue in several ways.

The *first synthesis* involved the level of medicalization and psychologization research, which has thus far either been studied individually or been merged into concepts such as therapeutization. In Chap. 2, we made a case for the benefits associated with studying both processes simultaneously and comparing them. To that end, we revealed that the two disciplines share many interests, subject areas, and scientific methodologies. Moreover, in practice, the two disciplines often work together professionally. However, these disciplines differ significantly in terms of their theoretical attribution of responsibility, their diagnostic and treatment techniques, the institutions in which they primarily work, their professional power, and their driving forces that have been identified in the literature.

The *second synthesis* involved linking these two processes and the welfare state. In our conceptual model of the biopsychosocial welfare state, we suggested that medicalization and psychologization in the welfare state can be understood by adapting the framework created by Halfmann (2012) by adding three commonly applied categories from welfare state research: ideas, institutions, and actors. We applied this framework in the empirical analyses in Chaps. 4–6 and revealed how it enables the versatility of medicalization and psychologization processes in the welfare state to be measured. This framework allowed us to select the level and dimension on which the medicalization and/or psychologization of the welfare state should be studied. Our findings demonstrated that the empirical study of medicalization and psychologization processes not only is possible by using a variety of qualitative and quantitative methods, but also benefits from the use of these methods. While qualitative methods have been more common in medicalization and psychologization research, both theories formulate hypotheses that require quantification (Conrad, 2007). For instance, we showed that quantitative research methods—such as factorial surveys with case vignettes—are a fruitful method of linking both research on medicalization/psychologization (e.g., McLeod et al., 2004) and research on welfare attitudes (e.g., van Oorschot et al., 2017). Another example is our use of bibliographical methods to examine medicalization and psychologization in scientific discourses on social problems (see also Krayter & Reibling, 2020).

The *third synthesis* involved examining how medicalization and psychologization can be understood as processes in the context of welfare state restructuring based on neoliberalism and social investment thinking. While there are many examples of scholars pointing to the influence of neoliberalism for medicalization and psychologization (e.g., Adams et al., 2019; Barbee et al., 2018; Madsen, 2014), little research has been conducted on the link to social investment. Moreover, neoliberalism has been used in this work as a form of discourse, whereas we looked more specifically at the associated policy changes that resulted from these discourses in Germany and at the extent to which these changes included or resulted in medicalization and/or psychologization.

In summary, the medicalization and psychologization of social problems unfolds in, through, and due to the welfare state. Therefore, on the one hand, future medicalization and psychologization research should look more specifically at the welfare state as a concrete social entity and use theoretical and methodological expertise from welfare state scholarship, such as welfare state typologies, data on the development of social rights and services, and welfare cultures and narratives. This step would result in more detailed analyses of how institutions, power resources, and cultural narratives stimulate, shape, and inhibit the medicalization and psychologization of specific problems in the welfare state. For instance, studies from Anglo-Saxon countries have indicated that reforms that have eliminated the non-medical receipt of income benefits have resulted in medicalization processes (e.g., being sick may be the only way to access support) (e.g.,

Hansen et al., 2014; Pulkingham & Fuller, 2012; Wong, 2016), whereas in our German case, being on sick leave seems to be a solution for dealing with the conditionality of benefits and the strict activation regime that is implemented in the German minimum income system.

On the other hand, welfare state research has largely ignored the role of medicine and psychology outside the healthcare sector even though the welfare state heavily relies on both disciplines and professions in various fields of action. Our results corroborated the hypothesis that medicine and psychology matter across various social problems and are present on various levels as well as across several dimensions. Thus, future welfare state research could benefit from more explicitly studying medicalization and psychologization processes in various fields in addition to in the welfare state overall. To that end, welfare state research could draw on the rich theoretical and methodological tools applied in medicalization and psychologization research. For instance, medicalization research shows a strong link to the actor-centered perspective in welfare state theory, while psychologization research relates more strongly to the role of ideas and culture in the welfare state. Most importantly, such research could help to broaden our understanding of the changes that many welfare states have experienced since the popularity of neoliberalism and social investment began. As we showed, both paradigms are often reduced to an economic idea of human capital in social policy research even though existing discourses and policies have increasingly often included medical and psychological ideas, tools, and actors.

8.2 Policy Implications

Above, we outlined the idea that the implications of medicalization and psychologization have an inherently double-edged nature. Nevertheless, concrete policy implications can be drawn from our findings that could contribute both to supporting the productive consequences of medicalization and psychologization and to mitigating the repressive and constraining implications of these processes. In terms of the role that medicine and psychology play in social policies, three important fields of action exist: (1) *science and the use of evidence*, (2) *professions as self-reflective agents*, and (3) *solidarity and welfare state institutions.*

(1) *Science and the use of scientific evidence*: In Chap. 5 of this book, we revealed how medicalization and psychologization can be viewed quantitatively in the scientific discourse on poverty. Medicine and psychology are

not only professions, but also scientific disciplines. One important way in which medicine and psychology have become more important for social problems is by generating scientific evidence on certain topics (Bell, 2012). While an interdisciplinary perspective on social problems mostly constitutes a scientifically and socially desirable development, it is important to also consider the structural inequalities between scientific disciplines. These inequalities in both resources and prestige (e.g., perceived credibility and scientificity) likely lead to differential output and influence (both within and outside of science). For instance, there are visible differences in the resources dedicated to certain disciplines or research areas, with medicine, for instance, receiving a disproportionate share of research funds compared with the social sciences (which here include psychology) (Deutsche Forschungsgemeinschaft, 2021). Moreover, Comte's (1830) idea of the hierarchy of the sciences (i.e., the physical sciences are at the top, the life sciences are in the middle, and the social sciences are at the bottom) as well as the notions of *hard* and *soft sciences* are still used in research on scientific fields (Fanelli, 2010; Simonton, 2006). More notably, this hierarchy can also be identified in the attitudes of professionals (O'Brien et al., 2022) and students (Munro & Munro, 2014), who consider the natural sciences and medicine to be more credible and scientific than the social sciences. Thus, such conceptions could likely also shape science policy and the use of evidence in (social) policymaking. For example, medicalization and psychologization could be the result of what happens when medical or psychological evidence based on randomized clinical trials is given greater weight than sociological and economic evidence based on observational studies.

(2) *Professions as self-reflective agents*: Medicalization and psychologization within the welfare state occur due to the increasing importance of the medical and psychological profession in various fields of the welfare state. The impact of the work of these professions depends on both their professional habitus and their concrete practices. Knowledge about the existence and implications of medicalization and psychologization processes is an important prerequisite for self-reflexive professional practices (Adams et al., 2019; LaMarre et al., 2019; Madsen, 2014). In our analyses of press statements in Chap. 6, we found that on the associational level, pediatricians are aware of medicalization dynamics and act as advocates for educational policies. Aside from advocacy, scholars from critical psychology have also highlighted the way in which professional practice can take the downsides of psychologization into account, for example, by implementing a

stepped diagnosis approach and reducing pathologization (Batstra & Frances, 2012), thereby making people aware of structural limitations rather than exclusively focusing on what the individual can do (LaMarre et al., 2019). Moreover, psychological research could engage more in cross-cultural and de-colonial research in order "to *denaturalize* taken-for-granted assumptions about supposedly natural tendencies of human beings in general" (Adams et al., 2019, p. 207; italics in original). In the context of the welfare state, both professions also need opportunities to reflect on their assigned, perceived, and possible role in concrete policy contexts. However, at this point, the curricula of medical education and psychology seem to provide little opportunity for such reflection (Madsen, 2014).

(3) *Solidarity and welfare state institutions*: The medicalization and psychologization of social problems is also the result of the institutional structure of welfare states. Access to the healthcare system has a relatively low threshold and is largely free, at least in Germany. Thus, the fact that unemployment, poverty, and problems in childhood show up in medical and psychological practices indicates that alternatives are non-existent, more difficult to access, or less attractive. Considering the results of our vignette study on children in Chap. 6, medical doctors and psychologists are not generally the first or most important point of contact; rather, educational professionals fill this role. However, in the educational system in Germany both resources and qualifications to deal with such issues seem to be limited. Moreover, access to services for children with difficulties is tied to medical or psychological diagnoses in a number of instances. Thus, medicalization and psychologization might in certain areas be the result of the welfare state's restructuring toward less generosity and higher levels of conditionality. Thus, our results highlight the current critique that social investment reforms have become alternatives rather than complements to traditional social security policies (Cantillon & van Lancker, 2012; Olk, 2007). The takeaway for policymakers is that it is critical to consider that a lack of social services and shortages in the educational sector might result in a higher level of the medicalization and psychologization of problems and consequently also in higher costs for the healthcare system.

8.3 A Glance into the Future

While social crises are a general characteristic of modern, differentiated societies, recent crises—including the COVID-19 pandemic, contemporary international conflicts and refugee movements, and the progressing issue of climate change—represent crises of a new magnitude, speed, and global reach. These crises have posed—and will continue to pose—great challenges to modern welfare states that require substantial financial investments and societal efforts to mitigate the consequences for citizens' health, living expenses, social integration, and quality of life. However, at the same time, these crises can also be viewed as windows of opportunity that enable political action by giving greater attention to certain issues and that thus also offer the potential for building new coalitions and political majorities for political change. From the perspective of the biopsychosocial welfare state, the interesting question involves how contemporary crises have shaped medicalization and psychologization processes in the welfare state. As these crises developed during and after our research, our results do not directly speak to their influence. Nevertheless, we can develop some theoretical expectations as to how these crises may have impacted—or may in the future impact—medicalization and psychologization in the welfare state, and these expectations could be tested by future research.

First, as a crisis that originated due to a disease, the COVID-19 pandemic has certainly been particularly important with respect to medicalization and psychologization. In fact, societal changes related to the pandemic can be considered a momentous example of the medicalization of social life:

> Virtually our entire existence became medicalized in the spring of 2020. How we worked, shopped, washed, loved had suddenly been transformed into actions with a profound impact on our own health as well as the health of our nations, essentially into matters of life and death. Medicalization is obviously not a new phenomenon; many of the activities just mentioned have been subject to medical expertise and language. Yet the intensity and scope of the medicalization we have experienced during the pandemic is novel—at least in terms of recent history. Most of us had not known what it is like to have our public and private lives framed in terms of medicine. In some ways, we have shared what was already the reality of many chronically ill people. (Degerman, 2020, p. 61)

As the above statement illustrates, never before has social life been so heavily influenced by medicine in so many ways. In the early period of the pandemic, medicine dominated public and political discourses. Medical researchers and doctors became top-level policy advisors, and medical technologies and categories such as tests, quarantines, and immunization statuses became central to the organization of social life. While a controversial debate exists on whether this strong medicalization at the beginning of the pandemic was necessary and/or useful, it certainly put medicine in an unprecedented position as a discipline and profession. Moreover, this strong medicalization created a window of opportunity for bringing long-standing issues to the forefront, such as the need for innovation and for more resources in the public health service in Germany (Ewert & Loer, 2022). While this need resulted in new investments in the public health service, a systematic analysis of political changes in Germany after the COVID-19 pandemic by Ewert and Loer (2021) came to the conclusion that the pandemic had not led to a paradigmatic change in prevention policy. However, our focus in this book was limited to advanced welfare states in Western, democratic countries. Medicalization and psychologization in other parts of the world—that is, in places with less well-established welfare states or different political systems—might look different. For instance, the question of medically legitimized social control and surveillance caused by the COVID-19 pandemic might be of particular importance in autocratic countries, such as China.

However, the pandemic may have had an important impact in another way: namely in terms of the widespread tendency to medicalize and psychologize the negative repercussions of the pandemic and infection control measures, such as loneliness, fear, and depression (Arora et al., 2022; Ravens-Sieberer et al., 2021). Even though the experiences of the pandemic are known to have been the result both of a collective crisis situation and of specific social measures, such as school closures, these experiences have nevertheless been primarily framed and operationalized in existing research with medical and psychological vocabulary, concepts, and measurement tools (Johnstone, 2021; Rajkumar, 2021). Moreover, despite the widespread concern about the (long-term) implications of the pandemic on children, at least in Germany, resources in early childcare and schools have not been substantially increased, which suggests that many existing problems and experiences might end up in the jurisdiction of medical doctors and psychologists.

The sustainability of political changes that have resulted from the pandemic is also doubtful given that new challenges have emerged with the war in Ukraine and with the resulting levels of inflation and exploding energy crises. In the current situation, rather than health, costs of living and personal security have come into public focus. As a result, current political initiatives have re-focused on the classic welfare state function: social security. As poverty has become legitimized through an external source, various monetary payments have been administered, and political initiatives in support of increasing less conditional welfare benefits have been launched. Thus, in this constellation, the medicalization and psychologization of social policies have become less important.

While these social crises may have represented windows of opportunity for medicalization and psychologization and may have re-oriented the welfare state toward social security, the role that medicine and psychology have played in Western welfare states over the course of the last 150 years suggests that the biopsychosocial welfare state and its dynamics will continue to be a vital subject matter for years to come.

References

Adams, G., Estrada-Villalta, S., Sullivan, D., & Markus, H. R. (2019). The psychology of neoliberalism and the neoliberalism of psychology. *Journal of Social Issues, 75*(1), 189–216. https://doi.org/10.1111/josi.12305

Ariaans, M., & Reibling, N. (2021). Die Rolle von Gesundheit und Krankheit im deutschen Armutsdiskurs. *Zeitschrift für Sozialreform, 67*(2), 123–152. https://doi.org/10.1515/zsr-2021-0005

Arora, T., Grey, I., Östlundh, L., Lam, K. B. H., Omar, O. M., & Arnone, D. (2022). The prevalence of psychological consequences of COVID-19: A systematic review and meta-analysis of observational studies. *Journal of Health Psychology, 27*(4), 805–824. https://doi.org/10.1177/1359105320966639

Barbee, H., Moloney, M. E., & Konrad, T. R. (2018). Selling slumber: American neoliberalism and the medicalization of sleeplessness. *Sociology Compass, 12*(10), e12622. https://doi.org/10.1111/soc4.12622

Batstra, L., & Frances, A. (2012). Diagnostic inflation: Causes and a suggested cure. *The Journal of Nervous and Mental Disease, 200*(6), 474–479. https://doi.org/10.1097/NMD.0b013e318257c4a2

Bell, K. (2012). Cochrane reviews and the behavioural turn in evidence-based medicine. *Health Sociology Review, 21*(3), 313–321. https://doi.org/10.5172/hesr.2012.21.3.313

Brase, J., Krayter, S., & Reibling, N. (2022). *Scientific discourses on three social problems: What is the role of medicine and psychology?* Working Paper.

Brickman, P., Rabinowitz, V. C., Karuza, J., Coates, D., Cohn, E., & Kidder, L. (1982). Models of helping and coping. *American Psychologist, 37*(4), 368–384. https://doi.org/10.1037/0003-066x.37.4.368

Buffel, V., Beckfield, J., & Bracke, P. (2017). The institutional foundations of medicalization: A cross-national analysis of mental health and unemployment. *Journal of Health and Social Behavior, 58*(3), 272–290. https://doi.org/10.1177/0022146517716232

Cantillon, B., & van Lancker, W. (2012). Solidarity and reciprocity in the social investment state: What can be learned from the case of Flemish school allowances and truancy? *Journal of Social Policy, 41*(4), 657–675. https://doi.org/10.1017/S0047279412000359

Comte, A. (1830). *Course de philosophie positive.* Bachelier.

Conrad, P. (1980). Implications of changing social policy for the medicalization of deviance. *Contemporary Crises, 4*(2), 195–205. https://doi.org/10.1007/BF00728366

Conrad, P. (2007). *The medicalization of society: On the transformation of human conditions into treatable disorders.* Johns Hopkins University Press.

de Swaan, A. (1988). *In care of the state: Health care, education and welfare in Europe and the USA in the modern era.* Polity Press.

Degerman, D. (2020). The political is medical now: COVID-19, medicalization and political theory. *Theory & Event, 23*(4 Supplement), 61–75. https://doi.org/10.1353/tae.2020.0081

Deutsche Forschungsgemeinschaft. (2021). *Förderatlas 2021: Kennzahlen zur öffentlich finanzierten Forschung in Deutschland.* Deutsche Forschungsgemeinschaft e.V.

Ecclestone, K., & Brunila, K. (2015). Governing emotionally vulnerable subjects and 'therapisation' of social justice. *Pedagogy, Culture & Society, 23*(4), 485–506. https://doi.org/10.1080/14681366.2015.1015152

European Network of Public Employment Services. (2020). *Activation of the Inactive: PES initiative to support the activation of inactive groups.* Brussels.

Ewert, B., & Loer, K. (2021). Die Corona-Pandemie als Wendepunkt in der deutschen Präventionspolitik? *Dms – Der Moderne Staat – Zeitschrift für Public Policy, Recht und Management, 14*(2–2021), 305–333. https://doi.org/10.3224/dms.v14i2.14

Ewert, B., & Loer, K. (2022). COVID-19 as a catalyst for policy change: The role of trigger points and spillover effects. *German Politics*, 1–24. https://doi.org/10.1080/09644008.2022.2088733

Fanelli, D. (2010). "Positive" results increase down the Hierarchy of the Sciences. *PLoS One, 5*(4), e10068. https://doi.org/10.1371/journal.pone.0010068

Foucault, M. (1979). *Discipline and punish: Michel Foucault; The birth of the prison. Transl. from the French by Alan Sheridan*. Vintage Books.

Friedli, L. (2015). The politics of tackling inequalities: The rise of psychological fundamentalism in public health and welfare reform. In K. E. Smith, C. Bambra, & S. E. Hill (Eds.), *Health inequalities: Critical perspectives* (pp. 206–221). Oxford University Press.

Furedi, F. (2008). Medicalisation in a therapy culture. In D. Wainwright (Ed.), *A sociology of health* (pp. 97–114). SAGE.

Goijaerts, J., van der Zwan, N., & Bussemaker, J. (2022). Health and the social investment state. *Journal of European Public Policy, 1–21*. https://doi.org/10.1080/13501763.2022.2038239

Halfmann, D. (2012). Recognizing medicalization and demedicalization: Discourses, practices, and identities. *Health (London, England: 1997), 16*(2), 186–207. https://doi.org/10.1177/1363459311403947

Hansen, H., Bourgois, P., & Drucker, E. (2014). Pathologizing poverty: New forms of diagnosis, disability, and structural stigma under welfare reform. *Social Science & Medicine, 1982*(103), 76–83. https://doi.org/10.1016/j.socscimed.2013.06.033

Holmqvist, M. (2008). *The institutionalization of social welfare: A study of medicalizing management. Routledge advances in sociology*. Vol. 30. Routledge. https://doi.org/10.4324/9780203937358

Jo, Y. N. (2013). Psycho-social dimensions of poverty: When poverty becomes shameful. *Critical Social Policy, 33*(3), 514–531. https://doi.org/10.1177/0261018313479008

Johnstone, L. (2021). Does COVID-19 pose a challenge to the diagnoses of anxiety and depression? A psychologist's view. *BJPsych Bulletin, 45*(5), 278–281. https://doi.org/10.1192/bjb.2020.101

Klasen, H. (2000). A name, what's in a name? The medicalization of hyperactivity, Revisited. *Harvard Review of Psychiatry, 7*(6), 334–344. https://doi.org/10.3109/hrp.7.6.334

Krayter, S., & Reibling, N. (2020). Medicalisation and psychologisation of poverty? An analysis of the scientific poverty discourse from 1956 to 2017. *Journal of Poverty and Social Justice, 28*(3), 361–381. https://doi.org/10.1332/175982720X15979441697421

LaMarre, A., Smoliak, O., Cool, C., Kinavey, H., & Hardt, L. (2019). The normal, improving, and productive self: Unpacking neoliberal governmentality in therapeutic interactions. *Journal of Constructivist Psychology, 32*(3), 236–253. https://doi.org/10.1080/10720537.2018.1477080

Linden, P., Reibling, N., & Krayter, S. (2018). Lieber krank und arbeitslos als "nur" arbeitslos? Die Auswirkungen der Medikalisierung von arbeitslosen Personen auf Stigmatisierungsprozesse. *Zeitschrift für Sozialreform, 64*(4), 431–461. https://doi.org/10.1515/zsr-2018-0022

Lupton, D. (1997). *The imperative of health: Public health and the regulated body.* SAGE.

Madsen, O. J. (2014). *The therapeutic turn: How psychology altered Western culture. Concepts for critical psychology.* Taylor and Francis.

McLeod, J. D., Pescosolido, B. A., Takeuchi, D. T., & White, T. F. (2004). Public attitudes toward the use of psychiatric medications for children. *Journal of Health and Social Behavior, 45*(1), 53–67. https://doi.org/10.1177/002214650404500104

Medina, T. R., & McCraine, A. (2011). Layering control: Medicalization, psychopathy, and the increasing multi-institutional management of social problems. In B. A. Pescosolido, J. K. Martin, J. D. Mclead, & A. Rogers (Eds.), *Handbook of the sociology of health, illness, and healing: A Blueprint for the 21st century* (pp. 139–158). Springer.

Munro, G. D., & Munro, C. A. (2014). "Soft" versus "Hard" psychological science: Biased evaluations of scientific evidence that threatens or supports a strongly held political identity. *Basic and Applied Social Psychology, 36*(6), 533–543. https://doi.org/10.1080/01973533.2014.960080

Nolan, J. L. (1998). *The therapeutic state: Justifying government at century's end.* New York University Press.

Nye, R. A. (2003). The evolution of the concept of medicalization in the late twentieth century. *Journal of the History of the Behavioral Sciences, 39*(2), 115–129. https://doi.org/10.1002/jhbs.10108

O'Brien, T. L., Hawkins, S. L., & Loesch, A. (2022). Scientific disciplines and the admissibility of expert evidence in courts. *Socius: Sociological Research for a Dynamic World, 8*, 237802312211080. https://doi.org/10.1177/23780231221108044

Olafsdottir, S. (2007). *Medicalizing mental health: A comparative view of the public, private, and professional construction of mental illness* [Dissertation]. Indiana University, Bloomington, IN.

Olk, T. (2007). Kinder im "Sozialinvestitionsstaat". *Zeitschrift für Soziologie der Erziehung und Sozialisation, 27*(1), 43–57. https://doi.org/10.25656/01:5602

Pulkingham, J., & Fuller, S. (2012). From parent to patient: The medicalization of lone motherhood through welfare reform. *Social Politics: International Studies in Gender, State & Society, 19*(2), 243–268. https://doi.org/10.1093/sp/jxs007

Rajkumar, R. P. (2021). Suffering and salutogenesis: A conceptual analysis of lessons for psychiatry from existential Positive Psychology (PP2.0) in the setting of the COVID-19 pandemic. *Frontiers in Psychology, 12*, 646334. https://doi.org/10.3389/fpsyg.2021.646334

Ravens-Sieberer, U., Kaman, A., Erhart, M., Devine, J., Schlack, R., & Otto, C. (2021). Impact of the COVID-19 pandemic on quality of life and mental health in children and adolescents in Germany. *European Child & Adolescent Psychiatry, 31*, 879–889. https://doi.org/10.1007/s00787-021-01726-5

Rose, N. S. (1996). *Inventing our selves: Psychology, power, and personhood. Cambridge studies in the history of psychology*. Cambridge University Press. https://doi.org/10.1017/CBO9780511752179

Simonton, D. K. (2006). Scientific status of disciplines, individuals, and ideas: Empirical analyses of the potential impact of theory. *Review of General Psychology, 10*(2), 98–112. https://doi.org/10.1037/1089-2680.10.2.98

Stenner, P., & Taylor, D. (2008). Psychosocial welfare: Reflections on an emerging field. *Critical Social Policy, 28*(4), 415–437. https://doi.org/10.1177/0261018308095278

Stone, D. A. (1984). *The disabled state. Health, society, and policy*. Temple University Press.

van Oorschot, W., Roosma, F., & Reeskens, T. (2017). *The social legitimacy of targeted welfare: Attitudes to welfare deservingness*. Edward Elgar Publishing.

Wilfer, T., Braungardt, T., & Schneider, W. (2018). Soziale Probleme in der hausärztlichen Praxis. *Zeitschrift für Psychosomatische Medizin und Psychotherapie, 64*(3), 250–261. https://doi.org/10.13109/zptm.2018.64.3.250

Wong, S. (2016). Geographies of medicalized welfare: Spatial analysis of supplemental security income in the U.S., 2000–2010. *Social Science & Medicine, 160*, 9–19. https://doi.org/10.1016/j.socscimed.2016.05.018

Appendix

Chapter 4

How Institutions Shape the Dynamics of (De)-medicalization of Unemployment and Institutional Complexity

For this chapter, we analysed both primary and secondary data. First, to outline how institutions shape the form and dynamics of (de-)medicalization of unemployment in international comparison, we used OECD data on public spending on incapacity (OECD, 2017, doi: 10.1787/f35b71ed-en, last accessed on 10th of June 2022). Second, we illustrated the institutional complexity in the German context as well as the challenges at the interfaces to other social systems (health and pension insurance), by compiling the central sections of paragraphs §§ 8 (1), 10, 15, 31, 31a, 31b, 32 Social Code Book II, §§ 145, 146, 156 (1) No. 1 & 2, 311 Social Code Book III, § 47b Social Code Book V & § 43 Social Code Book IV. Third, to demonstrate the relationship medical case reports by the medical service agency of the Federal Employment agency among all unemployed people in Germany, we have drawn data on medical assessment services and annual reports on unemployment and minimum income benefits for jobseekers in Germany from 2006 to 2018 (Statistics from the Federal Employment Agency, 2006–2018). Both data sources are provided by the Federal Employment Agency.

N. Reibling, M. Ariaans (eds.), *Toward a Biopsychosocial Welfare State?*, https://doi.org/10.1007/978-3-031-32793-3

The Consequences of Medicalizing Unemployment

Fourth, we exemplified the consequences of the category ***sick leave for unemployed*** on re-employment opportunities and health across time by analysing representative data (N = 20,196 cases) from the Panel Study Labor Market and Social Security (PASS). The data (Version 0619 v3, DOI: 10.5164/IAB.PASS-SUF0619.de.en.v3) was accessed via a scientific use file provided by the Research Data Centre of the Federal Employment Agency at the Institute for Employment Research (IAB). Since 2007, PASS conducts an annual survey of households in which at least one person receives a benefit under the German Social Code Book II (SGB II). In addition, households that are not in receipt of SGB II benefits are also surveyed to examine the dynamics of the receipt of social benefits and the effects on the economic and social situation of the households and persons concerned (for a documentation of the data, please refer to Bähr et al., 2021; Berg et al., 2020; Bethmann et al., 2013; Dummert et al., 2020; Trappmann et al., 2013).

Public Perceptions and Attitudes Towards Welfare Benefits

Finally, we investigated how public perceptions and attitudes towards welfare state benefits change when unemployment is justified with a sickness by designing, programming, and implementing a factorial survey[1] within the YouGov panel Germany across two waves. Factorial surveys are widely used for assessing attitudes in both medicalization and welfare deservingness research (e.g. Pattyn et al., 2013; van Oorschot et al., 2017). The appeal of this approach lies in the connection of the strengths within both methods. It combines the identification of causal effects through experimental design with the stronger external validity of survey research when using large, representative samples (Aguinis & Bradley, 2014; Atzmüller & Steiner, 2010; Dülmer, 2016). Moreover, the design allowed us to present highly sensitive and complex phenomena in simple understanding and realistic situational descriptions, thereby reducing social desirability (Auspurg & Hinz, 2015).

YouGov recruited a sample of $N = 2621$ respondents with a follow-up sample of $N = 1843$ respondents. Both samples were representative of the adult German population. In the survey, participants were asked to rate hypothetical people who become unemployed for various reasons using

[1]The study involving human participants were reviewed and approved by the Council of Research Ethics (Ethics Council) of the University of Siegen and the Ombudsman System for the Safeguarding of Good Scientific Practice. The participants of the YouGov panel Germany provided their written informed consent to participate in this study.

so-called vignettes. Vignettes are small case descriptions of situations or people. They consist of a basic text describing the situation or environment. In addition, we varied different factors related to the CARIN model of perceived deservingness (van Oorschot, 2000, 2006; van Oorschot et al., 2017) for welfare state recipients (age, marital status, migration status, and motivation to seek work). Moreover, we added the reason for unemployment status: Personal misconduct and employer bankruptcy thereby reflected non-medical reasons for unemployment, while we also described individuals who were unemployed for medical (chronic back pain) or psychological (depression) reasons. To measure perceptions of deservingness, respondents could select how much unemployment and minimum income benefits they would allocate to the person described. To measure perceptions of social control, the survey also asked what obligations beneficiaries had to meet to receive full benefits. Finally, the survey described the individual's failure to keep appointments with Federal Employment Agency officers. The survey then asked by what percentage minimum income benefits should be reduced if this obligation to cooperate was not met. The data and documentation of the vignette study are available from the Data Archive for the Social Sciences (Reibling 2023).

CHAPTER 5

Scientific Discourse Analysis

Data for this analysis were drawn from a longitudinal dataset including scientific literature citations from the Social Sciences Citation Index (SSCI) in the Web of Science (WoS). The SSCI provides data back to 1956. We collected data with the focus on poverty and closely linked concepts. The following search terms were used: poor, poverty, low-income, low income, or depriv* (with * as a lemmatization of the basic form to search for deprivation or deprived). We only included peer-reviewed journal articles in our analysis. In order to exclude non-relevant articles that used the search terms in another way, then indented for our analysis (e.g. poor sleep), we carried out a manual exclusion process by screening the titles of all articles. Additionally, we excluded articles referring to countries outside the EU or OECD area, as the definition of poverty in those countries differs to some extent. Our subject of analysis are the research areas, that each article in the SSCI is assigned to, exploring how the research areas develop in the research on poverty. As one article can be assigned to more than one research area, we weighted the research areas for each article according to the total number of research areas, that one particular research article is assigned to (e.g. 0.5 each when two research areas are assigned or 0.25 each if four research areas are assigned). Finally, we controlled the observed trend for the overall trend of these research areas without a focus on poverty. For a more detailed overview about methodological approaches, see Krayter and Reibling (2020).

Analysis of German Parliamentary Debates
The analysis is based on a comparison of parliamentary debates on ALMP reforms in Germany at two time points: 2002 and 2003 (grouped together under the year 2003) and 2016. The first set of reforms are an example of workfare policies during a time of macroeconomic hardship; the second set of enabling policies during macroeconomic stability. The laws for the first time point are called "Laws on modern services in the labour market" (in short: Hartz legislation after the head of the reform commission). The laws for the second time point are called "Law on strengthening vocational further training and the insurance coverage of the unemployment insurance" (in short AWStG) and "the ninth revision of the social codebook II".

All debates of the first parliamentary chamber on each law were included. We developed a quantitative coding scheme, which is grounded on publications on (German) labour market reforms but also includes inductive elements. The coding units are the paragraphs that already exist in the official transcripts of the debates. Only paragraphs which have a clear focus on (un-)employment, and the labour market are coded. One paragraph can have multiple codes. The codes allude to scientific disciplines. The coding scheme was pretested at a 2.3% and two 5% random test samples separately by both authors to discuss challenges of the coding and refine the coding instructions. The reliability based on kappa values for the final pre-test is 0.60 for the thematic level of the coding scheme.

Chapter 6

Analysis of Press Releases

The question if and how paediatricians and educators medicalize or (de-) medicalize is answered by an analysis of the press releases of both German professional associations. The VBE (Verband Bildung und Erziehung, Association for education and upbringing) is the occupational association representing teachers and kindergarten teachers, the BVKJ (Berufsverband der Kinder- und Jugendärzte, Association of pediatricians) is the occupational association representing paediatricians in Germany. All press releases of both associations between 2009 and 2019 are analysed. The VBE issued 505, the BVKJ 442 press releases during this time. For all press releases, titles were checked if they relate to deviant child behaviour or disorders. The remaining press releases (104 VBE and 48 BVKJ) were read, summarized, and then coded by an inductive thematic coding scheme. To evaluate the level of medicalization we used (Conrad & Schneider, 1980) three levels on which medicalization—and (de-)medicalization—can unfold, doctor-patient interaction level (micro level), the institutional level (meso level), and the conceptual level (macro level). The conceptual level mainly deals with the definition of social problems in medical terms. The institutional level refers to organizations and programmes. On the doctor-patient interaction level, the medical definition of a problem by a physician and the treatment as well as the patient stand at the centre. Halfmann (2012) adopts similar levels and adds that medicalization and (de-)medicalization can happen at the same time and by different degrees in all these levels.

Public Perceptions and Attitudes Towards "Problematic Children"
In addition, we researched public opinion regarding "problematic" children by analysing findings from our own vignette study (see Chap. 4). In the same survey we also described eight-year-old children and their behaviour in school. We varied other factors such as gender, immigrant and family background, and parental education level to explore whether respondents associated these factors with their assessment of the child. In addition, we varied the description of the child and his behaviour. Normal children were described to have minor social issues (shyness, harmless fight in class). We furthermore described a child with clinical, yet latent symptoms of hyperactivity (difficulty concentrating, forgetfulness, and impaired attention). The development of the vignettes was co-developed and evaluated by three psychologists. We then asked respondents to give their assessment of (1) what they considered plausible reasons for the behaviour, (2) what behavioural recommendations they would make to parents, and (3) what courses of action are possible for social interactions by society. Response options on a 7-point Likert scale ranged from 1 = very unlikely to 7 = very likely (for attribution of cause) and 1 = disagree at all to 7 = agree completely (for recommendations and courses of action). The data and documentation of the vignette study are available from the Data Archive for the Social Sciences (Reibling 2023).

References

Aguinis, H., & Bradley, K. J. (2014). Best practice recommendations for designing and implementing experimental vignette methodology studies. *Organizational Research Methods, 17*(4), 351–371. https://doi.org/10.1177/1094428114547952

Atzmüller, C., & Steiner, P. M. (2010). Experimental vignette studies in survey research. *Methodology, 6*(3), 128–138. https://doi.org/10.1027/1614-2241/a000014

Auspurg, K., & Hinz, T. (2015). *Factorial survey experiments. Quantitative applications in the social sciences: Vol. 175.* Sage.

Bähr, S., Beste, J., Coban, M., Dummert, S., Friedrich, M., Frodermann, C., Gundert, S., Müller, B., Schwarz, S., Teichler, N., Trappmann, M., Unger, S., Wenzig, C., Berg, M., Cramer, R., Dickmann, C., Gilberg, R., Jesske, B., & Kleudgen, M. (2021). *Panel Arbeitsmarkt und soziale Sicherung (PASS) – Version 0619 v3.* https://doi.org/10.5164/IAB.PASS-SUF0619.de.en.v3

Berg, M. et al. (2020). *Codebuch und Dokumentation des Panel 'Arbeitsmarkt und soziale Sicherung' (PASS).* https://doi.org/10.5164/IAB.FDZD.2012.de.v1

Bethmann, A., Fuchs, B., & Wurdack, A. (07/2013). *User Guide "Panel Study Labour Market and Social Security" (PASS): FDZ-Datenreport.* Institut für Arbeitsmarkt- und Berufsforschung (IAB) der Bundesagentur für Arbeit.

Conrad, P., & Schneider, J. W. (1980). Looking at levels of medicalization: A comment on strong's critique of the thesis of medical imperialism. *Social Science & Medicine. Part A: Medical Psychology & Medical Sociology, 14*(1), 75–79. https://doi.org/10.1016/S0271-7123(80)90804-4

Dülmer, H. (2016). The factorial survey. *Sociological Methods & Research, 45*(2), 304–347. https://doi.org/10.1177/0049124115582269

Dummert, S., Beste, J., Frodermann, C., Schwarz, S., Trappmann, M., Bähr, S., Coban, M., Friedrich, M., Gundert, S., Müller, B., Teichler, N., Unger, S., & Wenzig, C. (2020). *Panel Arbeitsmarkt und soziale Sicherung (PASS) – Version 0619 v1.* https://doi.org/10.5164/IAB.PASS-SUF0619.de.en.v1

Halfmann, D. (2012). Recognizing medicalization and demedicalization: Discourses, practices, and identities. Health (London, England: 1997), 16(2), 186–207. https://doi.org/10.1177/1363459311403947

Krayter, S., & Reibling, N. (2020). Medicalisation and psychologisation of poverty? An analysis of the scientific poverty discourse from 1956 to 2017. *Journal of Poverty and Social Justice, 28*(3), 361–381. https://doi.org/10.1332/175982720X15979441697421

OECD (2017). *Social protection: Public spending on incapacity (indicator).* https://doi.org/10.1787/f35b71ed-en

Pattyn, E., Verhaeghe, M., Sercu, C., & Bracke, P. (2013). Medicalizing versus psychologizing mental illness: What are the implications for help seeking and stigma? A general population study. *Social Psychiatry and Psychiatric Epidemiology, 48*(10), 1637–1645. https://doi.org/10.1007/s00127-013-0671-5

Reibling, N. (2023). MEPYSO Vignettenstudie. *Datenfile Version 1.0.0*, https://doi:org/10.7802/2456

Statistics from the Federal Employment Agency. (2006–2018). *Minimum income benefits for jobseekers in Germany: Annual reports 2006–2018.* Federal Employment Agency. https://www.arbeitsagentur.de/datei/sgbii-jahresbericht-2018_ba043368.pdf

Trappmann, M., Beste, J., Bethmann, A., & Müller, G. (2013). The PASS panel survey after six waves. *Journal for Labour Market Research, 46*(4), 275–281. https://doi.org/10.1007/s12651-013-0150-1

van Oorschot, W. (2000). Who should get what, and why? On deservingness criteria and the conditionality of solidarity among the public. *Policy & Politics, 28*(1), 33–48. https://doi.org/10.1332/0305573002500811

van Oorschot, W. (2006). Making the difference in social Europe: Deservingness perceptions among citizens of European welfare states. *Journal of European Social Policy, 16*(1), 23–42. https://doi.org/10.1177/0958928706059829

van Oorschot, W., Roosma, F., Meuleman, B., & Reeskens, T. (2017). *The social legitimacy of targeted welfare.* Edward Elgar Publishing. https://doi.org/10.4337/9781785367212

Index[1]

A

Access, 2, 10, 12, 45, 64, 69, 71, 78, 82, 83, 92, 93, 98, 108, 109, 136, 144, 148, 151, 154, 174, 180, 192, 195, 198, 201
Activating, 14, 80, 135
Active labor market policies
Actors, v, 3, 6, 7, 10, 11, 14, 24, 28, 30, 34, 41, 42, 56, 57, 59–61, 63, 65–67, 69, 71, 78, 80, 83–91, 102, 107, 108, 110–119, 122, 132, 137, 138, 144, 150, 166–168, 179, 181, 191–193, 197, 199
Acts for modern services on the labor market, 116n4, 212
Administration, 4, 5, 13, 68, 167
Advocacy, 150, 200
Agent, 6, 35, 41, 137, 199, 200
Anglo-Saxon, 198
Assessment, 31, 32, 47, 56, 69, 70, 79, 82, 87–91, 87n3, 102, 136, 152, 153, 168, 173, 191, 195, 209
Attention-deficit/hyperactivity disorder (ADHD), 25, 80, 130, 132, 136–139, 141, 143, 144, 149, 150, 192
Attitudes, 4, 93, 97–102, 110, 144, 196, 198, 200, 210–211, 213

B

Benefit, 4, 5, 10–13, 28, 36, 42, 43, 45, 48, 58, 62, 64, 65, 69, 71, 77–79, 81, 83, 84, 84n2, 86–97, 100–102, 108, 115, 119–123, 131, 151, 152, 167, 168, 171, 172, 174, 176, 192–199, 204, 209–211

[1] Note: Page numbers followed by 'n' refer to notes.

N. Reibling, M. Ariaans (eds.), *Toward a Biopsychosocial Welfare State?*, https://doi.org/10.1007/978-3-031-32793-3

Bibliographic, 14
Biopsychosocial, v, 5–6, 8, 9, 14, 15, 23–48, 60, 66–71, 102, 119, 140, 154, 183, 191–204
Boundary, 14, 24, 37, 39, 121, 140

C
Capable to work, 86–89, 96
Case, 9–11, 13, 29, 44, 46, 61, 67, 77–102, 109, 118, 121, 122, 138, 139, 142, 144, 146, 148, 149, 152, 153, 168, 171–173, 193, 196–199, 209–211
Character skills, 3, 47, 131, 154
Childcare, 11, 58, 133, 134, 140, 176, 177, 180, 203
Children, 3, 4, 11, 15, 28, 45, 47, 58, 61, 62, 71, 113, 117, 118, 120, 123, 129–155, 167, 168, 173–176, 178, 179, 201, 203, 213
Compensatory, 43, 44, 140
Conditional
Conditionality, 10, 11, 64, 83, 194, 195, 199, 201
Conrad, Peter, 7, 11, 25, 26, 29, 41, 42, 44, 45, 47, 56, 56n1, 60, 80, 92, 97, 110, 149, 196–198, 213
Conservative, 10, 11, 58, 60, 62, 64, 81, 82, 119
Consultation, 3, 118, 122
COVID-19, 45, 98, 99, 101, 132, 155, 202, 203
Credibility, 200
Crises, 202, 204
Critical, 7, 25, 26, 28, 30, 32, 33, 35, 40, 45, 80, 141, 144, 152, 196, 200, 201
Cultural, 5–8, 30, 35, 42, 43, 61, 62, 64, 173, 198
Culture, 32, 34, 40, 47, 62, 63, 198, 199

D
Dialogue, 6–9, 197
Dimension, 8, 14, 24, 28, 31, 37, 43, 56, 56n1, 59–63, 66–71, 80, 90, 109, 113, 114, 114n3, 123, 132, 137, 150, 151, 153, 169, 170, 191, 192, 198, 199
Disability, 2, 10, 13, 14, 56, 65, 66, 78n1, 84, 85, 113, 120, 121, 151, 195
Driving forces, 37, 41–42, 197

E
Economic, vi, 2, 6, 8, 40, 59, 64, 66, 78, 92, 95, 107–110, 113, 119, 122, 123, 131, 133, 134, 137, 167, 169–172, 175, 178, 195, 196, 199, 200, 210
Economy, 116, 131, 167
Education, 3, 4, 9, 15, 31, 65, 101, 109, 114, 130, 133–136, 138, 139, 141, 142, 144, 152, 168, 173, 175–178, 192, 201, 212, 213
European, 80
European Commission, 2, 4, 65, 66, 131, 133, 168, 169, 172, 178
Expert, 32, 36, 70, 87, 115, 118, 119, 123, 140, 152, 171

F
Federal Employment Agency (FEA), 13, 83, 84, 86–88, 90, 91, 94, 95, 97, 209–211
Field, v, vi, 1, 6–9, 12–15, 24, 25, 29, 30, 36, 39, 40, 44, 46, 57, 58, 107, 111, 113n2, 114n3, 130, 137, 138, 167, 179, 191, 197, 199, 200
Future, 15, 84, 88, 120, 121, 130, 131, 133, 154, 171, 173, 176, 198, 199, 202–204

G

Generosity, 10, 78, 201
German pension insurance (DRV), 78, 83, 209
Germany, 3, 4, 10–14, 33, 62, 64, 78–83, 85, 90, 91, 93, 96, 99, 102, 108, 109, 115, 118–120, 132–137, 142, 149–154, 166, 171–174, 179, 180, 183, 192, 193, 195, 196, 198, 201, 203, 209, 210, 210n1, 212, 213
Governmentality, 7, 30, 32, 65, 179, 192

H

Halfmann, Drew, 26, 28–30, 42, 56, 56n1, 59, 62, 63, 194, 197, 213
Health, 2, 3, 6, 9, 11, 14, 28, 28n1, 29, 32, 35, 37, 40–42, 45, 57, 60, 65, 66, 68, 69, 78–80, 87, 88, 90–97, 100, 101, 107, 109–111, 113–115, 117, 118, 123, 131, 134, 135, 139, 141, 142, 154, 155, 167–183, 195, 196, 202, 204
Healthcare, 1, 2, 8, 10, 12, 23, 29, 33, 39, 46, 55, 57, 60, 79, 130, 135, 140, 141, 143, 150, 151, 169–171, 178, 179, 191, 193, 199, 201
Health insurance, 10, 13, 23, 83, 86–89, 136, 150
Historic, 36, 41, 130
Holmqvist, Mikael, 9, 10, 23, 30, 57, 61, 65, 79, 92, 98, 102, 118, 149, 166, 173, 197
Human capital, 65, 92, 114, 130, 134, 169, 175, 176, 178, 199

I

Ideas, v–vii, 2, 5–8, 10, 11, 14, 15, 24, 28, 29, 31, 32, 34–37, 42, 44, 46, 48, 55–57, 59, 61–63, 65–68, 70, 71, 78, 80, 84, 102, 107, 108, 110, 114–116, 118, 119, 122, 123, 130, 132, 134, 135, 137, 138, 144, 150, 153, 167–170, 172, 176, 191–193, 195–197, 199, 200
Ill, 25, 44, 79, 83, 85, 86, 89, 101, 122, 141, 172, 174, 202
Illness, 2, 5, 6, 9, 14, 40, 41, 44–47, 62, 64, 66, 68, 79, 84, 86–88, 90, 93, 94, 109, 120–122, 136, 137, 142, 154, 169, 174, 176, 182
Incapacity, 4, 78, 78n1, 79, 81–83, 86–89, 92–94, 96, 172, 174, 180, 192, 193, 195
Individualization, 15, 92, 167, 169, 170, 179, 196
Individualize, 46, 179, 196
Inequality, 2, 3, 47, 66, 119, 135, 149, 154, 174, 177, 179, 183, 196, 200
Institutions, v, 4, 6, 14, 23, 24, 27, 28, 30, 35, 36, 42, 43, 47, 57–59, 61–67, 69–71, 81, 88, 90, 107, 110, 119–123, 130, 132, 141, 144, 150–153, 167, 168, 172, 181, 191, 192, 197–199, 201, 209
Interdisciplinarity, 6
Interdisciplinary, vi, 7, 8, 37, 39, 154, 155, 200
International Classification of Disease (ICD), 3, 25

J

Jurisdiction, 28, 34, 46, 71, 89, 140, 203

L
Labor market, 61, 79, 80, 84, 86, 91–94, 96, 102, 116n4, 120, 121, 168, 173, 175, 177, 179, 180, 183, 195
Layering, 8, 192
Learning difficulties, 62, 132, 136, 138, 149–154, 192
Legitimization, 35, 62, 192
Legitimize, 7, 44, 62, 68, 178, 195
Level, 11, 14, 24, 26, 45, 56, 56n1, 58, 59, 66–71, 77, 82, 86, 89, 93, 95, 96, 101, 102, 114, 114n3, 116, 118, 119, 121–123, 131, 135, 152, 154, 155, 168, 170–173, 177, 191, 197–201, 204, 212, 213
Liberal, 7, 9, 10, 30, 36, 58, 64, 79, 119, 179

M
Macro, 24, 56, 66, 71, 191, 213
Material, 2, 30, 40, 47, 107–123, 134, 179
Medical, v, 1–5, 7, 8, 11–13, 15, 23, 25–30, 33, 39–48, 56, 57, 60–63, 65, 67–69, 71, 78, 80, 82, 84, 86–92, 87n3, 98, 102, 107, 108, 110, 111, 112n1, 116–123, 132, 134–137, 139–143, 145, 146, 148–151, 153–155, 166, 170, 181, 192–196, 199–203, 209, 211, 213
Medicalization, v, 3, 5–11, 13–15, 23–31, 37–39, 41–48, 55–71, 78–81, 83–102, 107, 110–119, 122, 123, 130, 132–143, 149–155, 165–183, 191–204, 210, 213
Mental health, 109, 110, 155
Mental illness, 2, 25, 41, 79, 88, 136, 137, 146, 154
Meso, 24, 56, 66, 71, 191, 213
Micro, 24, 56, 66, 71, 191, 213
Minimum income, 62, 77, 80, 82–86, 84n2, 88–91, 93–96, 100, 121, 123, 130, 174, 194, 196, 199, 209, 211
Model, 4, 6, 10, 11, 27, 39, 43–45, 48, 56, 58, 66–68, 70–71, 98, 101, 133, 134, 191, 197, 211
Modern, 1, 7, 8, 30–35, 41, 42, 45, 48, 57, 60, 62, 116n4, 194, 195, 202, 212
Multidimensional, 14, 107, 109–111, 123

N
Need for assistance, 35, 59, 60, 63, 65, 135, 171, 176, 196, 203
Neoliberal, 8, 11, 15, 79, 83, 91, 98, 102, 115, 116, 119, 166–179, 181–183, 194

O
Obligation, 4, 11–15, 43, 45, 83, 86, 88, 90, 100, 101, 121–123, 147–149, 211
Organization, 5, 10, 23, 31, 34, 35, 44, 47, 60–62, 65, 66, 68–71, 80, 85, 87n3, 118, 133, 137, 138, 142, 150, 154, 168, 169, 176–178, 181, 195, 203, 213
Organization for Economic and Co-operation and Development (OECD), 12, 78, 81, 82, 108, 109, 133, 168–171, 173, 176, 177, 209, 211

P
Pandemic, 45, 132, 155, 202–204
Paradigm, 8, 11, 15, 48, 63, 65, 66, 115, 116, 130, 134, 135, 166–168, 175–179, 181, 182, 199

Parenting, 32, 66, 131, 134, 135, 146, 148, 179, 193
Pathologization, 46, 201
Patient, 3, 12, 33, 34, 40, 44, 170, 195, 213
Personality, 2–4, 6, 32, 34, 172, 175–181
Physician, 3–5, 10, 12, 13, 46, 86–88, 139, 140, 154, 213
Policy, 8, 10, 11, 15, 24, 43, 58, 60–62, 65, 66, 68, 69, 78, 79, 84, 114, 116, 117, 119, 130, 132–135, 137, 138, 144, 152, 153, 155, 166–183, 192, 198–201, 203, 212
Policymaker, 60, 118, 136, 144, 201
Political system, 13, 42, 48, 203
Poor, 2, 26, 58, 71, 90, 108–110, 113, 115, 119–121, 123, 139, 174, 178, 211
Poverty, v, 2, 3, 9, 11, 14, 15, 56, 57, 63–65, 92, 107–123, 129, 131, 133–135, 138, 139, 141, 154, 165, 174, 176–178, 180, 183, 191–193, 195–197, 199, 201, 204, 211, 212
Power, 10, 28–31, 33, 35, 36, 40, 43, 45, 48, 59, 60, 71, 114, 122, 167, 194, 195, 197, 198
Practice, 3, 6, 7, 11–13, 24, 28, 30, 36, 37, 40–43, 46, 48, 56, 58, 60, 61, 63, 65, 68, 69, 78, 79, 118, 139–141, 149, 154, 192, 193, 196, 197, 200, 201
Prevention, 40, 135, 139, 141, 155, 169, 170, 174, 176, 177, 180, 203
Preventive, 2, 135, 142
Principle of promoting and demanding
Psychiatrist, 150
Psychologist, 1, 3, 4, 12, 13, 23, 31, 33, 35, 39, 40, 46, 57, 60, 69, 88, 102, 132, 135, 136, 144, 146, 148, 150, 152, 153, 173, 179, 181, 194, 195, 201, 203
Psychologization, v, 3, 5–11, 13–15, 23, 24, 30–36, 41–42, 44–48, 55–71, 79, 80, 92, 94, 97–99, 101, 102, 107, 110–119, 122, 123, 130–137, 149–155, 165–183, 191–204
Public health, 10, 23, 40, 41, 83, 111, 112, 112n1, 115, 118, 174, 176, 177, 196, 203

Q

Qualitative, 5, 6, 14, 93, 112, 116, 138, 198
Quantitative, 14, 58, 112, 113, 115, 193, 198, 212

R

Reflection, 201
Reflective
Reform, 8, 10, 11, 14, 63–65, 70, 79, 80, 82–85, 91, 102, 108, 115, 116, 116n4, 118, 119, 121, 123, 131, 166, 167, 171–174, 177, 179–183, 194, 196, 198, 201, 212
Rehabilitation, 65, 79, 89, 91, 169, 172, 180, 181
Rehabilitative, 2, 13, 100, 181
Responsibility, 2, 15, 25–27, 32, 38–39, 43, 44, 46, 48, 57, 98, 100, 101, 110, 167–175, 181, 196, 197
Restructuring, 15, 55, 63–66, 165, 195, 198, 201
Rose, Nikolas, 7, 9, 24, 30–34, 36, 40–42, 44, 60, 98, 110, 193

S

School, 1, 3, 4, 13, 31, 36, 39, 60, 131, 135, 139, 141, 142, 144, 148–152, 168, 173, 183, 203, 213
Scientific discourse, 14, 110–112, 115, 130, 192, 198, 199
Scientization, 5, 37
Sick leave, 3, 4, 12, 46, 65, 82, 86–88, 90, 91, 93–96, 172, 174, 192, 194, 195, 199, 210
Sickness, 14, 37, 46, 78, 83–88, 87n3, 92, 94, 96–98, 101, 102
Social code
Social control, 7, 25–27, 32, 33, 36, 43, 45, 46, 195, 203, 211
Social-democratic, 9, 10, 58, 60, 79, 119
Social insurance, 3, 5, 10, 11, 58, 81–83, 119, 120
Social investment, 2, 8, 10, 11, 15, 48, 63, 65, 66, 78, 98, 115, 116, 119, 130, 131, 133–136, 154, 165–183, 194–196, 198, 199, 201
Social legitimacy, 14, 144
Social life, 57, 175, 202, 203
Social policy, v, vi, 1–2, 5, 6, 8–11, 14, 15, 48, 57, 62, 63, 65, 78, 119, 122, 133–135, 166, 167, 169, 175, 181, 183, 191–204
Social problem, v, vi, 2, 3, 5, 6, 8, 10–15, 25, 26, 30, 32, 41–42, 44–46, 56–59, 61, 65, 71, 77, 92, 97, 98, 122, 129, 131, 138–140, 154, 165, 166, 176, 183, 191–194, 196–201, 213
Social rights, 4, 5, 10, 14, 15, 58, 66, 69, 102, 134, 150, 198
Social Science Citation Index (SSCI), 111, 130, 211
Social stratification, 8, 149
Social work, 4, 31, 40, 192
Student, v, vi, 6, 12, 13, 70, 133, 141, 142, 149–153, 168, 173, 200
Synthesis, 14, 197, 198

T

Therapeutization, 7, 24, 28n1, 31, 62, 197
Therapist, 1
Therapy culture, 7, 24, 31

U

Unemployment, v, vi, 2–4, 8–11, 14, 30, 56, 57, 61–65, 77–102, 109, 115, 116, 116n4, 120–122, 129, 165, 168, 171–174, 176, 180, 183, 191–196, 201, 209–212

V

Vignette, 14, 93, 98, 99, 144, 145, 196, 198, 201, 211, 213

W

Web of Science (WoS), 111, 112, 112n1, 211
Welfare state, v, 1, 2, 4–11, 13–15, 23–48, 55–71, 77–81, 96, 101, 102, 107, 110, 119, 120, 122–123, 129–155, 165–168, 171, 173–176, 178–182, 191–204, 210, 211
Window of opportunity, 203
Work, vi, vii, 1, 4–7, 9, 11–14, 23, 25, 30–32, 34, 35, 37, 39–46, 58, 59, 63, 77, 78, 82–84, 84n2, 86–90, 97, 100, 101, 110, 112, 121, 122, 131, 132, 135, 136, 138, 140, 166, 176, 178, 197, 198, 200, 211
World Health Organization (WHO), 4, 41, 169, 176–178

Kolibri 360 GmbH
Ferdinand-Jühlke-Straße 7
99095 Erfurt, Deutschland
produktsicherheit@kolibri360.de